TOLSTOY REMEMBERED

By his son

TOLSTOY REMEMBERED

By His Son

SERGEI TOLSTOY

Translated by

MOURA BUDBERG

WEIDENFELD AND NICOLSON

20 NEW BOND STREET LONDON WI

First published in 1949 by
Mezhdunarodnaja Kniga, Moscow
Second edition 1956
English translation © 1961 by
George Weidenfeld and Nicolson Ltd

Printed in Great Britain
by The Whitefriars Press Ltd
London and Tonbridge
17/6132

Contents

Translator's Note

ANOTHER book about Tolstoy? Certainly; but of a very unusual kind. Though the author, Leo Tolstoy's eldest son, was an old man when he wrote these memoirs, he has successfully recaptured the child's point of view. The book has the intimacy and charm of a family chronicle: we see the great man at home, a family man, playing games with his children; we discover that the Tolstoy family, like so many other families, has its own private language and slang, its private jokes. The distinguished men around Tolstoy are seen through a boy's eyes: the poet Tiutchev is simply ' a funny man who did not know how to behave with children '; a great composer is highly thought of for reasons that have nothing to do with his music; the children liked Turgenev because he made them laugh.

The Tolstoys suffered from the jealousies, prejudices and self-torments, and enjoyed the laughter and fun of large families everywhere; some were favourites, others felt left out in the cold—Sergei Tolstoy understood these feelings very well.

The book is composed, as one can easily see, of a series of autobiographical articles, leaving large gaps—for instance between 1910 and 1919. I have excluded a certain number of passages which seemed to me either repetitious or of merely local and ephemeral interest. More autobiographical material has been found among Sergei Tolstoy's manuscripts and this will be published in Russia shortly.

MOURA BUDBERG

Part I

FAMILY LIFE

1862-1881

Part I

Family Life

My parents were married on September 23rd, 1862, at the Palace church in Moscow. My father was thirty-four, my mother eighteen. It is clear from contemporary documents that my father was very much in love with his bride. But reason also played a part in his choice. Firstly, my father had determined to marry a very young girl whom he could mould to his own design; secondly, it was a matter of principle that he should marry out of his own noble class.

Sofia Andreevna Bers answered both requirements: she was very young and the Bers family did not belong to the aristocracy. Her father, Andrei Evstafovich Bers (grandson of the military instructor who had come from Germany under Elizabeth*), was an intelligent and distinguished physician, but he did not belong to the real Russian nobility who at that time looked down on the medical profession. Sofia Andreevna's mother, Lubov Alexandrovna, daughter of A. M. Isleniev, although of ancient lineage, was born of a marriage which was considered illegal. Thus, she and her brothers and sisters bore the improvised name of Islavin and were considered not to belong to the nobility but to the merchant class.

My mother's early marriage and her semi-noble origin had a great influence on the subsequent life of our family. Being so young and malleable, she completely surrendered to her husband's will; she absorbed his views on marriage and encouraged his ambitions to make money and acquire fame. But later in life when he repudiated these ideas, she was unable to change with him and abandon the opinions acquired in her youth. Owing to her semi-

*The Empress Elizabeth, 1741–1758.

2

noble origin, she attached a certain value to so-called high society and tried to keep up appearances with her aristocratic friends according to the standards of the Tolstoy family.

My parents were engaged for a very short time as my father put pressure on my mother's parents when they wanted to delay the wedding. Immediately after the ceremony, the couple went to Jassnaia Poliana in a postchaise. There they were met by my father's aunt and governess, Tatiana Alexandrovna Jergolskaia, his brother, Sergei Nikolaevich, the teachers of the schools of Jassnaia Poliana and the whole domestic staff.

At first young Sofia Andreevna did not feel at ease in Jassnaia Poliana. She had always lived before in a town or in a suburban villa in Pokrovskoe, never in the country. For instance, she was unpleasantly surprised to find that it was dark at night in the country, that there were no lamp-posts. Everybody in Jassnaia Poliana treated her with great friendliness and kindness. But of course there was a big difference between town and country people.

She took some time to get accustomed to her husband and in the early days of her marriage addressed him with the formal ' you '. She was jealous by nature, jealous of his past, and the resultant frictions grew more severe with time; in the first years they were not so pronounced, because of my father's infatuation and my mother's devotion to him; and because they both had a high ideal of family life.

During our continuous stay in Jassnaia Poliana until we moved to Moscow in 1882, there was no sharp disagreement between my parents. Misunderstandings began to occur only in the last two or three years (1878–1881); but at that time my father had not yet begun to expect his family to change their way of life, nor had he himself much altered his habits. The consequences of the change in his outlook on life had their effect on the family much later—after 1881.

I was born on June 28th, 1863, in Jassnaia Poliana, on a leather sofa. On that leather sofa my father, too, had been born, as were also his brothers and sisters and—later—some of mine. To this day it is part of the furniture of my father's study.

My birth was slightly premature. On the 27th, when my mother felt her first labour pains, my father said to her: ' Darling, try to wait until midnight.'

3

He wanted his firstborn to come into the world on the 28th: he is known to have thought this number was his lucky one; he himself was born on August 28th, 1828. Nature seemed to have granted his wish as I was born after midnight.

My father wished to call me Nicholas, in memory of his father and his favourite brother, but my mother protested that in the Tolstoy family Nicholas was an unlucky name.

Then my father suggested that if in the saints calendar there should be a St. Sergius on June 28th, I should be called Sergius in honour of his second brother, Sergei Nikolaevich. It turned out that the June 28th celebrated the memory of the 'Valaam miracle-workers Sergius and Herman ', and so I was baptised Sergei.

My godfather was Uncle Sergei Ivanovich, my godmother Aunt Tatiana Alexandrovna Jergolskaia.

My mother started by nursing me herself, but she developed an inflammation of the nipples, and Evlampia Matveevna, wife of our driver Philip Rodionov, who later became our coachman and then bailiff, came to her help; later I became friends with my milk brother Misha, their son. Evlampia was followed by Natalia Kasakova and after that I was given the bottle. I was a delicate child. My first nanny was my father's old nanny—whom I don't remember—and the next, Maria Afanassievna Arbusova, a former serf of the landowner Vojeikov. She was a kind, gentle woman. After me, she was nanny to my brothers Ilya and Liova and my sisters Tania and Masha. She was greatly attached to us and we loved her. She did not tell us fairy tales, as nannies usually do, but she spoilt us and when she was promoted housekeeper, she used to take us secretly to the pantry and give us raisins, almonds, jam and honey.

Apart from my parents and nanny, there emerges from the misty memories of my childhood, the image of my aunt Tatiana Alexandrovna Jergolskaia. I now realise she was typical of that strange past era, a woman in whom romantic ideas and sensibility mingled with the cruelty of serf ownership. At that time she seemed to me to be merely a very kind but rather dull aunt. I called her Auntie and so did my parents. She was small and neatly dressed, with a shawl round her shoulders and a bonnet on her head. She showed particular affection for me, her godson, plied me with sweets and liked to show off her possessions to me: miniatures, boxes, embroideries, etc.

4

Auntie had a personal maid, a former serf, Aksinia Maximovna, who was very devoted to her mistress. She also had a friend, an old lady only a little younger than herself—Natalie Petrovna Okhotnitskaia, who belonged to the small gentry. She, too, was small, with flabby cheeks; she mumbled rather than talked, took snuff and liked to have a glass of vodka before dinner. She was a great chatterbox and would tell far-fetched but rather boring stories about the lives of landowners, army officers and monasteries.*

In addition to the permanent inhabitants of Jassnaia Poliana— my father, my mother, we children and Auntie—my father's nieces Varia and Lisa Tolstoy used to spend a lot of time in Jassnaia Poliana; and almost every summer my mother's sister, Aunt Tania, who in 1867 married A. M. Kusminski, came to our manor house with her husband and her growing family. All these young people brought great animation to the house. In November 1866 a new recruit to our household was a young Englishwoman, the daughter of the gardener at Windsor Castle—Hannah Tardsey. She had been sent for by my father from England to be governess to us three children: I was three years old. Tania was two, and Ilya a few months.

With the help of a dictionary my mother and Hanna soon learnt to understand one another; my mother's knowledge of French and German was a great help. Two days after Hanna's arrival she and my mother were already close friends—they were about the same age. We children soon learnt to love her and she was like one of the family.

Servants play a far more important part in the lives of children than of grown-ups. This was so with us. Nanny—Maria Afanassievna—had two sons, Paul and Sergei Arbusov. Paul was a cobbler. He settled down for good in Jassnaia Poliana and built himself a house near the outskirts of the village, and eventually

---

*It is known that my father wrote a story ' The Dream ', signed it ' N.O.', and sent it to I. Aksakov to the paper *The Day*, as from Natalia Petrovna Okhotnitskaia, asking him to publish it. Aksakov replied to Madame Okhotnitskaia that ' for a first literary effort the style is . . . passable ', but that the essence of a story lay not in the style but in the contents and that therefore her story could not be published in his paper.

5

taught my father the craft. Sergei was a footman by training and also did some carpentry work. Occasionally he would be employed as a footman in our house and just as often was discharged for bad behaviour. Then he would go to Tula and work in a factory which made cases for harmonicas. He was of medium height, with bandy legs, bright red hair and side-whiskers (he shaved off his moustache) and a face full of expression. He had a lot of energy and talent and was even educated to some extent; later he wrote his memoirs of my father. He was a prey to wild passions, and was especially addicted to wine and women. In spite of all this, he was devoted to our house and close to us as the son of our nanny, so that a lot was forgiven him. Sometimes he used to get dead drunk; he would spend all his money on drink and would disappear for several days; on his return, he would say to his virtuous wife, Arina, whom he loved and respected in spite of his dissolute living: 'Never mind, Arina. Just keep a stiff upper lip!' And then he would return to his job in our household.

Most of the servants in our house were former serfs who had not yet lost contact with the estate. Before Serge Arbusov, my father's servant was Alexei Orekhov, one of the boys about whom he wrote in his memoirs: ' My aunt, who was also our guardian, had the silly idea of giving each of us, the four Tolstoy brothers, a boy serf who was eventually to become our devoted servant.'

Alexei was with my father in the Caucasus and shared with him the dangers of the Sebastopol seige. I remember him as far back as the sixties, not as father's servant, but as a respectable-looking bailiff of Jassnaia Poliana; he was married to the clever and cheerful Duniasha, who had been my mother's personal maid. Alexei was quiet, sensible and very devoted to my father.

In their memoirs, my father, my sister Tatiana and my brother Ilya all wrote about Agafia, my father's grandmother's maid, who became our housekeeper, and later the ' dogs ' governess '; so I will not repeat their stories. I would only like to say that Agafia looked like an aristocrat, and that there is some reason to think that the blood of the Princes Gorchakov flowed in her veins.

I shall also say little about our cook Nikolai, a real pre-reform serf, dirty, often drunk, but good-natured and devoted to our family, or about his son Semion Nicolaevich, who also served as cook in our house for many years after his father (almost to the year of my mother's death in 1919), though there was nothing to be gained by doing so.

Very typical, too, were the two brothers Suvorov—Ivan and Vassili. Ivan, or *Jean le cuit* as we called him for some reason, was, like Alexei, one of the boys attached to the Tolstoy brothers by their aunt. Ivan knew some French, like Vaniusha in *The Cossacks* (he had been taught in the Caucasus by Leo and Nicholas) and at times he would pronounce very distinctly with a sly, proud look: '*C'est très joli; bonjour; la femme*'; etc. He continued to be a valet by profession but only occasionally served in our house.

Ivan's brother, Vassili, was a coppersmith and made samovars. He collected orders and material in Tula and worked on the separate parts of the samovars at home. He was a carefree person and a drunkard. Yet his wife, Pelageia, was remarkably energetic and hardworking; she was our laundress, washed all the linen from our house and at the same time found time to work for her numerous daughters and her dissolute husband. On the whole my memories about the Jassnaia Poliana servants are very mellow. I formed close friendships with some of those who were of my age.

My father's attitude to them was calm and controlled. I don't remember that he ever struck any of them or even raised his voice to them; he could of course be angry with them, but he restrained himself. My mother was not so self-controlled and sometimes lost her temper with them, but in spite of that had far less authority over them than my father.

I think that my earliest recollection is our trip to Moscow in the winter of 1866: I can see myself sitting with my mother and someone else in a closed box, the box is moving, we are thrown against its walls, and I feel sick. We were travelling to Serpukhov in a horse-drawn coach; the Moscow-Kursk railway was being built at the time and it functioned only from Moscow to Serpukhov. But I have a more vivid memory of our visit to Moscow in 1868; I remember the porch crumbling down in the house in which we were living; and that grandfather Bers was dying. I was afraid of him and was deeply moved by the suffering I could see on his face.

Two painful impressions of my early childhood are engraved on my memory. The first was in Tula where I saw a cart slowly moving along the street, with a high seat on which a woman in a convict's garb sat huddled. On her back was a poster which was inscribed in large letters: ' Husband killer '. In those days criminals were subjected to public exhibition of this sort. People ran after the cart and threw coppers on the high seat.

The second was my first experience of panic. I was an independent child, and one day I escaped supervision to explore new places, this time a meadow near the river Jassenka, where I saw a peasant leading a foal. Suddenly he stopped, pulled out a long knife and plunged it into the foal's neck. Crimson blood poured out like a stream, and I ran as fast as my legs would carry me. I was sure the peasant was a terrible monster who would knife me as well. At home they explained to me that he had killed the foal so that it should not sap the strength of its working mother.

In those days, tame bears which were led from village to village were a great entertainment. The appearance of one in Jassnaia Poliana was first of all heralded by the desperate barking of all the dogs of the neighbourhood. Then, approaching along the alley, came the leader with the bear on a chain, a ' goat ' and, usually, a boy. All the inhabitants came running to gather round them and then the performance started. The bear-leader issued commands, pulling the chain:

' Mikhail Ivanovich, make a bow to the masters.'

The bear grunted, rose on his hind legs and, clattering his chain, bowed deeply.

' Show how the priest's children steal the peas.'

The bear dropped down and crawled to the imaginary peas.

' Show how a young lady titivates herself.'

The bear got down on his haunches, a mirror was held up to him and he stroked his snout with his front paws.

' Drop dead!'

Grunting again, the bear lay down and remained motionless.

Then the bear would dance with the ' goat ', who was a man with a blanket over his head, out of which protruded a rattle. The rattle rattled, the leader or the boy would beat the drum and the bear and the ' goat ' danced. I could never understand why this disguise was called a ' goat '.

After the performance was over, it was usual to offer vodka to everybody, including the bear, which when he had drunk some of it, became very jovial and rolled over on his back and seemed to smile.

Of course the bear was amusing; but at the same time he was pathetic, with a ring in his cheek, his moth-eaten skin, and forever tied to a chain. In later years this entertainment was forbidden.

Our great distraction in the country was pedlars. There were two kinds: strolling pedlars and those who travelled in caravans. The first transported their meagre collection of stuff, chiefly haberdashery, on a pushcart. The others called themselves ' Hungarians '; their caravans were pulled by two horses and they brought whole shops with them: fabrics, both cotton and wool, shoes, ties, stationery, ribbons, buttons, etc., and even musical scores. Their wares were of good quality. I remember my father buying once the score of Strauss's *Accelerationen-Walzer* and playing it afterwards with great delight.

Up to 1871 a joyful, radiant atmosphere pervaded the house in Jassnaia Poliana. My parents were fairly well in health and on good terms with one another; Aunt Tatiana was still up and about and introduced a note of soft, old-world sentimentality into the family; we children were in the charge of Hannah Tardsey, whom we loved and who loved us; the guests and relations, Aunt Marie, her daughters and the Kusminski family made up a very lively company. It was the exciting time, when my father was writing *War and Peace*, and in the intervals supervised the estate and hunted, while my mother copied *War and Peace* over and over again, gave birth to and nursed children and was busy in the house. The following notes show how deeply engrossed my father was in his work and how intensely my mother also was working at the time.

On January 23rd, 1866, my father wrote half-jokingly to the poet Fet: ' I'm glad you like my wife. Though I love her less than my novel, she's my wife, you know, all the same.'

And my mother wrote to her sister (June 27th, 1866): ' I keep weaning or nursing or washing or boiling and apart from that there are the children, the pickling, the jam-making, the sweet-making, copying for Liova, but for *les beaux arts* and for reading, I can hardly spare a moment and then only if it is raining.'

It would be impossible to gather from these notes that there was any friction between my parents at that time. I was not the only one to consider that in the first years of their marriage my parents were an exceptionally united couple. Both my father's

9

and mother's relations thought the same. In her diary for 1864, Varia, my Aunt Marie's eldest daughter, wrote: 'Mamma told us that we shouldn't hurry to get married, that Sonia and Liova were an exemplary couple, but that they are hard to find and that all one hears about it a husband leaving his wife, or a wife divorcing her husband.' My mother's brother, Stepan Bers, wrote the following about his sister and brother-in-law: 'The mutual love and understanding between this couple have always been my ideal and model of marital bliss.' My grandparents used to say: 'Sonia couldn't wish for more happiness.' My father often used to write to his friends about his happy family life.

In September 1869 an event occurred which, it seems to me, played an important part in my father's life.

He went to Pensa with the intention of buying an estate and spent the night on the way in Arsamass in a bad hotel. He underwent there the indescribably dreary sensation which he called later the 'Arsamass misery'. He wrote to his mother on September 4th, 1869, 'I spent the night before last in Arsamass and something remarkable happened to me. It was two o'clock in the morning, I was very tired, I wanted to sleep and I had no pain. But suddenly such a dreary sensation overcame me as I had never felt before. I'll tell you the details of it later, but I had never felt anything like it and hope never to feel it again. I jumped up, ordered the horses to be harnessed. While they were doing that I fell asleep and woke up quite restored. Yesterday the same feeling returned in a much smaller degree during the journey, but I was prepared and didn't succumb to it, especially as it wasn't so intense.'

I wouldn't undertake to explain the reason of the 'Arsamass misery', but it seems to me that there was something unhealthy about it. Perhaps it was a liver complaint, from which he suffered constantly, perhaps—mental exhaustion. The 'Arsamass misery' passed and did not disturb the active and cheerful run of life in Jassnaia Poliana.

1871

From this year my recollections become clearer and I will put them down in chronological order.

I remember how in 1871 we looked at illustrations representing the French being shot by the Germans and how my father's and all our sympathy were with the French.

At the beginning of the year clouds gathered on the Jassnaia Poliana sky. On February 12th my mother gave birth prematurely to a delicate, blonde little girl, Masha, and was struck with puerperal fever. Her head was shaved and a wet-nurse was engaged for Masha. My father was gloomy, he did not feel well; he was afraid of consumption and in the spring went to Samara to drink mare's milk with his brother-in-law, Stepan Bers.

Stepan Bers, one of my mother's younger brothers, was educated in the Law School. He spent all his holidays in Jassnaia Poliana, from 1866 when he was eleven years old up to 1878 when he finished at the School. He was an alert and physically strong boy and worshipped my father. He was only eight years older than I and treated me with condescension, but as a friend. I liked him, but his unreasonably quick temper put me off at times.

On his return from Samara my father recovered completely. Mare's milk always did him a lot of good. He and Stepan spoke enthusiastically of their Robinson Crusoe life in a Bashkir caravan. My mother's health had also improved.

In the same year the new building of the wing to the house in Jassnaia Poliana was started. The plan was to add a large room to it and make two rooms in the basement below. Up to then the house in which we lived was one of two quite similar wings and on the northern side three small rooms with a covered terrace over them had been added. Now my father decided to make a two-storied additional building on the other, the southern, side. According to tradition my father wanted to wall into the foundation a golden coin and as he had none at the moment, he took from me a golden sovereign given to me by Hannah. He had it walled in, behind the backs of the builders, while they were eating, and afterwards made up the money to me.

The building turned out to be successful, one of the rooms below served as a hall and the other one was for a long time my father's study.

In the autumn my great-grandfather on my mother's side, Alexandr Isleniev, arrived at Jassnaia Poliana. He was a very young-looking old man of seventy-eight, tall, bald, clean-shaven, with large features, brisk movements and the manners of a pampered gentleman. He was the prototype of Nikolenka's father in my father's *Childhood* and *Boyhood*. My father was very polite and respectful to him and in order to remind him of the past, organised a hunt with hounds. Although I was a little more than eight years old at that time, I could ride quite well and was taken to the hunt. I was given a big, quiet horse called Kashkirian —after his place of origin. My father had taught me and my brothers to ride without a saddle and stirrups so as to learn to keep our balance. He also considered that it was less dangerous to fall from an unsaddled horse. So I went to the hunt riding on a saddle-cloth, tied up with a strap. My father, great-grandfather, two other sportsmen and I spread out across the fields, at a certain distance from one another, in order to start up a hare or a fox.

As I circled away from the others, behind a wide swamp, and was wondering how I should ever get back to them I suddenly heard cries coming from their side: Tally ho! Tally ho! Someone had raised a hare and the pursuit began. My father, great-grandfather and the other two galloped after the hounds and the hare and, at the sight of the chase, my Kashkirian, who had known many a hunt, started without further ado to gallop straight across the swamp. He almost sank in the slime, got through to the other side with a great effort and then, feeling his feet on firm ground, suddenly stopped short. He had evidently lost his breath in the endeavour and stopped to recover it. But I failed to keep my seat and flew over his head.

The Kashkirian was big and I was small; there were no stirrups and without help I was unable to mount him again. So I had to walk, leading the Kashkirian. The others had disappeared behind the hillock and when I reached them at last, the chase was over, the hare had been caught, killed and fastened to the saddle. This was my first real hunt—and, what is more, with my great-grandfather—and I hadn't been able to see anything! I was in despair.

I spent the winter of 1871–72 in already quite strenuous study. My mother taught me Russian and French, a little history and geography, and to play the piano; Hannah Tardsey gave me English lessons and my father—also Russian (but no grammar) and arithmetic. At that time he was composing his *Alphabet* and tried it out on us children. He told us the stories and made us re-tell them in our own words. They were mainly stories that were afterwards included in his *Books for Reading Aloud*. He considered himself to have no talent for mathematics and therefore to be a good teacher of them. He used to say that as he had absorbed his knowledge of mathematics with great difficulty, it had sunk deep enough and remained so clear in his memory that he was able to give adequate explanations. In teaching as in everything else, he searched for new methods. He taught us for instance to count on the abacus. He made us learn the multiplication tables by heart only up to five. We multiplied from six to ten on our fingers, in the following manner: the figure five had to be extracted from each multiplier, the remainder to be kept on the bent finger of both hands. The bent fingers when added up, would form so many tens of the total. Then the remaining fingers of both hands had to be multiplied and added to the tens. For example, to multiply 7 by 9: by subtracting 5 from both figures you get 2 and 4. You bend two fingers on one hand, four on the other. Adding them up you get 6. Those are the tens, making 60. The other unbent fingers are multiplied: 1 by 3 = 3. Thus you get the final answer: $7 \times 9 = 60 + 3 = 63$.

I don't remember whether it was then or later that my father set us his favourite popular sum about the geese: a herd of geese comes flying, another goose is met on the way. The goose says: ' Hullo, you hundred geese!' The geese reply: ' We are not one hundred geese, but we would be one hundred if we were that and once more that and then half that and then a quarter that and you into the bargain.' This sum, easily solved algebraically, is more difficult to do arithmetically. ($100 = x + x + \frac{x}{2} + \frac{x}{4} + 1 = x = 36$.)

1872

At the end of 1871 and the beginning of 1872, there was great animation in Jassnaia Poliana. D. A. Diakov arrived with his daughter and her governess ' Sophèche ', Aunt Marie with her children—Varia, Lisa and Nikolai—and Uncle Kostia Islavin. We were for ever on sleighs, enjoying it most when we capsized. We had fancy dress parties during Christmastide. D. Diakov dressed up as a bear-leader, Uncle Kostia, with his sheepskin turned inside out, walking on all fours, represented the bear, my father was the ' goat '. Nicholai Tolstoy dressed up as an old woman, Sophèche as an old hunchback with a beard. All the people of the estate crowded into the hall and danced to the sound of *Barinia*, duets played on the piano and afterwards to the harmonica. My mother dressed me in a girl's blue dress, pinned something like a powdered wig on to my hair and I was to be a *marquise*. Sister Tania was dressed as a man, also in blue, and was the *marquis*. We danced an intricate polka which my mother had taught us, but the success of it was doubtful: the *marquise* costumes and intricate polka somehow didn't tally with the usual type of Christmas entertainment in Jassnaia Poliana.

On May 14th my father went to our other estate, Nikolskoe, and took me with him. It made a great impression on me. The thick forests, the deep ravines, the hilly fields, the ancient poplars and a magnificent fir-tree in the apple orchard, the river running into space and sparkling between the trees, the steady beat of a watermill, the long view on the river, the wooded slopes, the far away villages and church spires, the huge stones on the highest spots of the estate—all this was new to me and seemed remarkably beautiful, which, indeed, it was. Owing to my extreme youth I paid no heed to the poverty of the peasants at Nikolskoe: all I saw were the old-fashioned home-woven dresses of the women, their linen petticoats, their embroidered shirts, the head-dress and the ribbons in their ears instead of earrings.

My father drove round the whole estate examining particularly the conditions of the forests, and on the whole seemed satisfied with the bailiff, Orlov.

On our return to Jassnaia Poliana, on the road to the station Chern, we saw a distressing scene in one of the villages: an old dog sitting on the site of a smouldering fire, amidst burning beams, heaps of bricks, coal and ash. It was a brown dog with white spots and long hanging ears and it wailed, its head thrown up in the air. The house and the whole family with it had just burned down, so we learnt, and all that was left alive was the old dog.

While father was in Nikolskoe, an accident had taken place in Jassnaia Poliana: a bull had gored the shepherd. The story went that the bull had gone wild and begun attacking people because a boy had teased him. One day it rushed at the boy and the old shepherd, unafraid, hit it with a whip. Then the bull turned on the shepherd, chased him and nailed him to a tree. The shepherd died the same day and the bull was killed.

There was a lawsuit as a result. The young judge issued an order that my father should not leave the estate until the trial. He was 'liberal-minded' and enjoyed demonstrating his power over a rich landowner and a count. My father was enraged by the order and lodged a complaint demanding that the order be annulled. He had to pay a fine of one hundred roubles but the judge's order was cancelled.

That summer the Kusminskis (Aunt Tania with her husband and their three small daughters) went to the Caucasus. Kusminski, who had been assistant public prosecutor in Tula up to then, had been transferred to Kutaiss. Jassnaia was empty all the summer. My mother felt particularly strongly the absence of her favourite sister.

In July my father went again for a few weeks for a cure of mare's milk.

In the autumn a great change occurred in the life of us children. Hannah Tardsey began to cough and lose weight: she had caught consumption. My mother decided to send her to some place with a warmer climate. At that time the Kusminskis were looking for a governess for their children. They asked Hannah to come and she left in the autumn for Kutaiss. I still have an affectionate letter from her from Kutaiss describing her journey: she was particularly surprised at the passengers (herself included) being actually thrown from the boat in Poti, into Turkish feluggas.

A short time after Hannah's departure, we boys (I was nine years old, Ilya six and Liova three) got a German tutor, or rather supervisor, Fedor Fedorovich, recommended by the poet Fet. He was a semi-educated man about thirty-five. He wore a wig, which he carefully but unsuccessfully tried to conceal. He stayed with us for two years. An English governess, Miss Dora, was engaged for our sisters. She stayed a short time in Jassnaia, but long enough to conquer the heart of Fedor Fedorovich.

In the winter of 1872–73 my father tried out the experiment of the so-called Lancaster education. I, my sister Tania and even my brother Ilya, who was not yet seven, were entrusted with teaching the village children to read and write. Uncle Kostia also taught them. The children came to our house, we gave our lessons each to our own group, in the hall and the rooms adjoining it. The experiment was rather successful. My pupils and my sister Tania's did learn the elementary rudiments of reading and writing. Ilya, however, was too small and for the most part fought with his pupils. In our leisure hours between lessons we had great fun playing on improvised toboggans with our pupils. They, in their turn, were our teachers at that sport. We loved to scramble on a long board belonging to a deaf and dumb man, Makarov; seven of us found room on it and drove at great speed down the slope and rolled with shrieks of laughter into the snow at the bottom of the hill.

Such close contact with our contemporaries in the village created a friendly relationship with them, which continued all our lives.

1873

This was the year when Aunt Tatiana seemed suddenly to grow very old and frail. She moved from her room on the second floor near the living-room into a small room on the ground floor, in the wooden wing. She said to my father: ' I'll move there so as not to spoil your nice top room by dying in it.'

Aunt Tatiana felt a particular affection for me, her godson, and demanded that I should visit her in her room at least once a day; but these visits bored me and I tried to avoid them in spite of the sweets that were offered me.

I felt ashamed when a day passed and I hadn't been to see my aunt. I remember one evening lying in bed and going through my agony of remorse which was mixed with the emotion pro- duced in me by music—my father was playing something very beautiful on the piano in the hall on the second floor.

On May 31st the disaster of the previous year was repeated in Jassnaia: another bull gored the cowman. The bull was chained in his stable and the cowman, as he fed him, very imprudently stood in front of him. The bull got angry for some reason and butted him in the stomach with his horns. The cowman rushed out of the cowhouse holding his intestines with both hands; he developed peritonitis and died three days later. My father was greatly upset by his death and from then on his interest in cattle breeding waned. He wasn't sued this time but generously com- pensated the family of the dead cowman.

On June 2nd Fedor Fedorovich, Stepan Bers, Nanny and Serge Arbusov and I went to the estate near Samara which my father had recently acquired. He had bought these eighteen hundred dessiatines* for eight roubles a dessiatine on the money he made out of his books.

We went through Moscow to Nijhni by train and from Nijhni to Samara by boat. The great spaces of water, the dark forest slopes, the yellow sand beaches, the spray that splashed up from the ship's wheels, the fish and the smell of fish, the trading at the ports, the different types of vessels, barges, cargo boats and rafts—all these were new and vivid impressions.

There was no railroad further than Samara and we had to travel one hundred and twenty versts* by road to the estate. Shortly before our journey an old friend of my father, Sergei Urussov, in order to make the journey easier for my mother, presented her with his large *dormeuse* that seated six people. It was the classical vehicle of these times, in which our ancestors travelled before the railroad existed. It was pulled by six horses—two in front and four in a row behind; a boy, the so-called *Vorreiter*, rode on one of the front horses. A kind of trunk was fixed on the roof of the carriage; behind was a two-seated bench, and the coachman's seat was large enough to hold three people. In the carriage sat all our women with the youngest children, the others drove in wicker carts with straw carriage-bodies. Halfway we stopped for the night in a large hut where we suffered greatly from bedbugs. I don't remember whether it was the first time or later that Hannah Tardsey came to stay with us near Samara from Kutaiss. My parents had invited her to undergo a cure of mare's milk for her lungs.

Our house there was like a large peasant's hut. There was not enough room in it for all of us; so Fedor Fedorovich, my two brothers and I spent the summer in an empty shed, and my father and Stepan Bers in a Bashkir caravan, a sort of felt tent, which my father had bought.

At that time the Samara steppe was still practically uncultivated. The rich, deep black earth was covered with thick grass, various herbs, feather grass, spear grass, wormwood and oats. Brown buzzards as large as turkeys flew over the steppe, large white-beaked eagles and hawks soared everywhere, reed-sparrows fluttered about noisily and the air was filled with the prattle of

*A dessiatine is about two acres, a verst about two kilometres.

17

grasshoppers. In spite of the intense heat, it was easy to breathe on the steppe; the air was dry and even on the hottest days there was a breeze.

Our property was divided into twelve fields of which only two were sown: the first, on hard soil, with Turkish wheat, the second with Russian wheat. Sometimes corn would be sown in the third year. The other nine or ten fields were left for pastures and meadows. The first two years after ploughing, the fields were overgrown with coarse, wild grass, but the next years they gave very good hay. The hay was gathered into stacks spread all over the steppe. There was no wood in that neighbourhood, and bricks of dried manure were used for fuel. Pyramids of these bricks were stacked around the villages and huts.

My mother was at that time nursing Peter and she bore with difficulty the discomforts of life on the farm. The house was draughty, the roof leaked, the bricks stank and burnt badly, the incredible number of flies made eating and sleeping a misery, the post came rarely, and had to be fetched by messenger from Samara. There were no neighbours, except Bashkirs and peasants, and the doctor lived far away.

My father, on the contrary, enjoyed this primitive life. To provide the mare's milk, an old Bashkir, whom my father knew from his former trips, came to stay. His name was Mukhamed-shah Rakhmatullin. He put up his felt tent close to the house and brought ten milking mares. They fed in the steppe and their foals were tied up near the tent. Mukhamedshah himself didn't work, his wife and daughter-in-law managed all the house chores, milked the mares, hung and shook the mare's milk, which turned in large leather bottles into *kumiss*. These women lived behind a curtain, which cut off a third of the tent. When men came to see Mukhamedshah the women hid behind the curtain. Mukhamed-shah, a handsome old man, who looked like a hawk, in an oriental cap and a silk Bukhara dressing-gown, under which one could see a clean white shirt, stepped softly in his oriental shoes, welcomed guests, shaking their hands with both of his, sat down on the carpet, arranged a cushion behind the guest's back and offered *kumiss* from cups made of birch bark. There were no chairs or tables in the tent, only carpets, but it was clean and cosy.

Mukhamedshah was an intelligent and, in his way, a well-educated man. He could speak Arabic, read the Koran, and he had perfect manners and a great deal of tact. His favourite subject of conversation was how the Bashkirs used to live in the old days and how much worse they lived now. In the old days each had his tent, now they lived the year round in huts; before they had had large herds of horses, now there were some who had none; before, dozens of caravans gathered at weddings and feasts; they ate several horses and many sheep; they organised races, drank *kumiss* to the full, sang, played on the flute and on a sort of horn that was put down a man's throat as he lay on his back.

My father liked the original, beautiful way of life of this nomad people, now dying out. He said that it reeked of Herodotus, but he saw that it was being rapidly supplanted by the way of life of the Russian peasant-labourer.

I was always surprised at the way the Samara peasants husbanded their soil. All their efforts were concentrated on sowing as much wheat as possible. They sowed little corn, and no oats or hemp, no vegetables or potatoes. Therefore if there was a bad crop of wheat, which depended on whether it rained in May, they not only suffered great losses but even hunger. It was an irregular form of agriculture.

The peasants were all ' state peasants ', that is, for a long time they had not experienced serfdom under landowners. This showed in their confident and independent attitude to us. They did not treat us as masters, but as rich farmers; they shook hands with us, invited us to visit them and were completely at their ease. As early as 1871 my father wrote about them that ' the simplicity, honesty, naïvety and intelligence of these people are very attractive '. We became close friends with some of the peasants. Among them was Vassili Nikitin, a steady, sensible, garrulous man, of about sixty, with a red beard and lots of freckles on his face and arms. He would visit us and we would return the visit to him, drinking innumerable cups of tea. Some of his mannerisms were incorporated in the peasant in *Fruits of Enlightenment*.

We bought our provisions at a market, where during the harvest there was a crowd of workmen, who had come from some distance to offer their services. The wage for working a dessiatine of land was determined on the spot and varied greatly—from three to twenty-five roubles according to the harvest.

The year 1873 was a very poor one for the harvest and so the wage was low. The following winter there was famine in Samara and my father sent out an appeal for help for the starving population. The appeal attracted the attention both of society and the State and over two million roubles were collected.

In the summer my father organised races on the farm, like the ancient Bashkir races. I won't write about these because the races which my father organised in 1875 were much more spectacular than the first and put them in the shade.*

Apart from the races, the chief events of that summer were the digging of a hill where some remains of a Scythian tomb were found and also the triumph of Fedor Fedorovich who killed a buzzard; this is a very rare occurrence, as these birds are very alert and seldom allow anyone to approach as close as that. At the end of the summer we returned to Jassnaia.

In the autumn the painter Kramskoy came to Jassnaia. P. Tretiakov had commissioned him to paint a portrait of my father for his gallery. Kramskoy lived five versts away from Jassnaia and came to us every day. My mother commissioned another portrait of my father for the house in Jassnaia and it is still there. My father did not like sitting, and Kramskoy, modest as he was, did not like to insist. My mother told me that, in fact, he never completed the portrait ordered by Tretiakov, that he finished only the head and to paint the rest of the body had to fill father's grey blouse with tow.

On November 9th my brother Peter died of croup. My mother was deeply upset by this first death of a child. She wrote to her brother Stepan, Peter's godfather, on November 18th; 'Our little Petia died on November 9th. His voice grew very hoarse and he died two days later, very quietly passed from sleep to death, almost indistinguishably and quietly. All my joy went with him, as if the light had gone out, everything seemed stifling and dark.'

1874

Our family went on living their busy, quiet life throughout the winter of 1873–74. My father was working on *Anna Karenina* and particularly *The Alphabet*.

Reading Aesop's fables in the original, he compared them with

*See page 23.

those of La Fontaine, not to the advantage of the latter. He used to say that there was a lot that was superfluous and artificial in La Fontaine, whereas Aesop was a model of succinctness. For instance, in La Fontaine's fable a crow holds a piece of cheese in its beak. La Fontaine needed the cheese for the rhyme:*fromage* and *plumage*. Krilov, who did not know Greek, also wrote about the crow and the cheese. Yet neither crow nor fox are likely to feed on cheese. Aesop did the right thing: he wrote that the crow was holding in its beak a piece of meat.

We three elder children, I, Tania and Ilya, had our lessons according to a weekly schedule, taught by mother, Fedor Fedorovich and the English governess, Miss Emily. We called Leo and Masha the little ones and did not allow them to take part in our games. Leo always tried to butt in but we all, and I in patricular, kept him away, teased him and called him ' Milksop with gravy ', because he had one day poured some gravy over his clothes. At that time Leo, or Lelia as we called him, was a pretty boy with chestnut curls; he was Fedor Fedorovich's favourite and Ilya and I were jealous. Masha was an ugly, pale, delicate little girl; she played an insignificant part in our family life, and our mother liked her less than the other children; she was a sort of Cinderella.

My father used to spend a lot of time with us; he taught us mathematics and composition, but never gave us abstract subjects to write about. I remember he once told me to describe Uncle Kostia and I didn't know how to do it.

In the evenings he told us stories, read aloud *The Children of Captain Grant, Journey to the Moon* and other books by Jules Verne in their illustrated editions. We loved these stories.

In the spring we got the news that Hannah Tardsey had married the Georgian Prince Matchudatze and was to remain in the Caucasus. On April 22nd my brother Nicholas was born.

Aunt Tatiana was gradually leaving this life. Towards the summer she kept entircly to her bed. While still conscious, she was sweet and friendly with everybody. She died on June 20th, at the age of seventy-nine; she passed away very quietly, as my mother wrote to her brother. Shortly before her death, her maid Aksinia died.

After Aunt's death her friend Natalia Okhotnitskaia left our house to live on Turgenev's estate, in an old people's hostel which he had founded, where she died. With the departure of these old women our house lost the special, old-fashioned, pre-reform, gentle, if rather musty atmosphere which they brought into our lives.

In July my father went again to our Samara farm and took me with him, which delighted me, of course. On this trip I was surprised to hear my father reprimand a local peasant very angrily for appropriating about thirteen dessiatines to his plot. Altogether the affairs on the farm were not too prosperous. My father had appointed an ignorant peasant, Timofei, as bailiff and he proved totally inadequate. My Uncle Sergei used to say about it: 'Leo can allow himself the luxury of taking on bad bailiffs; for instance, Timofei will cause him one thousand roubles damage; Leo will describe him in a book and receive two thousand roubles for the description—so he'll be one thousand to the good. I can't allow myself such luxury.'

We stayed a short time in Samara and returned to Jassnaia in August.

At the end of October my sister Tania, running along a polished parquet floor, slipped, fell and broke her collar-bone. My father took her at once to the doctor in Moscow, and she soon recovered; there were no bad consequences from her fall.

My mother went on nursing Nicholas this autumn, but felt poorly.

1875

In this year my father continued to work on *Anna Karenina* and *The Alphabet* and also devoted some time to music. At one time he used to play the piano for about three hours a day: sonatas of Mozart, Haydn, Weber, some of Beethoven's sonatas, some Schubert and Chopin. He also played duets with my mother: symphonies, overtures and quartets by Haydn, Mozart, Beethoven and Mendelssohn.

On February 20th, after two weeks of suffering, my youngest brother Nicholas, aged ten months, died of meningitis.

In the winter of 1875 my father's aunt, who was destitute, came from the Tula convent where she had been living, to live in Jassnaia in the room below, where Aunt Tatiana had died. She was seventy-six years old, and very capricious; she demanded a lot of nursing and was constantly ailing.

In the early summer of that year, the whole family and Stepan Bers went again to the Samara farm. Again Mukhamedshah came with his mares and foals, his old wife, his daughter-in-law and grandson Hasis, and settled down near by. The chief events of that summer were the journey to Busuluk, the races and the attempt made by the Kirghiz to steal our horses.

On June 29th there was always a fair in Busuluk. My father went there partly to buy mares for the stud-farm he intended to start, partly because he liked to see new places. My mother, Stepan and we three older children went with him. My impressions of this trip were: a bad hotel with bedbugs, brown ewes with funny crinolines on their backs, herds of untrained horses, their wild galloping, the ardent, hoarse voices of the Bashkirs and the Kirghiz; general animation and dust, dust, dust. Behind Busuluk was a monastery where a hermit, a simple peasant, lived in a cave he had dug himself. My father was very much interested in him and talked to him at length.

At the end of the summer my father informed the Bashkirs as well as the other people living in the neighbourhood that on August 6th, his Saint's Day, he would organise races on a course of fifty versts. The prizes were: a young bull, a gun, a watch, a Bashkir gown. A great crowd foregathered; the whole steppe was agog. The grey Bashkir caravans sprang up on it like large mushrooms, carts and wicker carriages stood about with the shafts raised in the air, horses grazed on the meadows, bonfires burned and Bashkirs, mounted and on foot, roamed around. To feed them my father gave a fat, limping foal and a few sheep; *kumiss* flowed in abundance and the Bashkirs rejoiced like children, played the flute and the horn, sang and danced and talked endlessly.

Before the races my father suggested to those who wanted, to fight and tug with a stick. I and my friend, Timrot, the son of a neighbouring farmer, began the competition. He was victorious which was a cruel disappointment to me. This is how one tugs with a stick: you sit down opposite each other, heels touching: each grasps the stick with both hands and tries to lift the other. My father lifted everyone except the fat village elder; he couldn't lift him simply because the elder weighed no less than ten *pouds* (four hundred pounds).

On an even place in the steppe a circle of five versts was

23

marked out with a deep furrow, which had to be raced round ten times. Thirty-two horses were in the race, among them one of ours, four or five belonging to Russian peasants, and the rest were Bashkir horses. The jockeys were young boys who were distinguished by the various coloured kerchiefs they wore round their heads.

The organisation of the race was not very efficient. When the horses had already started, my father moved the finish to a considerable distance from the start (so that the distance should be exactly fifty versts) and this upset the calculations of the participants. Then the mounted Bashkirs who were not in the races dashed about the circle, encouraging their horses and bewildering the others. Only seven horses reached the end, the others having moved out of the circle. The first prize was won by a Bashkir horse that had raced the distance in one hour thirty-nine minutes; the second winner was our horse; the other prizes were won again by Bashkir horses and only one Russian horse got a prize. The Russians were disgruntled and said that the Bashkirs had upset their horses. But on the whole a lot of fun was had by all.

My father had planned to have a large stud at the Samara farm. By crossing trained English and Russian trotters with wild Kirghiz, Kalmik and Bashkir animals it was hoped to get strong, enduring horses, particularly suitable for cavalry. The conditions in the Samara steppes for such a stud were very favourable. The steppe hay, grown on almost virgin soil, was as nourishing as oats, and there were plenty of meadows. To fulfil this plan my father bought several beautiful pedigree horses and a great number of steppe mares.

One evening, towards the end of the summer, the grooms who were looking after the grazing horses, came tearing home to the farm with the news that some Kirghiz men had pounced on the horses and galloped away with about forty of them. The method of the Kirghiz horse-thieves was to chase the horses behind the Ural—about two hundred versts away—regardless of the fact that some of the animals could not survive such a distance; for behind the Ural it was impossible to retrieve the stolen horses.

The farm was alarmed. A chase was organised on the remaining horses. Several Russian grooms went with them and the Bashkir Lutai, a good, primitive man and a ' tough ' who was not with the horses, but at home when they were stolen. The Kirghiz were caught. Lutai, with wild cries, quite fearless, rushed upon them. There was a fight with whips, Lutai was badly beaten up, but the Kirghiz left the horses and galloped off.

The wheat crop that year was good. During the harvest the harvesters lived for whole weeks on the steppe. It was a tremendously busy scene, with tents, horses, bonfires. Some of the harvesters came from long distances. There was an old Tartar who had come on foot from Kazan, one thousand versts away, with his wife, a little girl of eight with a mouth askew, and a suckling baby whom he and his wife pushed all this distance in a little cart. My mother took an interest in this family and helped them with food and clothes. One day she gave the little girl a bun; she liked it so much that every time she met my mother she would say: ' Auntie, give bun.'

At that time the watchman at the farm was also an old, bedraggled, dirty and good-natured Tartar Babai. In the evenings he sang his Tartar songs and banged an old pail with a stick. Sometimes he would come to Mukhamedshah, stop timidly at the door of his caravan, pray as befits a Moslem, holding his hands over his face, and greet him respectfully. Mukhamedshah would tell him to sit down and offer him mare's milk. When he saw this, my father said: ' How reverently the Moslems keep the laws of hospitality. Mukhamedshah, an aristocrat by comparison, tells the beggar, Babai, to sit down and offers him refreshments. We Christians don't behave like that with beggars.'

In August we returned to Jassnaia.

My mother was pregnant and feeling very ill. She had a sort of fever and in the autumn we were all stricken with whooping cough and she caught it from us.

I remember an odd event connected with that period. My father usually washed and undressed in the room under the sitting-room, which had been his study. Then, in his dressing-gown, he would go to the bedroom he shared with my mother. I and my brother Ilya slept at that time in the room between the pantry and the vaulted room. One autumn night I woke up about midnight hearing my father's desperate screams: ' Sonia, Sonia!' I peeped out of the door. The hall was dark. He screamed again. I walked out into the hall and heard my mother running down the stairs with a candle.

Very upset, she asked: ' What happened, Levochka?'

He replied: ' Nothing. I lost my way.'

After that my mother had a bad attack of whooping, with wheezing and breathlessness and for a long time she was unable to settle down. It turned out that my father had no matches and passing from his study upstairs he lost his way in the hall. I can't explain this otherwise than by a pathological condition. Evidently on that night he was in the state of mind which he called the ' Arsamass misery '.

Soon after that my mother had to take to her bed. The conscientious doctor Knertzer, who came from Tula, found that she was suffering from some kind of fever as her temperature rose every day, and filled her with quinine which seemed to do her no good. Then my father wrote to Dr. Zakharin asking him either to come himself or to send a good doctor from Moscow. Zakharin sent his assistant Chirkov. Knertzer's diagnosis proved to be wrong. Chirkov diagnosed peritonitis, prescribed an appropriate treatment and my mother's condition improved immediately. But owing to this illness she gave premature birth to a girl, Varia, on November 1st, who lived only for an hour.

On December 22nd my father's aunt Pelagea, who lived below in the wing, died at the age of seventy-seven. Her death was caused by a fall when she was hanging something in her room. She died in great suffering and kept saying to my mother: ' *Je suis si bien chez vous, je ne veux pas mourir.*'

My father was the one who was the most affected by her death. He wrote to A. Tolstoy in March 1876: ' It is strange, but the death of this old woman has affected me more than any other death. I will miss her, miss this last memory of the past generation of my father, my mother. I couldn't bear to see her suffer. But in this death there is also something else, which I can't describe to you, but one day will tell you about it. Not an hour passes without my thinking about her. It is all right for you believers but more difficult for us.'

Beginning with this autumn a music teacher, A. Michurin, started coming once a week to Jassnaia to give piano lessons to me, Tania and Ilya. Michurin was the son of a serf musician who taught himself to play the piano and the fiddle. The son played unimaginatively and coldly, but he loved music and was a conscientious teacher. He was a quick-tempered man and though I liked my music lessons, his irritability sent me into a sort of torpor. When I made a mistake he would pull my hands from the keys and say: 'Begin again.' When I repeated my mistake he said: 'Don't gaze at the keys with a vacant look, play the piece again.' I felt lost, muddled, and then he would stop the lesson and give me homework to do for a week ahead, during which week I played without anybody to direct me, and not only what he had given me to do.

During the school year of 1875–76 my father read to us Jules Verne's book *Round the World in Eighty Days*. That book was not illustrated and he added the illustrations himself, much to our delight. He did not draw very well, but his drawings were original. We loved them and waited impatiently for the next instalment. We were greatly intrigued as to whether Mr. Fogg would win his bet or not.

1876

During the winter of 1875–76 my father continued to work on *Anna Karenina*, played the piano a great deal and busied himself with the organisation of a teachers' seminar. Unfortunately his original scheme for a teachers' seminar did not materialise. His idea was to recruit and train village teachers from among the local peasants. Such teachers, living at home and continuing to work their land would content themselves with small salaries and would not strive to change their profession of teaching for something more profitable at the first opportunity.

I worked quite diligently at Latin, Greek and French with M. Rey, had Russian lessons, history and geography with my mother, mathematics with my father. My father decided to put my knowledge to the test and asked the director of a school in Tula to let me pass a trial written examination from the third to the fourth class in five subjects. I passed my examinations in Russian, mathematics, Greek and French, but got a bad mark for Latin. Those were my first examinations and after that I had some every spring with the schoolboys of Tula. My father took a great interest in them. He wrote on May 12th to Fet: 'I'm greatly taken up with Serejha's examinations that begin on the 27th.' For me they were a great event because here for the first time I made friends with boys of my own age. I greatly enjoyed that, but was upset when they treated me with a certain condescension, though they were quite friendly too.

My father, fearing that they might teach me some vice, warned me not to get too intimate with any of them except one boy, the son of Count Dmitri Tatishchev, with whom I became close friends but not for long. That fine boy died about two years after I came to know him. He fell under a train by accident, the wheels cut off both his legs and he died soon afterwards. Later I made friends with two other schoolboys, Khitrovo and Blioklov. Khitrovo played the fiddle and loved music passionately. Later he became a convinced democrat, in spite of being the son of a policeman; he died young. Blioklov became a radical and a local government statistician near Tver.

Apart from these two, I had another friend in Tula two years older than myself, Baron Anton Delvig, nephew of the poet. Our families were also on friendly terms. The Delvigs were a patriarchal, traditional, orthodox, provincial landowner's family of modest means. The family consisted of the father, the younger brother of the poet, his wife, an energetic little woman, a good housewife and the jealous mother of two daughters, of my friend, Anton, who was called the Turk at school because of his corpulence, and of three younger brothers. The Delvigs came to Jassnaia, and we went to Tula; we gave amateur performances with them, played rounders and other games, but there was no real intimacy between us.

From 1876 the Kusminskis began coming to us again every summer and lived independently in one of the wings. My cousin Varia came with her husband, Hippolite, and the latter's brother, Nicholas Nagornov. He was a virtuoso on the fiddle, not well-known in Russia but very successful abroad, especially in Italy. His powerful, deep way of interpreting music was one of my most vivid musical impressions. I remember his interpretation of the *Mazurka* and *Legend* by Weniavsky, Mozart's sonatas, particularly the delightful *adagio* in the G Flat sonata, the sonatinas of Schubert and Weber and the *Kreutzer Sonata*. In the easier pieces my father played the piano part and in the more difficult ones, Aunt Masha or Michurin. My father did not like Nagornov as an individual. I remember how angry he was when Nagornov, after having drunk too much, drove to a hunt with some other sportsmen, and shot a dog in the middle of the village because it

28

was pursuing our setter. The owners of the dog came to complain after Nagornov had left and my father had to pay compensation. Nagornov resembled the character of Trukhachevsky in my father's novel, *The Kreutzer Sonata,* and I am certain that he thought of him when he was writing it.

On September 3rd my father took his nephew Nicholas and left for the Samara farm, and from there went to Orenburg to buy horses. In Orenburg he saw the governor-general whom he had known at Sebastopol. He also became acquainted there with a merchant, Deiev, who traded with Turkestan. Deiev took 'a great fancy to him and presented him with a tiger's skin which my father gave to my sister Tania when he returned to Jassnaia. My father told us that Deiev's grandfather had made his fortune selling Russian girls to Central Asiatic harems.

In the spring of 1877 I had to have sixteen oral and written examinations in order to pass from the fourth into the fifth class and was working hard for them. From September onwards we worked according to a schedule, from six to eight hours a day. Now and then there were digressions: my brother Ilya and I would go for a day's shooting or take a walk after luncheon that lasted more than the preordained time. But on the whole we kept to the schedule. In the evenings my father read to us in French *Les Trois Mousquetaires* by Alexandre Dumas, omitting the passages unsuitable for children. We listened to him eagerly.

In the autumn the atmosphere in Jassnaia became gloomy. On September 15th my mother wrote to her sister: ' The snow has covered all the ground here and life has become dark and horrid. I am trying to tear myself away, but I don't know if I'll succeed. Leo is constantly disappointing me, constantly throwing cold water on my enthusiasms. That is probably why I have ceased to seek joy in the more serious interests I used to pursue, but interest myself only in momentary, trifling things, so long as they bring me joy for a few minutes. Leo keeps saying that everything for him is finished, that death is near, that nothing can bring him any more pleasure, that he has nothing more to expect from life. What joys can there be without him?'

As soon as the ponds froze Tania, Ilya, Leo, our two teachers and two governesses and I began to skate. Sometimes out parents joined us and also the boys of the village. We chased one another, jumped over sticks, rolled down the ice-hill on the pond, and there was much laughter and shouting. At the beginning of November Leo almost got drowned, falling through an ice-hole, on a spot where the ice was not thick enough. He was dragged out by the village women who were rinsing clothes nearby.

In December my father went to Moscow where he became acquainted with Tchaikovsky.

At Christmas there was a tree, as usual, many guests and fancy dress parties.

1877

The second part of the winter of 1876-77 passed uneventfully except for an accident out skating which almost cost me my life. Tania, Ilya and I swept several paths on the snow-covered pond and on January 23rd chased one another on skates. At one of the corners, trying to elude Tania, I butted into her and we both fell down. She was not hurt, but I struck my head so violently against the ice that I lost consciousness and began to have convulsions. I was carried home unconscious, ice-packs were applied to my head and a leech behind the ear. When I woke up after sleeping twenty-four hours I had completely lost my memory which, however, I recovered after a short time.

My father's health was on the decline at the beginning of the year. My mother wrote her sister: ' He has constant headaches and his blood pressure is very high. He went to Zakharin, who applied leeches, but his condition didn't improve. Though he looks well— that is, his complexion is pink—and has an appetite, his hands are cold and he gets tired as soon as he goes for a walk. He starts up in his sleep and I'm afraid of a stroke. According to Zakharin that is not impossible.'

In the winter my father read Xenophon's *Anabasis* with me. He was not very sure of his Greek grammar and we had to look it up sometimes while reading. But he knew a great number of Greek words and through a certain intuition managed to grasp the meaning.

The work on *Anna Karenina* was coming to an end.

There is no doubt that the change in Levin's outlook on life is derived from the mental and spiritual change in my father. He was trying to be a good orthodox and follow church rites. The main incentive for that was, I think, the desire to create a link through his faith with the peasants, for he always suffered from the spiritual abyss that existed between them. He decided to accept on faith the dogmas, the sacraments, the miracles—in a word, all that his reason rejected—and to accept them with humility, as the necessary act of submission of individual to collective reason—that of the church. His intellect soon overcame this imposed philosophy, but in 1877 he was a zealous orthodox. He did not try to force or persuade anyone in his family to believe as he did; true, no one opposed him, though no one encouraged him either. My mother considered herself an orthodox, but she had little interest in religion and we children had no conscious attitude to these questions. I tried to imitate my father and be a good orthodox, but something in me inwardly protested against it. I could not but feel the absurdity of such miracles as Joshua stopping the sun during the battle, or the ascent of Elijah to Heaven, Jonah and the whale, the resurrection of Lazarus, the resurrection and ascension of Christ and particularly the transformation of wine and bread into the flesh and blood of Christ. We said our prayers. My mother taught us to say ' Our Father ' before going to sleep and ' Hail, Mary '. Also a prayer for our family and all orthodox Christians. But this was done automatically.

In the spring, to the delight of my teachers and myself, I passed all the examinations which promoted me from the fourth class into the fifth, and I got a formal certificate saying so.

The Turkish war was in full swing and my father took a great interest in it. At first he was rather pessimistic as to its issue. I remember how upset he was at the news of the defeat at Plevna.

Before the start of the school year my father began to look for another Russian teacher. He was also looking for a bailiff for the Samara farm. He found both through a midwife in Tula; their names were Alexeev and Bibikov. My father used to say jokingly: ' The midwife has recommended two nihilists to me.' I'll speak of Bibikov, the bailiff, later. Now let me say a few words about Vassili Ivanovich Alexeev, my tutor; I wrote down at the time what he told me about himself.

His father was a landowner in the Pskov district, an officer of the times of Nicholas I, a man of the most old-fashioned conventional principles. His mother was a peasant, completely subjugated by her husband, an exceedingly kind woman, and mother of eight children. After finishing his Pskov gymnasium Vassili went to Petersburg university to read mathematics and finished his course brilliantly. He joined the party of *narodniks* (people's party) and led active propaganda among workmen and students. He became director of a technical college with a good salary. The students liked him and he had more of them than he could cope with. But as a man of great sensibility he felt that he was not worthy of such comfortable living. At the same time he became friends with a former revolutionary belonging to the same party, who had been in prison and deported, and now had become a preacher of a new religion, based on Christianity, but with a mystic slant and chiefly concerned with Christian ethics and the social and international relationship of peoples. The members of this creed had to reach a higher moral level than their disciples and demonstrate by their own behaviour the possibility of achieving their ideals. Alexeev became a member of this circle. It was decided to found an agricultural collective, in which everything would be common property; everybody would be equal and lead a highly moral life. In view of the fact that the Russian government would not permit the establishment of such a collective, it was decided to organise it in America. One of the girl students gave money to buy a farm in Kansas and about fifteen Russian intellectuals settled down there, among them Alexeev.

The collective farm lasted for two years. The colony lived at first on good terms with one another, but in the second year they began to quarrel among themselves, the harvest was poor and gradually the farm fell to pieces.

On his return from Kansas, Vassili Ivanovich lived in great penury, trying one thing after the other; in spite of that he first refused to come to us as a teacher, not wishing to live in the house of a count, where, he said, dinner was served by flunkeys in white gloves. My father, however, managed to persuade him and he started in the autumn, teaching us mathematics, Russian, history and geography. At first he lived in the village with his ' civil law ' wife and baby, Kolia, but moved into the house the next year. He was above medium height, gaunt and narrow in the shoulders, fair-haired and physcially not very strong. He had a scanty reddish beard sprouting in disorder under his chin, while no hair grew on his cheeks; his honest blue eyes looked kindly at the world, he spoke in a calm and even voice and never lost his temper.

His convictions were not original and were based partly on Christian ethics, partly on the social ideas of European thinkers. What came from him was his pure heart and search for truth and kindness. To live by his own labour, chiefly manual, to try to give the people more than you take from them, to follow the Christian rule: not to do unto others what you wouldn't have them do to yourself; to work out, with the help of science, the right views on social problems, to open men's eyes to the injustices of the existing social order—this is what his general outlook consisted of. He believed that the ways of life can improve only if people themselves become more moral. His attitude to church teachings was negative, but not hostile.

Before the appearance of Vassili Ivanovich the relationship between our teachers and ourselves was a more or less official one (except for Hannah Tardsey). They did their duty but without any pleasure. Vassili Ivanovich was the first teacher who sincerely wished not only to impart some knowledge to us, but also to give us a certain spiritual education. I became greatly attached to him, and fell under his influence. I am grateful, even now, for the good seed he sowed in my heart. He is not to blame if they did not all bear fruit.

At first he had, no doubt, a certain influence also on my father's outlook on Christianity, which was then in an embryonic state, but later it was Vassili Ivanovich who completely fell under my father's spell, so that he could be truthfully called the first Tolstoyan.

Apart from Vassili Ivanovich my father engaged two schoolboys from Tula to read classics with me and my brother Ilya; they came on Saturdays, gave us lessons that evening and early on Sunday, planned my work for the week and then returned to Tula.

1878

In January a great change occurred in the lives of my brothers and myself. M. Rey was discharged. My father went to Moscow to look for another tutor and on January 25th, Monsieur M. Nief arrived. While he lived in our house, I never knew that his name was not Nief at all, but Jules Montels, from an old French family, a viscount, I believe. He belonged to the communalistic government of 1871 and lived in Russia in hiding, under a pseudonym.

He must have told that to my father before he was engaged but I only learnt about it when he left. I remembered later a conversation I had with him on the Franco-Prussian war. I teased him one day: ' Fine people, the French! To launch a civil war when the Germans were at the doors of Paris! ' He got very angry and said: ' *Je vous defends de me parler de ce moment de l'histoire française.*' I fell silent. He never tried to inculcate in us any revolutionary or communistic ideas; but he had nothing good to say about Jesuits and advised us to read Proudhon's book *De la Justice dans la Révolution et dans l'Eglise.* My father had brought back this book in 1860 from one of his foreign trips. Ivan Turgenev, when he came to know him, said that he belonged to the rank and file type of ' Communards '. Nief was a very decent, gay, good-natured, but quick-tempered man.

That winter my father went on giving me lessons in Greek. We read the Odyssey. He did not demand any grammatical analysis, but merely a translation from the Greek into Russian. I remember what an artistic enjoyment I got from the description of the storm and of Ulysses on the Greek islands. At that period I read a lot and indiscriminately.

In the winter of 1877–78 my father began to detach himself from orthodoxy and studied the gospels. At the same time he was planning a novel on the life of the Dekabrists,* of the reign of Nicholas I and of the life of the settlers.

At the beginning of March he went to Moscow and to Petersburg. In Petersburg he signed the purchase deed for the estate of Bistrom, adjoining the Samara farm. He bought 4,500 dessiatines from Bistrom at twelve roubles the dessiatine, so that with the previous 1,800 dessiatines this became a big property. Besides this he gathered a lot of material in Petersburg for his future writings. He questioned the lady-in-waiting, Countess Tolstoy, about the intimate life of Nicholas I, examined the cells of the

*The Dekabrists were a secret revolutionary political confederation formed in 1821–1822, mainly composed of noblemen and officers. The revolt of the Dekabrists took place on the day of Nicholas I's ascension to the throne, December 14th, 1825. It was quashed on the same night and most of the members were executed or deported to Siberia. Their object was the abolition of autocracy and serfdom. They wanted an army revolution led by officers, for the people, but without the people.

Peter and Paul fortress where Dekabrists had been imprisoned, came to know some Dekabrists or people who had known them, and so on. He said that just as he had written *War and Peace* fifty years after 1812, now he could write about the Dekabrists about fifty years after 1825. He considered this lapse of time sufficient in order to consider the events from an historical point of view and at the same time not too distant to lose the freshness of memory about it. He repeated, for instance, a story that had been told to him by one of the Dekabrists, Svistunov. When Svistunov, his hands in chains, was going to Siberia on a troika with another prisoner, Zavalishin, the latter said to him, pointing to the chains: ' I should have become an ADC instead of being chained like this! ' ' Then I understood,' said Svistunov, ' that he was not one of us, for we were proud of our chains.' My father had a very high opinion of the Dekabrist Lunin and told us how Lunin, while he was chained to a cart, made jokes that made the guardian, a fat German major, laugh.

I can't remember whether it was in Moscow or Petersburg that my father met Alexander II. They met face to face on the stairs, coming from a photographer's shop. He made way to let the Emperor pass. The fear in Alexander's steely eyes surprised him: ' Like a tracked beast's,' he said later, ' Alexander must have thought that I, a man he knew nothing about, was going to kill him.'

On March 7th my mother wrote to her sister: ' Leva's health is not bad, but he is frail, something is wrong with his stomach, his general condition and mood, also he has become prone to colds. And what is more, he can't write or work. That poisons his life.'

That year my father again planned to go to the farm in Samara for his cure and to make arrangements about the newly acquired land. My mother did not want to go at all. She found it difficult and tiresome to travel so far with the whole family and the child, Andriusha, whom she was still nursing, and to live that sort of Robinson Crusoe life. And in addition it meant missing her sister and her family who had been coming to Jassnaia for the summer. ' I must admit that to me it is worse than prison,' she wrote to her sister. But she felt it was her duty to go for two months.

That spring I passed my written examinations into the sixth class and my mother decided to leave after my last examination, on

35

July 10th. My father, with M. Nief, Ilya and Leva, had gone before and lost his wallet on the journey.

This time we stayed in the house on the newly acquired property. It stood in front of a dirty pond with willows surrounding it and was larger than the other Samara house, but the landscape and the remoteness from other habitations was the same. Again Mukhamedshah was invited; he had by now married another wife. The bailiff was a friend of Vassili Ivanovich, also a ' nihilist '.

Bibikov was the son of rather a rich landowner, of ' good family ' as it was said at the time; he had finished a course of natural science in Kharkov university and was a liberal-minded magistrate in the government of Kaluga. After the attempt on the life of the Emperor in 1866 he had been arrested, imprisoned in the fortress where he spent six months and, though he was acquitted at the trial, deported to Siberia. After eight years in deportation he was allowed to live in his small estate near Tula, but without the right to leave it. There he gave all his land to the peasants, married a peasant woman, but soon left her and married another one, by whom he had several children. When I knew him, he had the right to live where he wanted, but was still under police supervision.

Bibikov was of middle height, sturdy, muscular and handsome. His kind blue eyes bulged slightly and his pleasant smile had a tinge of irony in it; he always walked hurriedly. In a Russian jacket and shirt and high soft boots, with a square, reddish beard, he tried to adopt the appearance of a peasant but I doubt whether he succeeded. The saying goes that ' you'd recognise a priest even in a sheepskin ', and you could see at once that he was of a different class. He was restrained and gentle in manner, never raised his voice and on principle addressed everyone as ' you ', which greatly surprised the peasants. When I got to know him, he was not a revolutionary and refuted the possibility of progress through a change in the way of life other than by a general improvement of morality. In this he agreed with Vassili Ivanovich and my father, and disagreed with the young. His aim was to live morally in this life, without expecting a reward in the next. He said that in a healthy constitution all demands must be satisfied normally, harmoniously. To live well means to live normally, harmoniously. He approved of the idea of an agricultural community of intelligent people, but considered that with the present level of morality it was not likely to succeed, for each individual had to improve first.

He leased a part of the land adjoining ours and built a farm on it, so that although he was our bailiff, he could also live quite independently. He was most conscientious as a manager, sometimes even to the detriment of his own interests.

There were many horses that year on the farm, more than one hundred and fifty. With the idea of starting a stud, my father had bought some fine pedigree stallions: an English trotter, a saddle-horse from the Rostopchin stud, a huge saddle-backed train-horse, a Bukhara and several Kabarda race horses. There was also one shaggy Bashkir stallion, that had a large number of steppe mares. Each stallion was given several mares, in the spring and the first part of the summer. Small groups consisting of one stallion and the mares appointed to him grazed freely in the steppe. The Bashkirs were very good with their mares, and gradually the pedigree stallions got used to the new rhythm of life. The white Bukhara horse two arshins three vershoks* in size, a beauty, with a lovely Arab head, a straight back, generous hocks and elegant legs guarded his harem with particular jealousy. In the spring, if someone came close to his group, he pounced at him, seized the rider by the teeth and dragged him down and started kicking and biting the horse, if it was of the male sex, and if it was a mare, chased it into the group. But he would be friendly with a pedestrian and obey him. The rest of the year he was a mild, easy horse. I loved riding on him for his steady, rhythmical trot.

Towards the autumn the stallions were put in the stables and the mares all collected into a herd. Some of the horses were completely untrained. This, for example, is how I saw one wild horse being trained. The herd was brought into a pen, a noose attached to a long stick was thrown over one of the wild horses, and then tightened. When the horse stopped, almost strangled, its mouth was twisted, that is to say a strap was tied round it and the knot strengthened with a stick. While the horse was completely absorbed by the unbearable pain in its mouth, it stood motionless and was bridled, saddled and tied with a long strap

*One *arshin* is just over a yard and there are sixteen *vershoks* to one *arshin*.

37

to another horse—a trained one, already saddled. Then a Bashkir jumped on each of them and the mouth was loosened. The horse did not come to its senses at once and stood for a second or two in bewilderment, after which it started to buck frantically and kick with both front and hind legs. The chief danger for the trainer of a wild horse is that it should fall and wallow on the ground. To protect himself from this the Bashkir who sat on it hit it with all his might and the one on the trained horse pulled it towards him.

After several critical moments the wild horse broke away and both Bashkirs galloped over the steppe and disappeared. They returned, very calmly, in half an hour. The horses were trotting gently, all covered with foam, and the Bashkirs smiled, revealing their dazzling teeth: a wild horse had been conquered by man.

One of my greatest enjoyments was to ride on the steppe on a semi-trained horse. Sometimes the horses would run away with me, but that wasn't dangerous: there were no obstacles on the steppe, no hedges, no ditches or trees. I would gallop along, holding on to the mane, my shirt blowing in the wind.

On June 29th we drove in a large company to the fair at Busuluk in various vehicles. My parents went and we three older children, N. Strakhov and Monsieur Nief. Busuluk is eighty versts away and it took us the whole day. When it grew dark and we were approaching the village the shaft of the wheel which hadn't been oiled by the coachman, took fire and we stopped in the middle of the field, wondering what to do. The drivers tried to cool the shaft by urinating on it, using Gulliver's method of putting out the fire in the Lilliput kingdom, as Monsieur Nief remarked. But this did not prove sufficient and the wheel had to be replaced by a lever which scraped along the earth mercilessly and forced us to move at a tortoise's pace. The usually imperturbable N. Strakhov suddenly lost his temper:

'You oafs! you idiots!' he roared. 'Going on a long journey and not oiling your shaft! You oafs!'

His well-groomed, spade-shaped beard trembled with wrath and we could hardly restrain our laughter.

At the beginning of August the whole family returned to Jassnaia where the Kusminskis had already settled in.

On August 8th Ivan Turgenev came to Jassnaia for the first time after his quarrel with my father. On September 2nd he returned again.

In September a bard, a teller of folk tales, a peasant from Archangelsk, called Shchegolenkov, came to us. He was a small, good-natured old man, bandy-legged, a cobbler by profession. He ate with the servants in their quarters and in the evenings he had tea with us. My father used to write down his stories, particularly the legends. Several of his popular stories have been drawn from Shchegolenkov's tales.

My father used to go shooting a lot that autumn; I was unable to go with him because of ill-health. The autumn was so warm that on October 7th, my sister Tania's birthday, we had a picnic in the forest, where we grilled *shashliks* and fried some eggs.

Our visits to our Tula friends became more frequent. One of them, the Vice-Governor Urussov, could be called one of the first Tolstoyans, though he didn't look like the later, downtrodden Tolstoyans. He agreed with my father especially on matters of religion and philosophy. He was always impeccably dressed, meticulously polite and spoke perfect French. He led a modest life, was kind to everyone and tried as far as it was possible to soften the harshness of his administrative functions. I did not much care for him, though; he seemed to me a somewhat artificial person. His face, though not young, was completely unwrinkled and lacked all expression and his philosophical deliberations were obscure and unoriginal. In society circles he did not have the reputation of an intelligent man, and my father, though he protested against this opinion, seemed to adapt himself to his limited understanding when he talked to him.

Urussov was not happy in his family life and in spite of having several children, he lived apart from his wife. His wife lived permanently in Paris.

1879

This letter of my mother's describes how we spent Christmastide that year:

' The Christmas holidays went off very gaily. The first day was quiet, with making the pudding, rehearsals and preparations for the show. On the second day we went to Tula to dine with the Delvigs. After dinner, again a rehearsal and then dancing. Suddenly someone mentioned the circus . . . We went to the circus. From there to supper and tea at the Delvigs. On the third day Nicholas Tolstoy with his wife came to stay and Strakhov from Petersburg. On the fourth day all the Delvigs came to us. In the morning a rehearsal, then dinner for twenty-two and in the evening everybody went sleigh-driving, three in each sleigh, without a coachman.

' There was a lovely Christmas tree on New Year's Eve, unusually well-decorated this year. We saw the New Year in with champagne. The show was on January 3rd, with many friends from town and all the staff in attendance. The first play *The Adventurous Grandmother* was a great success. Tania played the part of Glasha very nicely. The Delvigs also were excellent and Sergei played the part of a *jeune premier* very well. But in the second play, *The Uniform,* alas, there were many mishaps. Ilya kept fluffing his lines and this confused and muddled Sergei who had the main part of Rasgildiaiev. After the show everybody dressed up in fancy dress, danced a quadrille, a valse; the children were again allowed to stay up for supper and went to bed at 1 a.m.'

I remember what a mess I made that night of my part of Rasgildiaiev, but not because of anything Ilya did, simply because I lack talent for the stage. My sister Tania, on the contrary, always excelled at acting and played in many amateur shows.

At the end of January my mother went for ten days to Moscow and took Tania and me with her. We hadn't been in Moscow since our early childhood. ' My little jungle-dwellers found everything very exciting,' my mother wrote about us. We visited for the first time the Kremlin, the Palace, the cathedrals, the Arsenal, picture galleries, shops, and went for the first time to the opera. They were giving *Mascarade,* with Marius and Volpini. I was brought up on classical music and didn't much like the Italians, thought some of the tunes stuck in my memory. In the theatre Tania made us all laugh by asking, ' Is it true that Marius in real life is the husband of Volpini ? '

Back in Jassnaia we resumed a regular life and I began to prepare zealously for my examinations.

One day my father read in the papers about the attempt on the life of Alexander II and began to translate the paragraph for Monsieur Nief. When he came to the sentence: ' but God preserved his anointed servant,' he stopped, forgetting how to translate the word ' anointed '. ' *Mais Dieu a conserve son . . . son* ' he repeated, searching for the word.

' Son sang-froid! ' suddenly Monsieur Nief came to his help and we could none of us help laughing.

In the spring I passed the difficult examinations from the sixth into the seventh class. My father wrote to Fet on May 25th that he couldn't go to see him because he was detained: '... by various trifles: the tutors have gone, tomorrow I have to go to Tula to discuss Sergei's examinations, then the baby is ill, etc. The main reason is the boy's examinations. Though there is nothing I can do, I like to know about them. They are not progressing very successfully. Sergei in his clumsiness and absent-mindedness makes mistakes in his written examinations. And you can't correct them afterwards. Luckily the worst part of them is over.'

The summer passed as usual; the Kusminskis lived in the wing; now and then Strakhov and other guests and Shchegolenkov came.

At the end of July my father went with me to his mother-in-law, my grandmother Bers, at her small estate near Novgorod; we spent a fortnight there. It was a place remote from other habitation, ten versts from the railway station; the house was built on the shore of a lake and behind it spread an old fir tree forest. You could only drive through it in a dog-cart, the hay was transported in the summer on sledges, cattle grazed everywhere, the fields were hedged against them. The water in the lake and in the streams was dark red from ferruginous salts. Grandmother lived there with her youngest son, my Uncle Viacheslav, and a devoted servant, Nastassia. Viacheslav Bers was only two years older than I and we were great friends. I like remembering this kind uncle, this loving son, good friend and scrupulously honest man.

We swam with him, went sailing, shot partridges and woodcock. My father, wherever he went, was interested in the local peasants and talked to them. He found Novgorod peasants far better educated and more alert than our Tula ones, but spoilt by Petersburg where they went constantly to search for work. They had lost all their old songs and no longer wore national dress.

My father left before I did and I had to go home alone. In a third-class carriage I happened to sit next to a pretty girl, dressed in a simple black dress, travelling from Zurich. Our conversation began with Russian literature and turned later to political and

41

social subjects. At first in a restrained way but gradually opening up, she said that only revolutionary measures could force the Russian government to bring about reform, grant freedom, abolish classes, exonerate peasants from tax. I was glad that my rather vague radicalism, assimilated partly from Vassili Ivanovich, partly from my school friends, was being confirmed by this girl. We said goodbye before arriving at Moscow, without exchanging names, and I don't know now who she was. It seems probable that she had her stint of prison and deportation waiting for her.

In the autumn, some more shooting in our free moments—and study. One of the schoolboys who came this time to help us with our lessons was very revolutionary-minded and had some influence on me. Later on he became a self-sacrificing provincial doctor.

With the coming of winter my father started to study the gospels and theological criticism with great perseverance. He abandoned his work on the Dekabrists. My mother wrote to her sister: ' Leo is working, so he says, but alas! He keeps writing religious tracts, reads and thinks until his head aches and all this to prove how inconsistent the church is with the teachings of the gospels. There will hardly be a dozen people in Russia interested in that. But there is nothing to be done. I only wish that he would finish this as soon as possible and that it may pass like some sort of sickness. To guide him or govern his mental exercises, whatever they might be, is in no man's power; he himself is unable to do it.'

My father did not speak much to us children about his work, but discussed it with Alexeev and Urussov. At my still immature age I was not very interested in it, but was glad that he had abandoned orthodoxy, in which I already consciously had no faith.

On October 2nd, Monsieur Nief, having received a mysterious letter, suddenly left us and went to Moscow. The Communards had been pardoned and he returned to France. Later he became the editor of a Tunisian newspaper and sent from there a letter to my father and his photograph with a touching inscription, ' *De la part d'un français reconnaissant* '. To my shame I didn't write to him and our relationship came to an end with his departure.

On December 20th my mother gave birth to a healthy boy— my brother Misha.

1880

Misha's christening was on Twelfth Night. There was a beautiful Christmas tree. Strakhov came, and Uncle Sergei and friends from Tula. Then again, after the feasts, came studies, skating and a regular life.

At the end of January my father went to Moscow and Petersburg. He was more than ever amazed by the luxury of Petersburg life.

In February M. Loriss Melikov was appointed head of the commission for the preservation of government order and public safety with extraordinary powers. My father was surprised by this appointment.

' Why does the Emperor pass on his power to someone else? ' he said, ' And to whom? To a general, a military figure who knows nothing of civil affairs, not even a Russian. Have we no equally worthy Russian men? '

My mother found life in the country more and more difficult to endure. She wrote to her sister on January 30th: ' How hard I find it to bear my hermit's life! Imagine, Tania, I haven't been out of the house since September. It's like a prison, only brighter both morally and financially. But nonetheless I have the feeling of being locked up, held back, and I want to push through, break through and run away somewhere, as quickly as possible.'

In another letter of March 21st she writes, already in a different mood: ' Although you used to be angry with me, Tanechka, for preserving the peace around Liova, I consider that men are constantly straining their minds and therefore their brains and nerves should be preserved above everything else. Given that calm and that preservation of their nerves, they are able to engender a good atmosphere in the family and if we irritate them it's we ourselves who suffer from it.'

A few months later my mother wrote to my father on August 28th 1880: ' You probably think I am stubborn and persistent, but I feel that a lot of what is good in you is gently transferred into me and makes it easier for me to live on the earth.'

At the beginning of March Vsevolod Garshin* came twice to

---

*An outstanding Russian writer, author of *The Blind Musician*, *The Red Flower*, etc.

Jassnaia. He was already mentally unbalanced. The second time, in the worst possible weather, he arrived riding from Tula on an unsaddled horse which he had simply unharnessed from a droshky, and declared he was going straight to Kharkov. When he rode away, he kept waving his arms strangely. He was accused of horse stealing after that and sent to hospital after it was ascertained that he was mentally deranged.

In the spring Vladimir Soloviev* came to Jassnaia. He was still a handsome young man with dark hair. I was present when my father and he had a long philosophical discussion. My father spoke very calmly and neither he nor Soloviev interrupted one another. I understood but little but it seemed to me that Soloviev agreed with my father in most things but tried to maintain his independence. When he left my father gave a very appreciative criticism of his brilliant memory, erudition and general ability, but added vaguely: ' What will become of him? It is too soon to philosophise at such an early age.' Soloviev brought to my father or sent him later his books: *The Crisis of Western Philosophy* and *The Criticism of Abstract Foundations*, with warm inscriptions. At that time he was not so hostile to Tolstoyan ideas as he became later, in *The Three Conversations*.

In May I passed my written examinations into the eighth class. Ivan Turgenev came and other guests. In the evenings we ' made music '—the literal translation of ' *faire de la musique* '. My Aunt Tania excelled in that. She had a vibrant soprano with a pleasant timbre, liked music and sang enthusiastically, conveying this enthusiasm to her audience. A. Fet even wrote a poem under the influence of her singing and my father also liked it very much. We of the younger generation considered that no one could sing better than she did. She sang Russian, French and Italian songs to father's, my or her own accompaniment. Then we would sing *tsigane* and popular Russian songs all together, also ' The Key ', an old song mentioned in *War and Peace*. Sometimes my sisters Tania and Masha danced a popular Russian dance. Tania was very good at imitating the peasant women's manner of dancing. Masha was very graceful.

I consider the years 1879–80 the really happy ones of my life. I was well, strong, a satisfactory pupil, learning did not cost

*Prominent Russian philosopher.

44

me a great effort, I liked all sport, hunting and shooting, riding, fishing, swimming. I loved music and dreamt of having music lessons in Moscow and going to concerts; of my fellow students at the university and meetings; of doing things that would be of some use to humanity. I was of course in love, timidly in love, with a young girl about five years older than myself. She often came to Jassnaia with her mother and sister and took part in our amateur theatricals. But I was so shy that I didn't have the courage to tell her about my feelings and she remained only a bright memory of my youth.

As I had to pass next year my last examination enabling me to enter the university, my father engaged a philologist, I. Ivakin, with whom I was to study classics and to give other lessons to my brothers. From September 13th he came to live in the room previously inhabited by Monsieur Nief: a fair, frail, poorly clad, shy young man with a high voice and terribly thin hands. Later he wrote his reminiscences of his stay in Jassnaia which have not been published. A friend of his told him that L. Tolstoy needed a tutor and recommended him.

' What did you tell him ? ' asked Ivakin.

' I said that I knew of someone who would suit him but that he had one fault—indifference.'

' Indifference! ' exclaims Ivakin in his notes, ' I could not have had a better recommendation.'

Ivakin was erudite, but he was a looker-on at life rather than a participant. He was averse from the revolutionary trends of the young people of the time, but equally he did not pursue material gain. Eventually he became a school teacher in Moscow; he wrote a thesis on Vladimir Monomakh, and became a zealous follower of the orthodox church. He died at the age of forty. He came from an old Moscow merchant family; he loved Moscow and never wanted to go abroad. We were friends rather than pupil and teacher. My father had a great regard for him and often discussed the interpretation of gospel texts with him. My father was working a great deal that year on the gospels. I remember how he used to come out of his study, tired but happy, having found a new angle in his reading of them.

On October 28th N. Rubinstein* gave a concert in Tula to

*Son of Anton Rubinstein.

which we all went. My father sat in the first row, his eyes shut. He listened with such rapt attention that a lady, who did not know him, asked: ' Who is this gentleman who listens so intently to the music? ' And my mother wrote to her sister about the concert: ' I could see how his face twitched and how he kept blinking; his nerves have gone to pieces.'

I was greatly impressed by Rubinstein's playing, which had such clarity and precision, such a logically developed rhythm. He played Beethoven's C Sharp sonata, the E Flat polonaise and several nocturnes of Chopin, *Symphonic Etudes* by Schumann and the waltz from *Faust* in the Liszt variation.

On November 28th my mother wrote to her sister: ' Everything seems all right on the surface but Leo and I are cold and estranged. In the house nothing seems to interest me; it only provokes longing and regret, pain, tenderness for the children and a desire for death . . . Leo is deeply involved in his work, visiting prisons, magistrates, judges and recruiting offices, with a compassionate concern for all people and all underdogs. All this is very good, no doubt, and elevated, so elevated that one is all the more conscious of one's own inferiority. But alas, life makes its demands and pulls one to the other side, and so the misunderstanding grows more painful and stronger.'

On December 8th:

' My dear Tania,

My letter must have pained you. You must have thought your Sonia quite crazy. I can't pretend, and I babble away under the influence of the moment. That was a moment of crisis in my relationship with Leo. Now the ice seems to have melted, he is more natural and tender with me. Luckily I fell seriously ill . . . Leo got frightened and his love revived.'

1881

At the beginning of January I took part for the first time in a concert. My teacher Michurin organised a concert for his pupils in the Nobles' hall in Tula. The dances from *Life for the Tsar*, (now *Life of Ivan Sussanin*) were orchestrated for two pianos and a string quartet and I played the second *secundo*. I made a mistake in the Polish dance and stopped. Kislinski who was playing with me, whispered: ' Never mind, go on! ' and I started again,

missing a few bars so that my mistake apparently went un-
noticed.

On February 2nd, Mother wrote to her sister: ' Leo is working
hard, he can't stop. We have all been deeply upset by the death
of Dostoevsky. It made Leo think of his own death and he has
become remote and silent.'

In February Uncle Bers came to Jassnaia, with his beautiful
wife. On March 3rd my mother wrote: ' Sasha frightened me by
saying that Leo has changed for the worse. He is afraid for his
mind. You know how engrossed Leo gets in his ideas. But the
religious and philosophical mood is the most dangerous. Now
he is well and cheerful, he has put on weight and I see nothing
dangerous about it.'

This letter shows how ordinary people like Bers were surprised and horrified at the time that Tolstoy should be pre-
occupied with religious problems, that he should criticise the
gospels, repudiate the church, denounce luxury, etc., instead of
writing novels that brought him money and glory. This seemed
strange not only to Bers—the rumour spread in Tula at that time
that Tolstoy had lost his reason.

My mother decided to move for the winter to Moscow and have
her next child there. She did not want to let me go alone to town
for fear that ' I would have my head turned ' in the university, in
spite of my concentration on music. Also she had to be there for
Tania's ' presentation ' to society. So, like the Chekov three
sisters, we lived in the hope, my mother, my sister and I: ' to
Moscow, to Moscow.'

When I now recall the years before our move to Moscow I
understand better than I did then the important part my mother
played in the life of our family and the value of her care for my
father and for all of us. Then it seemed to me that our life went
on in its own rhythm and I took my mother's care for granted. I
did not realise that everything from our clothes and food to our
studies and the copying of Father's work was organised by her.
Father gave only directives now and then which Mother often
ignored. At the same time she was often ill and was either pregnant
or nursing a child.

We elder children did not have the timid and respectful
attitude to our mother which we had to our father, in spite of
addressing Father as ' thou ', and Mother as ' you '. I don't know

how it happened to be so. My mother certainly did not expect us to address her like that and later on my brothers used the 'thou' to her also. We sometimes made personal remarks about our mother. For instance, we would say in front of her: 'Mamma eats like a bird,' or 'Mamma doesn't understand jokes,' or 'While Mamma is buying three yards of material in a shop she manages to tell the assistant her whole life-history.'

My mother was not less energetic by nature than my father. Her movements and gait were quick, she was always busy, she could not be idle, sit doing nothing. If she had nothing on her schedule, nursing, children's studies, copying, household chores, etc., she would find other things to do: sewing, drawing, gardening, making jam, pickling mushrooms, etc. It was rare for her to take a stroll or just be spontaneously gay. She always had something on her mind.

In 1881 my mother was still young at thirty-seven and she looked younger than her age. Having lived eighteen years in the country, working hard all the time, she naturally wanted to enjoy some town life, to see people and go about; and above all, she considered it necessary to live in Moscow for the sake of her elder children.

My father had quite another outlook upon life in Moscow. In 1881 the change in his philosophy had already taken place. In spite of that, his way of life in Jassnaia had changed only slightly before the move to Moscow. He continued running the farms, he smoked, ate meat and even went out shooting. Only he did it all more reluctantly and worked more at his writing, not even resting in the summer. In 1881, of the great work he had set himself to do, consisting of four parts—(1) Introduction (*Confession*); (2) Criticism of dogmatic theology; (3) Study of the Gospels; (4) Statement of faith—the first two were written and he was working on the third.

The trend of his thoughts and the state of his mind made it clear that life in Moscow could not appeal to him. But realising that the idea of going to Moscow when the children began to grow up had been discussed long ago with his approval, he did not protest and regarded it as an inevitable evil.

On March 1st Alexander II was killed; we heard this the next day from a little Italian beggar who wandered into Jassnaia. He spoke in broken French: 'Life bad, nobody give money, Emperor

48

dead.' ' How is that? When? Who did it? ' we asked. He could tell us no more and we only learnt the truth from the papers in the evening.

On March 12th my mother wrote to her sister: ' We are having friction in the house all the time and I find it difficult to bear. The other day there was some trouble with Vassili Ivanovich and I had to tell him abruptly that I resent his interference. Leo is sulking and I implore God to put a quick end to this life, with its small narrow circle.'

My mother was afraid that under Vassili Ivanovich's influence my father had written a harsh letter to the Tsar which might cause his arrest and deportation. This is why she had the passage of arms with Vassili Ivanovich. Otherwise she liked him well enough but believed that my father's religious searchings were partly encouraged by him and she mistrusted these, because she did not understand them. The next day, however, she apologised to him for her behaviour.

My father did, in fact, write to Alexander III, appealing to him not to execute the murderers of his father. He wrote to the head of the Synod, Pobedonostsev, asking him to pass the letter on to the Tsar but Pobedonostsev refused. The letter reached the Tsar through another medium.

In February after a violent snowstorm a frozen man was found on the highroad. My father brought him into one of the huts: he, Urussov and Vassili Ivanovich tried to revive him; but it was in vain.

On April 9th my mother wrote: ' The atmosphere in the house is more peaceful, I think. But what will come next? ' A few weeks later she wrote: ' We often have little quarrals this year. I even wanted to leave home. Probably its because we have started living in a Christian way. In my opinion we lived better before, without the Christian way.'

In May I passed my last examination, with a new head of the school. The former one was very harsh with the pupils. He used to clip off their starched collars himself if he found them too high. One day he caught a pupil peeping through an eyehole in the door from the passage and hit the boy so hard on the head that he broke the pane with his nose and blood gushed out from it. The new director was a liberal man with literary tastes. It was said that one day, seeing two boys fighting, he cried: ' Go on, go on, it's good exercise.' He was lenient in the exams and almost all the pupils got their certificates.

In June my father went to the monastery in Optino and returned with even less faith in the orthodox church.

When I joined the university I had to decide what to read and, after a process of elimination, I chose natural sciences. I have never regretted that choice and believe that the natural sciences have helped to develop in me a certain sober reasoning.

From this time began my unfortunate arguments with my father. He wrote in his diary from June 28th: 'Talk with Sergei about God. He thinks that to say: " It can't be proved, therefore I don't want it," is a sign of intelligence and education, when it is only a sign of ignorance . . . We teach them church rites, etc., knowing that it will all vanish with adolescence, and we teach them many things not connected with one another, so that they remain uncoordinated, with contradictory knowledge and believe they've achieved something. Sergei admitted that he likes the life of the flesh and believes in it. I'm glad that the question is clarified.'

How was I not to like the life of the flesh? On that day precisely I had reached my eighteenth year!

In our childhood we three elder children had an unusual attitude to our father, quite different I think from that in other families. His judgments were law, his advice compelling. We believed that he knew all our thoughs and feelings but did not always tell us so. I could never stand the glance of his small, penetrating, steel-blue eyes and when he asked me something—and he liked to ask questions which one did not like to answer—I was unable to lie, or even avoid answering, though I often wanted to do so.

We not only loved him, he occupied a great place in our lives; but we felt that he obliterated our personalities, so that sometimes we wanted to escape. In childhood it was a subconscious feeling, later it became conscious and then both my brothers and I allowed a spirit of contradiction to creep into our relationship with him.

In our childhood all we wanted was for Father to be with us, to give us his time, either to take us for a walk, or round the farm or out shooting, or drive somewhere or tell us a story or do physical exercises with us. He was not affectionate in the usual sense of the word: there was no kissing, no presents, but we always felt he loved us and knew when he was satisfied with our behaviour. Sometimes he would come up quietly from behind and put both hands on my eyes. It wasn't difficult to guess whose hands they were. Or he would take me by both hands and say: 'Climb on me.' I would climb up his body to the shoulders; he would hoist me up and I would sit or stand on his shoulders. Propping me up he would walk about the room and then somersault me down and I would be on my feet again. We were fond of these exercises and whoever of us came first, the others would cry: 'Me too, me too!'

We liked Father's smell, the smell of his flannel blouse, healthy sweat and tobacco—at that time he still smoked. One of our favourite occupations with Father was gymnastics. This is what we did: we stood all in a row opposite Father, and had to imitate all his movements, rhythmically move our heads in all directions, bend and stretch our arms, lift and lower each leg alternately, bow down without bending our knees and touch the ground. There was also a 'horse' over which we jumped. Father attached great importance to physical development; he encouraged us in swimming, running, playing rounders and other games, and especially riding. Sometimes we would race each other; he ran faster than any of us. Then we would represent 'the Numidian cavalry'. Father would jump from the table and waving his napkin run round it, with us trailing behind. Why this was called the 'Numidian cavalry' no one, not even my father, really knew. It was very refreshing after a visit from boring guests.

My father rarely punished us or scolded us, and he never boxed our ears or slapped us; but we learnt to guess by various symptoms what his mood of the moment was. The greatest punishment was to be ignored by him, when he refused to take us with him or said something sarcastic. He had 'favourites of the moment', according to our behaviour and sometimes independently of it. He had no permanent favourites. Later when we grew up, what he liked best was that we should understand his point of view. Apparently he had no special educational system. He made ironical remarks about our faults, or indicated with a joke that we were not behaving as we should, or told an anecdote in which there would be a broad hint. At times he grew irritable and raised his voice, especially during lessons. But I do not remember him ever using a strong word though sometimes he would send us out of the room during a lesson.

What he disapproved of most was lying and rudeness to any-body—my mother, the teachers or the servants. Sometimes he would reprimand us for less serious reasons. For instance, he noticed if we ate with our knife or cut fish with a knife, which was bad manners. In *Anna Karenina*, Anna says about somebody: ' One can't say he is a nihilist, but he eats with his knife.' When I slouched he would say: ' Hold your back straight,' or push me in the back. Or, noticing that I tried to take part in games and entertainments and to listen to conversations which did not concern me, to poke my nose where it didn't belong, he would say: ' You're always afraid of missing something,' that is, missing the opportunity of having some fun or learning something interesting. He had, in fact, noted a feature of my character which led me later to take an interest in things that were not worth while.

When somebody among us tried to tell a funny or witty story and laughed himself as he told it, Father would say: ' There are three kinds of tellers of funny stories; those who laugh at their own joke, but the others don't; those who laugh together with their audience; the best are the third kind who don't laugh, only the audience does.' On the whole he advised us not to laugh for fear that the listeners would look bored and that would be embarrassing.

When I tried to be funny, he used to say: ' Your witticisms are like a lottery. The winning ticket seldom turns up, and more often you get a blank piece of paper with " lottery " written on it.' When I uttered some foolish remark, meant to be witty, he would say: ' Lottery ' and I knew that the joke had fallen flat.

When I did something accidentally—broke something or dropped something on my clothes, or forgot an errand and tried to justify myself by saying it was only an accident, he said: ' That's precisely what I blame you for. Nothing should ever be done accidentally.'

Another piece of advice he gave was: never try to do anything unless you do it well.

In the sixties and seventies, before the ' crisis ', Father was full of life, a dominating personality, not the man that he became afterwards. When I was a child there was even a sort of aristo-cratic aloofness in Father, though he did not put it into words. My mother expressed it more frankly. Father did attribute some importance to heredity, but aristocratic birth chiefly meant to him good manners in the best sense of the word, a feeling of dignity, education, restraint, generosity. With this went respect and love for the peasants—our 'providers' as he called them—and he inspired this respect in us. Later he repudiated completely the importance of aristocratic birth. He disliked familiarity in relations between friends, and even members of the family. He said: ' There are friends who clap each other on the back and add: " Ah, you dear old scoundrel " or " I love you, you old rogue ".'

As an example that good manners serve to make relationships easier, not more difficult, he would tell the story about Louis XIV who tested a courtier well known for his manners; the king invited the courtier to get into the royal carriage before himself. The courtier obeyed at once. ' That is a truly good-mannered man,' said Louis XIV. ' But when our Chichikovs and Manilovs crowd in a doorway to let one another pass,' my father used to say, ' that only makes things more difficult.'

His habits in those years were to smoke cigarettes (rolled by my mother), drink home-made herb tea out of a silver cup before dinner and a small glass of white wine during dinner; he ate meat and was a good shot. In spite of an almost total lack of teeth, he ate quickly but chewed little; knowing this to be unhealthy, he would say: ' Pour bien se porter il faut bien marcher et bien mâcher.' As far as I remember he always had a beard. Either he himself or Mother trimmed his beard once a month in the new moon. He had learnt that, he said, from the Muslims. He did not wear a starched shirt at home, but his traditional blouse—a grey flannel one in winter, a linen one in summer: an old servant Varvara or my mother made them for him. But when he went to town, he put on a starched shirt and a well-cut coat, made by a Moscow tailor.

The schedule of the day during all our life in Jassnaia until 1881 was comparatively regular and varied but little in the months from September to May; that is, while Father wrote and we had our lessons. In the summer there was more variety.

From September to May we children and our teachers got up between eight and nine o'clock and went to the hall to have breakfast. After nine, in his dressing-gown, still unwashed and undressed, with a tousled beard, Father came down from his bedroom to the room under the hall where he finished his toilet. If we met him on the way he greeted us hastily and reluctantly. We used to say: 'Papa is in a bad temper until he has washed.' Then he, too, came up to have his breakfast, for which he usually ate two boiled eggs in a glass.

He did not eat anything after that until five in the afternoon. Later, at the end of 1880, he began to take luncheon at two or three. He was not talkative at breakfast and soon retired to his study with a glass of tea. We hardly saw him after that until dinner.

My mother got up later, and had her breakfast about eleven. Luncheon was served to the children and teachers between mid-day and one o'clock, but our parents were never present then. So there were always the samovar, coffee and food laid on the table from nine to one.

When Father was writing, neither he nor his family said that he was *working,* but that he was *busy*. Until the so-called crisis he was not very busy in the summer, when he allowed himself three months of rest. During the remaining months except for a few autumn days when he went out shooting, he worked every day. When he was busy, no one was allowed to enter his room, not even my mother. He needed total silence and the assurance that he would not be interrupted. The doors in the adjoining rooms were locked. No one was allowed to play the piano, because Father said that he could not help hearing music or listening to it even when it was hardly audible.

After work Father would go for a walk or a ride, usually with some purpose: to supervise the work on the land, to shoot, or to visit somebody or go to the station. But when he just went out for pure relaxation he would concentrate on his work and collect material for further writing. The wild forest, that had once served as a defence against Tartar invasion, and the highroad were his favourite strolls. He loved the forest because of its primitiveness, its solitude and the splendour of the trees. He would choose untrodden paths in a wish to explore. The highroad to Kiev which went through Jassnaia led from the north of Russia to the Ukraine, the Crimea, the shores of the Black Sea. He remembered the time when there was no highroad—just a road. He would joke about his walk on the highroad and call it his entry into the *grand monde* or a stroll along the Nevsky Prospect.*

*Main street in Petersburg.

In the sixties and seventies the road was crowded with pilgrims on their way to various monasteries. Father said that piousness was seldom their main preoccupation; they went for other reasons: some because life at home was too hard, some out of curiosity to see the world, some because it was the right thing to do. The pilgrims usually walked at a pace of thirty versts a day, carrying bundles on their backs, in soft bast shoes; they walked in groups, they were fed on charity and spent the night wherever they could; they seldom washed and seldom changed their underclothes. They were the carriers of folk-lore, proverbs and legends —rumours, too—and had a certain influence on the popular outlook.

Father used to say that their tales were both literature and newspapers for the people. He loved talking to the passers-by, walking with them or sitting at the edge of the road. Some of the legends were transformed by him into works of art. The knowledge of popular life, popular language, dialect, proverbs—all this Father acquired on the highroad.

Local peasants also used to pass by, drunk or sober, with loaded or empty carts, friends or strangers. Father used sometimes to thumb a lift from them, which they readily gave. If there were stonebreakers on the road he would stop to talk to them or even start beating stone himself, saying it was hard work and made his hands sore.

At five we had dinner, to which Father often came late. He would be stimulated by the day's impressions and tell us about them. After dinner he usually read or talked to guests if there were any; sometimes he read aloud to us or saw to our lessons. About 10 p.m. all the inhabitants of Jassnaia foregathered again for tea. Before going to sleep he read again, and at one time he played the piano. And then retired to his bed about 1 a.m.

Part II

MORE RECOLLECTIONS
OF MY FATHER

Chapter 1

His Taste in Books

My father was a very selective reader, which is not very usual. He remembered everything he had read, and knew how to get the essence out of a book and what to discard. Thus he economised his time.

He read a lot of foreign novels, particularly English and French: Dickens, Thackeray, Trollope, Mrs. Humphrey Ward, George Eliot, etc. He thought Thackeray somewhat cold. Among other novels he praised *Adam Bede* and *The Vicar of Wakefield*.

He read Victor Hugo, Flaubert, Zola, Maupassant, Daudet, the Goncourt Brothers. He loved Hugo's *Les Misérables* and *Le dernier jour d'un condamné*. Among the realists he appreciated Maupassant most; Flaubert, Balzac and Daudet left him cold; Zola interested him, but he considered his realism contrived and his descriptions too detailed and petty. ' People eat a whole goose in twenty pages of Zola's books—it is too much,' he said about *La Terre*.

He did not read many German books, perhaps only Goethe, Schiller, Auerbach. He told us to read Schiller's *Die Räuber*, Goethe's *Werther* and *Hermann und Dorothea*. One cannot say that contemporary Russian literature occupied much of his time.

He read no political, topical literature and only glanced at *belles-lettres* when they came his way. He was interested in the works of Turgenev which were then appearing, but some of Dostoevsky's books, for instance *The Teenager*, I believe he never read. He did not like the popular Melinkov Pechersky, saying that he had a false approach, exploited popular speech and knew nothing of peasant life: ' It is false literature. Melinkov writes that the Russian man has no consideration for trees. He will hack down an ancient oak to make a bridle. He does not seem to know that a Russian peasant would never cut down an oak for a bridle, but would choose instead a young birch.' (In the domain of historical novels, imitations of Walter Scott whom he did not like, he pointed out the false interpretation of the life of the epoch.)

He advised us children not to read masterpieces too soon, so that the freshness of impression would not be lost later when we were old enough to understand them. That is why we read Pushkin, Lermontov and Gogol rather late. On the other hand, he did not like books specially for children: he encouraged us to read books interesting for the young as well as for the old, like *Robinson Crusoe, Don Quixote, Gulliver's Travels, Les Miserables,* the works of Alexandre Dumas the father, *Oliver Twist, David Copperfield,* and so on. In Russian literature he chose for us *A Sportsman's Notebook* and *Memoirs from a Dead House.* Among Pushkin's works—*Tales of Belkin.* He was a great admirer of Pushkin and considered *Pique Dame* a masterpiece. He never recommended his own books except *The Alphabet* and *Books for Reading.* But our mother encouraged us to read Tolstoy. *Childhood, Boyhood, Youth* was my favourite book because I identified myself with the hero.

He did not have much to say for poetry; he considered it limited by rhythm and scansion to which meaning was sacrificed, though sometimes, as with Pushkin, the search for rhythm brought unexpected discoveries. Only in the nineties when he wrote his article on art, did he express criticism of Pushkin. He said that the working people demand a serious attitude from a writer, while Pushkin writes poems about women's ankles and talks about dead gods. But he was full of admiration for him, and considered him, as a man, sincere and conscious of his own faults, a man, in fact, who if he did compromise at times, did so only in his actions, not in his opinions. I do not know who told him of Pushkin's words on meeting a friend on the Nevsky:

' I feel such a cad,' said Pushkin.

' Why? ' asked his friend.

' I've just met the Emperor and talked to him.'

In Jassnaia we were subscribers to a great number of reviews, both French and Russian, from which father used to read aloud to us; Schchedrin's stories delighted him particularly. He hardly ever read newspapers at that time. I believe we used to get only one Moscow paper, sent to us by Katkov.

Chapter 2

The Tales He Told Us

I CONSIDER myself happy because I have had the opportunity of hearing my father talk in his wonderfully alive, artistic rich language. With his remarkable memory and exceptional sensitivity, how well he recounted all he had seen, heard, read and thought about. What a lot of rarities he offered one, things that no one else had noticed or did not talk about. On the other hand, he never touched upon hackneyed subjects, nor did he gossip or tell tales about himself. One could feel that the story he told or the thought he expressed was essential to his work or to his outlook on life. He did not like to speak (or act) without purpose. He did not like the actual word ' purposeless ' and I don't think it ever occurs in his works. He loved and felt the beauty of nature, fields, forests, meadows, skies, more than most pepole do. He used to say: ' What a wealth of goodness there is in God! The variety of nature, every day differs from the one before, every year we have surprise-weather! '

He had the eye of a landscape painter, though he considered that the landscape is an inferior type of art. He said once: ' How lovely yellow corn looks against the background of a forest of oak; this is something for a landscape-painter.' He often said about the colouring of the sky and the clouds: ' If a painter could immortalise this, no one would believe him, they would think he had invented it.' He would bring some rare flower from his walks, an unusually long ear of corn, a strangely coloured leaf, admire them and proudly exhibit them to us. On clear nights he would talk to us about the stars; he was interested in astronomy, not the mathematical but the experimental side of it, and he explained to us the differences between stars, planets and comets. Often he would talk to us about the peasants' lives, especially those of Jassnaia, all of whom he knew. He used to visit them, unannounced, in their huts, talk to them, advise them and answer their questions. They had great confidence in him and he knew their family affairs and their secrets. Once he told us, in great confidence, that an escaped criminal was hiding in the house of a neighbouring peasant. Another time he told us that one of the peasants was buried under a sand-fall in a kiln by the highroad from where they took their sand. Together with the peasants he went to dig him out and said that the men worked without thought for their own safety, and risked being buried themselves. A crowd waited every day by the elder tree for him to leave the house; some came for advice, others begged for fuel, money, work. He was known in the district as someone who could give good advice and had an influence with the authorities. Later on, after the seventies, the type of visitor changed; the seekers of kindness and justice began to dwindle, beggars increased and so did people with religious problems and the openly inquisitive. He knew all about husbandry and used to examine us about the parts of a peasant's harness or those of a plough.

Or, suddenly, he would speak of the things that occupied his mind at the moment. In the seventies they were the thoughts expressed in *Confession* or *My Faith*, the philosophical thoughts chiefly inspired by Kant and Schopenhauer. One of the subjects was his deliberations on time. He said that there were two ways of calculating time, one subjective, the other objective. The objective one was measured by years, days, hours; the subjective, by the life behind us. A year lived by a child of three forms the third of his life by the number and effect of the impressions he goes through in that time, whereas for a man of thirty, a year represents only one thirtieth of his life. Everything is new and significant for a child and a year is a long span of time. This explains why the older we grow the quicker time passes.

He once expressed the thought that a country's cultural level should be judged not according to the literacy and education of the masses, but by the degree of erudition of the top layer of the population. In Russia the top layer is as cultured, if not more so, as in other European countries. Therefore one cannot say that Russia is less civilised.

About women he said that there are three categories: *la femme du foyer*, the housewife; *la femme du temple*, the woman of ideas; and *la femme de la rue,* the woman of the street.

60

His motto was: *fais ce que doit—advienne que pourra*. He always considered that duty came before everything else and that one's actions should not be governed by concern for their consequences.

About books, he used to quote in Latin: *Habent sua fata libelli pro capite lectoris* (books have their own fate, depending on the head (brains) of the reader). He used to say that only the first part of this saying is usually quoted, which makes it lose its real meaning: which is that the success of a book depends on the reader's capacity to understand it.

He hardly ever spoke of his literary plans, saying that it destroyed a work to talk of it. But while he was collecting material he told us episodes out of his own life which had been used in his books. Often his stories and ditties made us laugh till we cried.

> When a grain of coffee
> Gets into your nose
> Don't cry, don't cry, baby.
> You'll soon gulp it down.

was a song he sang to us when we cried and we would then laugh through our tears; or he would tell us a story. There was one about a German who could not climb on to his horse, although he begged one saint after the other to come to his help. At last he called them all together, and made a great effort and jumped so high that he found himself on the other side of the animal. Then he said: ' *Nicht alle auf ein mal* ' (not all at the same time). Or about the German prisoner, condemned to death, who begs the king to allow him to choose the way to die. When the king agrees to this plea he says: I want to die of old age. The king reprieved him. Another favourite was the one about the gypsy who teaches his horse to go without eating and had almost succeeded in training it when the horse died.

He liked to tell stories from the lives of mental patients. One madman, he said, imagined he was made of glass, and lived in fear of stumbling and breaking in pieces. Somebody playfully gave him a push. The madman bumped against the wall, said: ' Ping ' and died. Another one's delusion was that he was a mushroom. He sat down in a corner, opened an umbrella, refused to eat or move or answer questions. Then the doctor also took an umbrella, opened it and sat down beside the madman. They both sat silently for some time. At last the madman could bear it no longer and asked the doctor:

' What are you doing here? '

' I'm a mushroom,' replied the doctor.

The madman looked surprised but fell silent again.

After a certain time the food that the doctor had ordered was brought to him. He began to eat.

' Do mushrooms eat? ' asked the madman.

' But of course. Look at me: I'm a mushroom and I'm eating! '

Then the madman also asked for some food and began to devour it with appetite. After a time the doctor stood up, still holding the umbrella.

' Can mushrooms stand up? ' asked the madman.

' They can,' replied the doctor, ' you see I'm standing, although I'm a mushroom.'

The madman stood up. When the doctor walked, he walked, when the doctor folded the umbrella, he did the same. Gradually the activities of a mushroom developed so widely that the madman resumed his former way of life and finally forgot he was a mushroom.

There was another tale, a cruel one, about a madman who killed the stovemaker Semion, who worked in a mental home. Semion took snuff and often gave some to the patients. One day he went to sleep in the passage leaving his axe beside him. A madman crawled up to him and hit him on the head with the axe. Then he hid Semion's head under the bed and went to tell the other inmates with a cunning smile: ' When Semion wakes up and wants to take some snuff—he won't find his nose. It'll be under my bed.'

All my father's madmen had a meaning. The man of glass is the man who imagines that everyone is out to hurt him, he fears life, his fellow-men. Such people die when confronted with real life. The madman who knocked off Semion's head so that he should not find his nose is the egotist who'll do anything to satisfy a whim. The one who imagined himself a mushroom is the man who gets into a rut, is enclosed in a narrow circle created by himself, and refuses to go any further. The way to cure him is by widening his horizon.

I believe that these tales he used to tell us in the seventies were embryos of the thoughts which later on formed his outlook on life. He believed that false thinking is the reason for all evil in the world, that men were not evil by nature, but because of incorrect thinking and were therefore irresponsible like madmen.

One of my father's fairy tales was probably inspired by Gogol's story *The Nose*. This is how it ran:

The Nose

Somewhere at a crowded hall, Mr. X by mistake pushed against a Turk and hit him on the nose. Mortally offended the Turk swore he would have his revenge and cut off the nose of Mr. X. He challenged him to a duel and insisted that it should be with sabres.

Mr. X was a good fencer but the Turk sprang upon him with such violence that he was unable to parry the weapon and the Turk cut off his nose. The doctor who was present rushed to stem the blood, the seconds demanded that the duel should be stopped but when Mr. X asked where his nose was it turned out that the dog had eaten it.

Left without a nose Mr. X decided to have another one made and asked the advice of the best doctors. One of these advised him to find a man who would agree to have a nose made out of his body.

' But,' added the doctor, ' you will have to be tied to that man for six weeks.'

Mr. X agreed. He found a country lad who for a good remuneration was willing to have a nose made out of his arm. The doctor sewed Mr. X's face to the lad's arm and they lived like that for six weeks. Then when the face and the arm had grown together the doctor operated and made Mr. X a nose. The lad, pocketing the money, returned to his village, and Mr. X had a wonderful Roman nose, far better than the old one. But he did not rejoice over it very long. At times the nose, particularly on feast days, began to swell and grow red. He asked the doctor what it could be.

' Find out what your lad is up to,' said the doctor.

Mr. X found the lad and this is what he discovered: When his nose swelled it meant the lad was drinking hard. There could be no doubt: the boy's drinking affected Mr. X's nose. Then, as

63

he could well afford it, he engaged the lad as a doorkeeper and saw to it that he did not drink. But when he could get an opportunity, the lad drank all the same and on those days Mr. X's nose grew swollen and red and he could not show himself to his friends. Finally the lad could stand such control no longer and ran away. The nose began to grow redder and more swollen and lost its Roman shape. Evidently the lad had become an inveterate drunkard. Then, one day, the nose fell off. Mr. X decided to find out what had happened to the lad. And what did it turn out to be? The day the nose fell off, the lad had died. So Mr. X remained for the rest of his life with a flat spot instead of a nose.

Here is another fairy tale—*Toutou*:

There are large monkeys very similar to human beings, who live in the tropical jungle. One day the three-year-old son of a settler disappeared in the jungle. The father went with other men to look for him and after a long search found him. He was sitting under a tree eating a coconut. The father was on the point of taking him in his arms when a huge ape rushed to him, seized him in its shaggy arms and climbed up a tree. Neither the father, nor the other men had the courage to shoot, fearing to wound the child. The ape jumped from tree to tree, they pursued it, but it soon disappeared together with the boy. For a long time nothing was heard of the child. Then one day the father saw him again in the wood eating a coconut, the ape sitting on a branch near by. The settler began to crawl stealthily up to his son, but the ape saw him and ran, too, in the child's direction. Then the father aimed his gun at it, and wounded it in the arm. The boy rushed to the monkey's help, shouting ' Toutou, Toutou! '. The ape tucked the child under its arm and made a dash for the tree. But blood was flowing abundantly from the wound and it dropped the child. The child started sobbing bitterly and looked pleadingly upwards but his father carried him away. The others tried to track the ape in vain. Back home the child kept remembering the monkey and repeated amidst his tears: ' Toutou! Nanny Toutou! Give me Toutou! '

It was clear from his babble that the monkey had cared for him and fed him on bananas and coconuts and that he had grown attached to it.

Chapter 3

Travelling

FATHER always talked with tenderness of his elder brother Nicholas who had died of consumption in 1860. He used to say: 'Brother Nicholas knew how to " do nothing " which is a knowledge few people have attained.' Indeed, he could make himself pleasant to all, without actually doing anything concrete. He had tried to be a soldier, a writer, a landowner, but his impact on people did not depend on these pursuits. He somehow stimulated everyone wherever he went and he certainly sowed seeds in his young brother's mind which bore abundant fruit. Turgenev wrote about him: ' A heart of gold, intelligent, simple and charming.' Fet wrote that ' he was a remarkable man whom everybody not merely loved but adored.' ' The humility which Leo Tolstoy extols in theory,' wrote Garshin, ' was applied by his brother directly to life.'

Father told us a funny story about him. He came one day to see him in his country house and found him not at home, but in the orchard. He followed him there and this is what he saw: Nicholas was sitting silently under an apple-tree, making signs to his brother to be quiet.

' Sh . . . sh . . . don't make a noise.'

' What are you doing here? ' father asked in a whisper.

' Sh . . . I'm watching Father Akim stealing my apples.'

It transpired that Father Akim, a young priest just appointed to the parish had climbed over the hedge and after ascertaining that the watchman was not there, had filled his pockets with apples. The master of the house sat watching stealthily, afraid only of one thing: that Father Akim should realise that he had seen him.

One day my father, still a small boy, decided to surprise everyone with his dare-devilry. Walking beside a river with a large group of friends, he jumped into the water with his clothes on and his top boots. It was a narrow river, but very deep at that spot. He swam across, but could not get on to the shore; his boots, filled with water, kept dragging him down to the bottom. The peasant women, haymaking on the other side, pulled him out with peals of laughter.

Father liked to tell us about his adventures in the Caucasus, how he was pursued once by the natives and narrowly escaped, or how a bullet exploded against a big gun where he was standing.

He was often in danger at Sebastopol.

In the heat of the battle a staff officer, Count Olsufiev, rode to the moat of the fourth bastion. Seeing L. Tolstoy on the other side, he shouted:

' Count, here is a parcel from the C.-in-C.'

Leo shouted back:

' Ride up here with it.'

Olsufiev, evidently, had to make his way across the moat, but fell from his saddle. Meanwhile the shooting grew more fierce, the bullets whistled, the grenades exploded and he could not stand it any longer. He remained where he was with the parcel, jumped on the horse and galloped back.

My father and his fellow-officers used to send their batmen to Sebastopol on errands. My father's batman showed no fear when he had to cross a place under fire. But another officer's batman was terrified at the prospect. My father used to recall him with bitter self-reproach: ' How thoughtless we were and cruel! We would send to town not Alexei, who didn't mind, but the poor frightened batman, and laughed when we saw him crawling under the fire of grenades and bullets.' After the capture of the Malak-hoff hill and the Russian army's retreat to the north of the Sebastopol bay, it was decided to explode the battery on the Pavlov promontory, from which the allies could have opened fire on the town. The decision was made late and there was no time to bring away the wounded. Father said that he saw the officer who had just executed the order, sleeping the sleep of the just. He was a healthy, good-natured young man.

Father went twice abroad—in 1857 and in the winter of 1860–61. During his first trip he lived for a time in Paris. He saw a man being guillotined there and this left him forever disgusted with capital punishment and even with European civilisation.

66

He heard a lot of fine music there, and went to the theatres. He did not like the stilted style and pathos of Racine and Corneille.

In Switzerland he lived in Clarens, on the shores of the Lac Léman, in a modest *pension* where he was registered wrongly as M. Folstoy. As his title was unknown in the pension, people did not treat him as a wealthy Russian count and he became very friendly with the landlady and the lodgers. On the way home he stopped at Baden-Baden, where he prided himself on rubbing shoulders with the great, among whom was Count Olsufiev. When Father saw the latter bow low down before Prince William (later Emperor William) he realised the futility of his pride.

Father's second trip took place because of his brother Nicholas's illness and was saddened by his death. But my father had an interesting time nonetheless; he studied the situation of the schools in various countries and met many outstanding people like Froebel and Herzen and Proudhon.

After his brother's death he went to Italy. Perhaps because of his morbid state of mind, he did not react to the beauty of the country as he would have done otherwise and said that for us people of the north the southern climate was too disturbing.

He visited the Houses of Parliament in London and listened to a three-hour speech by Palmerston, which left him cold though he considered it a masterpiece of oratory. He went, too, to a public reading by Dickens and was moved to tears.

In the fifties Father had formed a preconceived hostile opinion of Herzen, but after 1861, when he actually met him in London, he changed his mind. They were photographed together on the momentous day of the proclamation of the emancipation of the serfs. Father considered Herzen to be a man of energetic, sanguine temperament, an eloquent conversationalist and a brilliant wit. He talked about Herzen's peculiar build—he was a short man and had a very broad body. They shared a hatred of Nicholas I and Father was often to quote Herzen's words on tyrants in general: ' Chenghiz-Khan was no doubt a menace and difficult to fight again. But how much more terrible it is when at the disposal of such a figure there can be guns, railways, telegraphs and telephones and all the other achievements of modern science. Nobody can fight against that.'

There was another story he told of Herzen. One day when Herzen was walking along a London street he came across a carpet spread on a pavement in front of a wealthy house. Two flunkeys stood on either side, forbidding passers-by to step on it, and people had to go out of their way to avoid it. It was clear that some important personage was expected to arrive. Herzen, however, did not go out of his way but pushing one of the flunkeys aside, stepped on to the carpet. The flunkey he had pushed shouted to the other one: ' Let him pass. He is a gentleman.'

' The English are an aristocratic people,' Father used to say. ' What they revere in their gentlemen is not only the question of heredity, of privileges and of wealth but also their physical and mental powers. They talk of their aristocracy as of " our betters ". No Russian would ever do that.'

He used to say of Herzen's personal tragedy that it was partly brought about by the fact that the men of those days, Herzen included, were light-hearted about betraying their wives with housemaids or prostitutes, whereas the women took such matters very much more seriously.

Later on he came to appreciate Herzen more and more. He said that the banning of Herzen's writings in Russia left Russian society unaware of an important trend in Russian letters and that this caused a distortion in Russian thought. He approved of Herzen's opinion of the slavophiles, who wished to remind the people of something they really wanted to forget; orthodoxy and autocracy. In his childhood and early youth Father's attitude to serfdom was as to something inevitable. Even his teacher and aunt T. Jergolskaia believed that there was no alternative. His reaction against it developed only after he left the university and began to manage the affairs of Jassnaia; but even then such criticism as one finds in *A Landowner's Morning* was unconscious. During the years in the Caucasus and in the Crimea he had little time to give to questions of this sort. But from 1885 his repudiation of serfdom became firm and determined and appeared with particular vividness in the story *Polikushka*.

When the time came to deal with the peasants, he behaved as did all the landowners of a liberal turn of mind, but no more than that, and indeed he reproached himself later for not having taken a more generous line. One day I asked him whether he had had the occasion of buying or selling ' souls '. He replied that sometimes he was, in fact, put in the position of having to do so, on the occasions for instance when girls of his village married peasants of other landowners or the other way round.

I remember a story my father used to tell as he himself had heard it from a peasant who at the end of the fifties foretold that freedom would be granted and gave the reason why.

' I was walking all by myself one day in the fields, in the twilight . . . Suddenly I see a dark, a very dark cloud cast over the sky; but the sky above it is still quite light. And coming out from under the cloud I see a pair of long, very long peasant's feet, in bast shoes, groping for the earth. They grope and grope and finally reach it. And as soon as they feel the ground under their feet they walk away in the bast shoes through the field. And so I knew—freedom would come.'

When he was a young man, Father had an exceedingly hot temper when roused to anger, and on occasion was known to resort to violence. This is one story he told us himself. In 1865 he was living with his wife and her then unmarried sister, Tatiana, on his second estate. My mother and her sister went one day to bathe in the river. In that year the forest adjoining the river had been sold to a merchant and the forestry offices were nearby. While they were in the water, a forestry official passed by. He stopped and began to make bawdy jokes at the two young women and in spite of their entreaties, refused to go away. When they finally got home, they told Leo Tolstoy about their adventure. He flew into a violent rage, rushed to the forestry offices and ' broke his stick ' across the offender's back.

Chapter 4

Farming

UNTIL the eighties, Father took a great interest in his estates. His way of farming was very characteristic of his nature. He became engrossed first in one aspect of it, then in another, searching constantly for new methods. But it was not the mainspring of his existence; he had not much time for it nor did he have sufficient patience. Besides men and the world of nature interested him much more than making money.

I remember when I was a small child in Jassnaia, we had numerous bee-hives, pigs and sheep and some beautiful cows. But the bee-hives did not last for long and my mother declared that, according to the veterinary surgeon, the pigs died from a strange disease caused by hunger. It proved to be unprofitable to breed sheep in such wooded land, they nibbled at all the young shoots and produced inferior manure. The cows yielded little milk for they were neither properly fed nor sufficiently milked. The only profit-making undertakings of Father's were the leasing of grazing land, the planting of new trees and the increase of the apple orchard—perhaps because these branches of agriculture did not demand the master's constant attention. In the sixties and seventies, oxen were sent from the Ukraine to Moscow and Petersburg, not by rail, but by road, and on the way they grazed on land specially leased for this purpose. About one hundred and fifty acres of our land were used for this. In the summer there would be several herds of smoky, phlegmatic, beautiful Ukrainian oxen with long horns, grazing on our land on their way to be slaughtered in Moscow and Petersburg. The men lived in tents, making bonfires to cook by. When, later on, it was forbidden to transport oxen this way because of epidemics, Father gave the land to the peasants; fertilized by many years of grazing, the land yielded good harvests and the prosperity of the peasants increased.

The forests were perhaps the estate's greatest asset. Father never felled the trees, for he considered that the forest was capital that increased through a natural process of accumulation. ' The forest is the daughters' dowry,' my mother used to say. In spite of its being well guarded, timber was often stolen by the peasants but Father never brought the cases to court, and sometimes even pretended not to notice that the pilfering went on. More and more apple trees were planted and yielded a huge harvest of apples. But there was not enough pruning and spraying of the trees and very soon the orchard became neglected. The estate on the whole ran at a loss, because the house absorbed too much of the land produce.

Father's other estate, Nikolskoe, came from my great-grand-mother Gorchakov, and after many ups and downs fell into my father's hands in 1860. It was situated near the estates of Turgenev and of Fet. Father lived in it during his quarrel with Turgenev* and the hill on which he wanted to fight a duel with the writer was halfway between the two estates. The village of Nikolskoe is described in *Resurrection*. Almost one-third of it was forest inhabited by wolves in great numbers. The old house had fallen down and in its place stood a thatch-roofed annexe. The farm buildings were in disrepair. Nearby stood a church built by my grandfather according to a vow he had made during the war. The man who ran the estate, Orlov, was of an ecclesiastic background and had managed it for twenty-eight years, at first with great zeal, but later he had taken to drink and had neglected it. He was exacting with the peasants, but he was a just man, and they had a great respect for him. When he was angry, he would seize a man by the nose and toss him from side to side. One of the peasants in the village was a well-known horse thief, feared by one and all. Orlov, presuming that a horse thief would not steal from his master, engaged him as a forest supervisor. True, there was no horse-stealing on the estate after Tikhon was hired, but the thefts of timber increased and he had to be discharged. One day Orlov met him in the wood and they had the following conversation:

' You did wrong when you discharged me,' said Tikhon, ' worse things might come to you . . . '

' What sort of things ? ' asked Orlov.

*See page 159.

'Well, who knows—maybe some of your animals will go . . . or there could be a fire!'

'A fire?' exclaimed Orlov. 'Let me tell you that if a fire breaks out on the estate, all your village will burn to the ground, and your house will be the first to go.'

I am certain that Orlov would never have carried out his threat, but it had its effect and no untoward incident took place.

He applied slightly original methods in his estate management. He believed insurance was an unnecessary expense, but planned the outbuildings far from one another, to prevent fire from spreading. As a result, there was a lot of thieving in the buildings farthest from the house and a great deal of money had to be spent on watchmen. Another idea was to spread straw in the field and plough it into the earth, which he maintained was more beneficial than using natural manure. The peasants used to carry away the straw to their homes each night. But in spite of these eccentricities his management proved successful; he planted crops of potatoes and sold them to distilleries and sold beet to the neighbouring sugar factory.

One day when I was returning from a ride on horseback with my father, he asked me:

'What are you thinking about?'

I don't remember what I replied to that but, summoning up my courage, I asked him, in my turn, what *he* had been thinking about. He smiled and said:

'I was wondering whether Orlov is honest or not and how unpleasant it was to suspect anyone of dishonesty.'

'And have you decided that Orlov is honest?'

'Yes, I have,' he replied.

He used to go from time to time to Nikolskoe to supervise Orlov; they corresponded continually and Orlov came often to Jassnaia to make his reports.

Chapter 5

Hunting and Shooting

In the old days many sportsmen considered hunting more of an obligation than a pleasure. I knew one poor landowner who used to put on fresh underclothes when he went to hunt boar, like a Roman general going into battle.

For my father, hunting was not simply an excuse for a social occasion, a picnic in the open air or for showing off his pack of hounds. The solitary aspect of it appealed to him, he loved to feel himself a part of the countryside, loved the exhilaration of hunting that makes the sportsman forget the petty trifles of life. He used to plan his future work on these occasions and often declared that only sportsmen and those who tilled the land were able to admire nature with any depth of feeling.

I remember from my childhood days our favourite Irish setter, the intelligent and affectionate Dora—my father gave her that name in honour of the heroine in *David Copperfield*. Another dog we had—Boffin—was also taken from Dickens. When Father went shooting duck, woodcock, snipe, quail, he would take Dora with him. He was a good shot and indefatigable and Dora tired sooner than he did; she would pant, her tongue hanging out of her mouth, and stare at him imploringly, begging him to send her back again into the swamp. When he did nonetheless order her to retrieve something she was very cunning and would rush about the field pretending to be on the look out for partridges.

Father at that time was not only not a vegetarian but he killed game mercilessly. When he had shot a bird but had failed to kill it, he would pull out a feather and pierce the bird's head with it, and he taught us to do the same.

Only the passionate sportsman knows the delight of following hounds on a clear autumn morning with the forest as a background, and the sudden thrill when all their voices are raised together and they are off after the scent of a hare or a fox. We did not have many hounds but those we had bore traditional names which were passed down from father to son. They were in the charge of Agafia Mikhailovna who was a great lover of animals, and of dogs in particular. She lived on a small annuity and spent a great deal of her own money on the dogs. If a half-trained dog should suddenly attack the sheep in a peasant's herd, my Father would beat it mercilessly with a whip, holding it by the hind legs so that it could not bite. He would pay three times the sheep's price. The peasants protested sometimes when we crossed their land and they were within their rights, but as a general rule the matter was settled perfectly peacefully.

After we moved to Moscow Father stopped hunting altogether. The hounds died one after the other and so did Agafia Mikhailovna. My younger brothers used to go out with a gun, but only to shoot hare.

It was a joy for me to go hunting with my father. He surrendered spontaneously to his passion for it and I was infected with his enthusiasm.

Part III

TOWARDS THE CRISIS

Chapter 1

First Winter in Moscow

In August 1881 my mother, in spite of her pregnancy, went to Moscow to find a house for us to live in. My father was moving to town because he had promised my mother to spend the winter in Moscow, but could not think of it without horror. My mother's heart was set on this move. For me it meant the long-awaited end of my school years and my entrance into the university. Tania was thinking of parties and balls and intended to learn painting for which she showed some talent. Ilya felt apprehensive about starting in a new school and missed the autumn hunting for which he had developed a passion. The others, Liova, Masha, Andrei, and Misha were too young to have any definite opinions at all.

At that time our financial situation was very satisfactory— I say 'ours' because Father considered that all he had belonged, in fact, to us. He had sold a mill on one of the estates, part of the forest in Jassnaia, and had received a large sum from his publisher.

At that time I had adopted a distant attitude to the rest of the family. I harboured vague radical notions, inspired partly by the books I had read, and by injustice and poverty. I violently criticized the government, bureaucracy, the wealthy classes and the clergy. Only very gradually was this trend transformed into what was called a liberal bourgeois point of view. But what was never to alter was my attitude towards science, especially towards the natural sciences which I considered to be true knowledge and enlightenment; and I could never agree with my father's attacks on it. On the other hand, I was attracted by the entertainments offered by a society in which my mother and Tania took such an active part, though I was a poor dancer. Throughout my life as a student, I rather tended to go from one extreme to the other— from the life of society to the life of the radical intelligentsia,

76

from Father's teachings of Christianity to the teachings of science and of atheism, from a simple way of life to one of drunkenness and revelry.

I loved music, particularly the piano, and wanted to enrol at a music school, but it was difficult to combine that with the university, and the latter was the more important to me. I lived the first month alone in Moscow quite independently, on the small allowance granted to me by my parents. I did not know my way about and had to ask people in the street to guide me to the university. The lectures had not started yet; I wandered about Moscow and found great pleasure in joining in the university life. In September our whole family moved to town and Mother engaged a new cook, Petr Vassilievich, who was a kind man, perhaps a little too fond of drink. Our old cook and the old nurse remained in Jassnaia and received a pension.

The first impression of the house was very unsatisfactory. This is what my mother wrote to her sister Kusminskaia:

' Soon after our arrival, everybody became wrapped in a deep gloom which increased every day. The house seems made of cardboard, and is so noisy that we have no peace in our bedroom and Liova cannot work in his study. I am in despair and the strain of keeping everyone from making a noise is considerable. Finally Liova burst out that if I loved him and was concerned with his mental condition I would never have chosen these rooms where he never had a moment's peace, where the price of a single chair would have made a peasant's happiness—allowed him to buy a horse or a cow, that it drives him to tears, and so on and so forth. But there is no going back. Of course he drove me to hysterics and I am walking about as in a vacuum; everything is a muddle in my head and I feel ill, as though suffering from shock. You can imagine how easy it all is, only a fortnight before the baby is due and so much to do.'

The house was indeed as though made of cardboard and one could hear everything going on in the next room. I had hardly any time to play the piano and when I found the time I was afraid of disturbing Father.

Ilya and Liova were supposed to enter a State gymnasium, and Father was asked to give a guarantee of their ' political stability '.

77

He was very angry and said: ' I can't give such a guarantee even concerning myself; how could I do so for my sons?' He arranged for them to go to a private school which made a better impression on him and where they asked for no such guarantees. Tania was placed in an art school and a music teacher was engaged for me.

But even after a month in Moscow my parents felt no better about it. My mother wrote to her sister:

' The first fortnight I cried all the time because Liova was not only gloomy but plunged in the most terrible apathy. He did not sleep or eat, and sometimes he wept and I thought I was going crazy. You wouldn't have believed how ill I looked. Then he went to Tver to see Bakunin, and after that he went on to a village where he stayed with a dissenter and finally he returned in a better frame of mind. Now he works in an annexe which he rents for six roubles a month, and goes out for long walks in the suburbs and saws wood with the peasants. He enjoys it and it agrees with him. We always have visitors in the evenings. But no one seems to be really content about the move and this is a great disappointment to me. Ilya longs to be in Jassnaia and so does Tania. I would feel better myself in Moscow if people were happier around me.'

My mother was only consoled by the fact that it was ' a blessing for Serejha, obviously, that we are in Moscow.' She was depressed not only because of my father's depression. She was on the verge of giving birth to her child and on October 31st the boy Aliosha was born without much discomfort.

Father was in a restless and gloomy state of mind. He wrote to a friend in November 1881:

' There are two alternatives: to give up and suffer passively, surrendering to despair, or to submit to evil and lull oneself into a semi-conscious state with trifles and card-playing. Luckily I cannot do the latter and the former is too painful so I am bound to seek some other solution. One possibility is: verbal or written preaching, but this opens the door to vanity, pride and perhaps self-deception as well, and one fights shy of it; another possibility is to distribute charity to the poor but here the huge figures of the needy oppress you.

It's not like in the country where immediately one is part of a natural community. The only solution I see is to lead a good life and show a kind face to everyone. But I have not found yet the way to do it, as you have. I always think of you when I go astray. It is very seldom that I succeed in achieving this happy state: I'm hot-tempered, angry, easily roused and continually dissatisfied with myself.'

Before his marriage my father knew almost the whole of Petersburg high society. Now he avoided his friends. My mother, on the other hand, in order to ' bring out ' Tania, tried to renew these ties and to take Tania to balls and parties.

Apart from the realisation that life had shaped itself quite contrary to his convictions, Father resented the disturbance of his habits and the loss of the freedom he had enjoyed in the country. When he first came to Moscow, for instance, he felt awkward in his traditional grey blouse. It did, indeed, seem strange amidst the elegant attire of our guests. Father could not both from habit and because of his new viewpoints, wear conventional clothes. So he chose a compromise: a black jacket that he wore over a soft shirt, buttoned up to the neck. It was neither a blouse nor a coat. He wore it for a whole winter, and finally returned to his old blouse.

It was not only the town atmosphere and the noise in the house that interfered with his works; he was upset by all the visitors. It would be unfair to say that he disapproved of them; no, some of them he liked; but there were so many of them and he was unable to organise himself sufficiently well to avoid them. One of his friends, Serge Yuriev, a left-wing slavophile, used to come often and Father expounded his religious views to him, to which the other listened sympathetically. He was very popular in Moscow and well-known for his absent-mindedness, a target for innumerable anecdotes. On one of the Thursdays when he used to receive guests, he left his flat and meeting a friend in the doorway, said: ' Don't go in there, it's terribly boring! ' One day he seized a cat instead of his hat and almost put it on his head. Another day he came to visit us and when I was seeing him out, I asked which was his coat. ' I don't know,' he replied. ' I've already tried two.'

Another friend was Nicholas Fedorov, a librarian and a man

79

of ascetic life. His room was so small that there was no room in it even for his bed—which consisted of a few boards. He distributed his small salary among the poor and refused every increase. His philosophy was expressed in a book called *The Philosophy of the Common Cause* and it consisted of a faith that science would sooner or later succeed in resurrecting the dead, the common cause of mankind being to encourage this aim and to preserve everything that remained after people's deaths.

In 1882 the well-known sectarian Siutaev came to Moscow. He was a small peasant dressed in a neat sheepskin coat, with a thin, reddish beard and kind grey eyes. He was gentle with human beings and animals and was a man of great intelligence. His faith, which he had arrived at quite alone, was based on Christianity, taken as pure, personal ethics. He was not a church-goer and was against military service. His son was a conscientious objector and was imprisoned for his beliefs in the Schlusselburg fortress. He did not pay taxes but did not object to them and had no keys to the doors of his house. He did not expect others to share his faith, in which he differed from my father, who was upset and irritated when anybody contradicted his beliefs.

In May my father finally purchased the Khamovniki house in Moscow. It was too small for our family and Father decided to build an annexe. It was he who supervised the work, made all the arrangements about wallpaper, decoration, and so on, bought furniture, and acquired a carriage. He realised he was acting contrary to all his convictions, but he did it to avoid the reproach that he left all practical matters to my mother.

We moved into the house in 1882.

At the time when I entered the university the students wore civilian clothes and uniforms were introduced only in 1885. Their appearance was varied; some wore clean suits and shirts with starched collars and cuffs, were properly shaved and beard-less, while others wore Russian blouses without ties and shabby jackets, throwing rugs across their shoulders instead of overcoats, had long hair and unshaven chins.

I took my work very seriously and conscientiously, though there was much I did not understand, having been insufficiently prepared for a scientific education . . . One of the reasons for this was my father's contempt for the natural sciences. He spoke ironically of 'small cells' and for a long time I was puzzled by his attitude. And one day when I said I was particularly interested in chemistry he declared that physics was the more interesting study because physical phenomena were more common in nature than chemical ones, with which I was in disagreement. I think probably that he had come to hold these opinions simply because in his youth the natural sciences were not as developed as they were to become in the eighties, and also because they did not fit in with his general outlook. Later I began to attend only those lectures that specially interested me.

Our professor of zoology was A. Bogdanov. He had a disconcerting habit of drawing various parts of animals on the blackboard, concealing them with his corpulent figure and then wiping them off.

I remember one amusing incident at an examination in zoology. We were being examined in ichtyology and one of my fellow-students got a question on the sheat-fish.

'Tell me what you know about the sheat-fish,' asked the professor.

'The sheat-fish is large and fat, with long whiskers and a slimy and hairless body.'

'This is a description of Ogarev, the Moscow Police Inspector in his bath, not a sheat-fish,' the professor replied.

Another similar incident occurred at an examination of physics and meteorology. At that time there were no typewriters and the lectures were copied in longhand and then lithographed. Thus it was quite easy to mistake 'cyclones' for 'cyclops' and this is what the same student announced at the examination:

'The cyclop is a system of winds, an area of low pressure, etc. Cyclops, anticyclops . . .'

The professor listened to the end and then asked:

'What is the science you are concerned with, mythology or meteorology?'

The student replied, most surprised:

'Meteorology, sir.'

'Where then did you gather your information on cyclops.'

'From your lectures, sir.'

'Your reference to my lectures is outrageous,' the professor answered and gave the student the lowest possible mark.

Chemistry enthralled me and I spent long days in the laboratory.

A great weakness in our chemistry classes was the absence of a professor of technological chemistry. I have no idea why this was so. It was said that the assistant took advantage of the situation to further his private fabrication of olive oil out of petrol.

Theology was another subject on our curriculum, although it has no connection with the natural sciences. I hardly ever attended the lectures and was unable to say anything at the examination. The professor, a priest, then asked me:

' What is the essence of the soul? '

I did not know how to reply and am still doubtful as to what the answer should have been—' divine ' I suppose. He gave me a bad mark, but this had no effect upon the general marks, although theology was a compulsory subject.

The period when I was attending the university was a period of rabidly reactionary tendencies; there were no riots, and the students' only activity was to distribute in secret forbidden pamphlets, which they themselves duplicated. I had expected to take part in revolutionary meetings, but in fact there were only three or four of them in the course of the whole four years.

In June 1884 I had an unpleasant encounter with our inspector Brisgalov. We were standing in the hall of the university, preparing to leave, having already put on our coats and hats. The prefect approached and said:

' Please take off your hats.'

I asked.

' Why? We're in the hall.'

He replied:

' You're in the professors' way.'

Nobody obeyed the order. But a moment later the director rushed in, shouting: ' Hats off! ' And all the students except myself and another student removed them. We were both summoned the next day into the director's room. He pretended not to notice us. After waiting for a few moments, I turned to him:

' Look here, you did have us brought here, didn't you? '

He jumped to his feet.

' What do you mean by " Look here! " '? How dare you address the director like that! You'll be reported for impertinence! '

I murmured: ' Is that all,' and left the room. As a result it was said in my certificate that my behaviour was good, but not excellent.

After I left the university there was some rioting, and repeated demands to expel the director. A student slapped his face and he had to leave.

I passed all my first university examinations in 1885. To become a candidate of natural sciences I had only now to write a paper and this I had decided to do on chemistry; and in particular on theoretical, atomic chemistry. I wanted to prove that the atomic theory had been arrived at purely from theory and not from experiment. But I found the subject was too vast for me and when I showed my paper to my professor he said: ' That's not chemistry, it's a kind of philosophy. I'd better look at your paper on naphtha, on heavy oils.' Which he did.

Having decided to postpone my finals for fear of failing to pass my examination in physics, I got a certificate of illness and had the whole summer before me to do as I wanted. It was the summer of the coronation of Alexander III. We decided, my former teacher and I, to take a boat down the Volga to Samara and from there to our estate, where my father was also going, and as we were quite indifferent to the celebrations we chose to go that particular day. It began to rain almost immediately and we anchored near a sandy beach covering ourselves with sails and tarpaulin. We spent the night there watching the illuminations and fireworks over Moscow, and shivering from the cold. We continued on our way the next morning and towards evening overtook a great barge, drifting along with five hefty peasants on board, blind drunk. We gathered from their shouting that they were intending to beat us up as students who had killed the Emperor Alexander II. They had probably decided we were students because I was wearing spectacles. We were in a tight spot as they would have no doubt beaten us up or thrown us into the water if they had caught up with us, but we pressed on our oars and made off as quickly as we could. Having reached Kolomna on our fourth day we decided to part with the boat. We had little money; our provisions had gone, and we were tired. We sold the boat at a small loss, took the train to Riazan, then a wretched little steamship as far as Nijhni-Novgorod, where we changed to a luxurious Volga steamboat as far as Samara; and from there we proceeded by carriage and horses to the estate.

My father was there before us. We found everything much as

usual, pyramids of bricks of manure, herds of oxen, sheep, horses and flies—clouds of flies. There was a new bailiff with his wife, who my father liked at first, but later on wrote about him that he was ' a bailiff of the grumbling kind ', who could always find some excuse to explain away his failures by unfavourable circumstances. There were about thirty people gathered to drink mare's milk. Among them was a young lad of twenty-eight who had been expelled from school in his last term for his ' red ' ideas and who since then had lived in either prison or banishment. Father often had arguments with him and his friends on the subject of revolutionary violence. I must admit that I agreed with Lazareff and his friends more than I did with my father. Father incorporated him in *Resurrection*, in the figure of Nabatov. Father had decided to lease the land to the peasants, after selling the inventory and taking some horses to Jassnaia. The land had to be surveyed and the boundaries set, but my father refused to get a surveyor, as he said he preferred to do it himself. He did indeed make a beginning with a measured piece of marked string but never finished the work. When my father left, the bailiff leased all the land to the peasants. Father wrote to his friends living near to collect the money from the lease and to use it for the poor, and for schools in the surrounding villages, etc. ' This, if God wills,' he wrote, ' will be done as soon as I can overrule the objections raised by my own family. I hope to live as long as that. Then I'll come and arrange it all as best I can. I've had the accounts from which it seems I am owed about ten thousand roubles. What shall I do about it? Forget it, or get it back from those who can pay and give it to those who can't? On the other hand perhaps all this is nonsense and just a kind of vanity on my part. Perhaps we'd better forget the whole thing and indeed I think that's the best thing to do.' His friends wrote to him that his claims could only be recovered if he went to law which of course he would never agree to do. The situation became uncertain and the problem of the Samara estate (the ' eastern problem ' as we called it) was settled only when my mother wrote to ask that the money from the lease should be sent to her direct, which the bailiff refused to do and, following which, another bailiff was appointed.

On my return I started working very hard for my examinations and in the autumn passed them all.

Chapter 2

The Discord

By the eighties the foundations of my father's outlook on life which he was to retain for the rest of his days were already firmly established. Somewhere I have read the words: ' Robert Burns was a poet and therefore an unhappy man.' Can it be that because a poet penetrates so much more deeply into life than the ordinary man he therefore becomes much more absorbed in all its wretchedness? That was certainly what happened with my father. He could see so clearly all the unhappiness in this world. He was too deeply aware of life's miseries and for that reason his own happiness was impaired for ever. The poverty in Jassnaia, the starvation in Moscow moved him to tears. I remember one day he came home from visiting Fedot, the poorest peasant of Jassnaia, who was dying, and said in a voice trembling with tears: ' Here was I, returning from Fedot by the short cut from the village when I heard Sercjha (that was me) playing Brahms's Hungarian dances. It is no shame on him, but it seemed so strange that almost next door there was a poor soul ill and dying and we did not know anything about it, we did not want to know, we just went on playing gay tunes.' After the ' crisis ' Father saw in his denial of everything he had previously loved and believed in the criterion of the rightness of his new opinions. Brought up as a churchgoer, now he was critical about the church rites; a farmer who had loved farming, now he denied the right to own land; a man of great culture himself, he now turned against European culture and knowledge; a great artist himself, he denied all art that did not correspond to his own conception of pure art . . . His opinion of the idle rich, including members of his family, was that they were a gang of madmen. He wrote in his diary in April 1884: ' It has suddenly occurred to me to write " notes of a non-madman." What is going to happen to us all? '

At the same time these years were his most prolific ones. He wrote: *What is my faith?*, *What is left for us to do?*, *On life;* also artistic works like: *The Death of Ivan Ilyich, The Employer and the Employee, The Kreutzer Sonata, Fruits of Enlightenment, Power of Darkness* and a number of folk stories. He was also learning Hebrew.

From 1881 his forbidden works began to circulate in manuscript and provoked an intense interest. People came rushing to him with problems of faith, with social and ethical problems and with their personal problems as well. He considered it his duty to see them all, though it took up a great deal of his time and wore him out; and in spite of my mother's efforts to limit the hours of the visits, the people came long before seven p.m. and stayed till long past midnight. My mother and sister Tatiana jokingly called my father's disciples ' the dark ones ', in contrast with their friends, who were ' light '. His whole order of life changed abruptly. He rose early, tidied his room himself, pumped water from the well and rolled it home in a barrel, chopped wood, made boots. He stopped drinking wine, became a vegetarian and tried to give up smoking, though it was only in 1888 that he actually succeeded in doing so. My mother considered vegetarianism unhealthy but in Father's case she was wrong, because for his liver complaint it was definitely very appropriate food. In Jassnaia, in the summer, Father gave a great deal of his time to helping a poor widow who owned a plot of land there and he took over from her all her hard work, cutting the grass, collecting the hay, the rye and the oats, manuring, ploughing and sowing for her.

As the censorship would not allow his books to be published he had *My Faith* printed at his own expense. But the thirty copies published in this way were confiscated and distributed among people of authority. Abroad there soon appeared translations in French and German. It was the voice of his conscience that was speaking now, urging everyone to devote himself to the truth and the spreading of it ' not only with one's tongue, but with one's belly, one's arms and one's legs.'

My mother could not accept his new views. Naturally she wanted security for herself and her children, who of course at that time could not earn their own living. I the eldest and nineteen in 1882, was still in the university, her youngest, Aliosha, was a baby. How far was she to limit expenses? Was she to go on

educating the children, or not? Should she keep a servant?
Should she live in Moscow or Jassnaia? Should she accept the
copyright money? She had to have definite answers to all these
questions, but she got none from my father, who considered that
the fewer material comforts a family could indulge in, the better.
My mother, on the contrary, as if by perversity, began to spend
more. She realised it, though, and wrote to my father on November 12th: ' As I'm a past master in grousing, I can't help grousing
and regretting all that has been; all that I used to grouse about,
how wonderful it all was! And I can't help reproaching myself,
for I am so much worse now than I have ever been and you, who
used to be good even then—you are so infinitely better now.'

Thus the discord between my parents was continually in-
creasing. I can't reproach either of them. They were both right
and wrong in their own ways. The dissension became acute in
1884 and 1885. My father wrote at that time in his diaries about
his loneliness within his family, the domineering character of his
wife, her sharp tongue, her hostility concerning the change in his
way of life, ' it is as if I was the only sane man in a madhouse,
run by madmen; my family does not understand the torment that
I live in.' He complained of the wickedness, the idleness of his
children, of his wife's unending criticisms; he was upset because
she had decided not to nurse the child she was expecting.* She
justified it by saying that she had to give too much of her time
now to looking after financial and domestic matters and she could
not do a man's work and a woman's work at the same time.

On June 17th after a stormy altercation, my father decided to
leave the family. My mother reproached him for not providing
the money to keep us all, my father reproached her for her
thriftless way of life and her refusal to live more austerely. In a
way, as far as the last winter was concerned, his reproaches were
justified, for my mother and sister had been leading a hectic
social life. But in her last month of pregnancy she certainly could
not be expected to bother herself with how to liquidate the
Samara estate or how to lead a more simple life.

After this conversation my father packed up a bundle of things
in a rucksack and made his way on foot towards Tula, determined
to leave us for ever. Fortunately by the time he had got halfway

---

*On June 18th 1884 their daughter Alexandra was born.

87

he had changed his mind and so he returned home. I was in Jassnaia at the time and only learnt of this much later.

In the eighties I sympathised very little with my father's point of view and often argued with him. I disagreed with his desire to alter our life, and in particular my life, with his attacks on science, and with his theory of non-resistance to evil. It infuriated him. He mentions his conversations with me in his diary:

' *March* 1884. Have argued with Serejha about his obtuseness . . . Have received letter from Chertkov with an outrageous note from an Englishman " for their own dear sakes " . . . All criminals are insane. A judge is a healer. Why does he judge and not testify? Why does he punish? I read it to Tania and Serejha. The latter is fiercely, liberally obtuse. It upsets me . . .

May 29th. ' Why don't I talk with Tania, with any of the children? Serejha is so obtuse he has his mother's castrated mind. If either of you two ever read this, forgive me, but it hurts very much.

' What is so terrible is that all the evil—the luxury, the sin in my life—is of my own making. And I too am contaminated and can never improve. I try to but it is a slow process. I cannot stop smoking, cannot find the right tone with my wife so that I neither offend her nor yield to her. I search, I try. Serejha has come. I haven't got the right approach to him either, just as with my wife. They cannot see; they do not begin to understand how much I suffer.

June 7th. ' I said to Serejha that everyone must carry his own burden and that his arguments, like those of many other people, are simply a shifting of the responsibility: " I'll carry it when the others do," he says, or " I don't see anybody else carrying it." That means me, of course, he means that *I* don't carry my burden either. That I only talk. That wounded me deeply. He is like his mother all over again, unkind and insensitive. Yes, it hurt me a lot. I wanted to get away at once. But that is weakness. Of course I have myself to blame if I'm wounded. I struggle, I try to dull the flame, but I realise that all this has upset the balance somewhere. In reality what do they need me for? Why should I suffer so? A tramp's life is supposed to be full of hardship (though it is not so in fact) but it could never compare with the torment I live in all the time.'

When I remember these talks, I realise that I should never have hinted that my father himself had altered his life only slightly, but I did not understand what it was he wanted from me. Perhaps if I had left the university and started working on the land like some Tolstoyans were to do later, then he might have approved of me. But I did not want to do that and did not think it necessary.

In one of the later notes in his diary he says:

' A man came to buy a horse. I broke my promise. Got 250 roubles. The lie in my life is wicked. I wanted to give the money to Tania. It turned out that the others, that is, Serejha, are envious. You'll read this one day Serejha; you must learn that you are very very wicked. You must work hard on yourself and most of all, you must learn humility.

' I talked to Serejha. He was rude without any provocation. I was upset and reprimanded him . . . For the bourgeois attitude, the obtuseness, the wickedness, the conceit. He suddenly said that no one loves him and burst into tears. God, how miserable I was. I could find no peace and after dinner caught him and said to him: " I'm sorry . . . " He began to sob and kiss me and repeated: " Forgive me, forgive me . . . " I hadn't felt anything like that for a long time. That is real happiness.'

I don't remember in what way I had been rude to him, but he was unjust in reproaching me with hating him. I never hated him, I loved him, but I could not curb my desire to contradict him. Now, after sixty years, I cannot remember all our arguments. But here is one of them, on the subject of science.

My Father: Science concerns itself with everything except the most important thing of all, that is—the secret of how to live. It is impossible and it is of no value to learn all the world's phenomena.

I: But science gives true knowledge and thus destroys superstition.

Father: Scientists don't discriminate between useful and useless knowledge; they learn and pass on unnecessary information on things like the sexual organs of the amoeba because it gives them the chance of living in comfort.

I: This is not an argument against science, but against the privileged status of scientists. You might as well say about people who deny church rites that they deny religion simply because of its dogma and its canons; it's like the proverb: 'Because one wants to be rid of the lice one throws a fur coat into the fire.' I can say as well that you decry science because of the scientists' privileged status.

Father (irritably): All scientists receive their salaries from the State and not only are they unable to teach truths unacceptable to the State, they have in fact to dance to the State's tune.

From 1883 my mother took over our entire financial affairs. We spent about 15,000 roubles a year, including the house in Khamovniki, clothes, theatres and concerts, transport, etc. The estates yielded little money, our only profitable source of income being the copyrights on Father's work. My father had given my mother the right to collect the income on all works published before 1881; all those published afterwards were out of copyright. In 1885 my mother undertook to have a fifth reprint of the *Complete Works of L. Tolstoy.* She had been advised to do this herself by the wife of Dostoyevski, and she borrowed 25,000 roubles for the edition. Thus in the wing of the house in Khamovniki there opened an ' Office for the publication of L. Tolstoy's complete works.' My father disliked the idea and frowned every time he had to pass the inscription.

In December 1885 relations between my parents suffered a turn for the worse. In November my mother went to Petersburg to try to get from the censor the right to include *Confession* and *My Faith* in the *Complete Works* but permission was refused. My father was against her journey; he considered it humiliating to beg people like Pobedonostsev for a permit to publish his work and was only too well aware that our family was going on with its luxurious worldly life, completely ignoring everything he believed in. All this depressed him. In an unsent letter in December he wrote to my mother:

' I am in despair and can't find a solution. There are three alternatives: (1) to take over authority and give all my possessions away to their rightful owners—the workers; give everything away, to save the young from temptation and destruction; but it will mean great conflict, I will provoke anger and irritation and frustrated desires, which is even worse; (2) to leave the family? But that means leaving them, relinquishing the influence which I still may have, creating loneliness for myself and my wife and breaking a commandment; (3) to continue to live as I do, trying always to develop the strength to fight evil with humility and kindness. That is what I do, but often can't achieve kindness and humility and suffer agonies of remorse. Must it go on like that, until I die?'

In another unsent letter to Chertkov at the same time he wrote:

' People don't read what I write; they don't listen to what I say or if they do, they become exasperated as soon as they understand what I am driving at; they don't see what I am doing, perhaps they try not to . . . But to break the chains, to free myself from falsehood without anger and irritation I am not able to do . . . When I look round at all the lies in which I live, and feel so poor in spirit, I hate myself and all those who place me in this situation . . . '

About December 15th my father, in a state of great disturbance, told my mother all he thought and felt and for a second time mentioned his desire to leave the family. My mother wrote to her sister:

' Liovochka is in a terribly nervous and gloomy state of mind. I was sitting writing a few days ago when he came in looking positively distraught. Until then everything had been going smoothly, with never a word, never an unpleasant word between us. " I have come to tell you I would like to get a divorce. I cannot go on living like this. I shall go and live in Paris or in America perhaps." I couldn't have been more surprised if the ceiling had fallen down on top of me. I asked him what the matter was? Nothing, he said, but if you keep loading a cart, the horse will refuse to move. What load is this? I asked. Then he started shouting and swearing and when he said: " The air is contaminated wherever you are," I told the servants to fetch me a trunk and I began to pack; I decided immediately to come and stay

91

with you for a few days. The children came rushing in, in tears. Tania said she would come with me. Then he began to beg me to stay, and finally burst into hysterical sobbing; it was horrible! Liovochka trembling from head to foot! I felt a great pity for him. All four children, Tania, Ilya, Lelia, Masha were weeping. I was turned to stone, could neither speak nor cry, afraid I might say something I would regret later. And that was the end of it all. But the feeling of estrangement, of pain, is always there. And I ask myself: Why is it so? I never move from the house, I work on the publication until late at night; my heart overflows with love . . .

'And then finally after all this we parted as friends. He went off with Tania, both of them on a tiny sledge, to visit the Olsufievs, sixty versts away . . . '

Later she wrote again to her sister:

'Yes, I want him to return to me, just as he wants me to follow him. The life I lead now is the happy life of the old days and I am content. His is a new life; a life of continual torment, that makes for nothing but desolation all around him. For me it is the abyss—and I will not allow myself to be lured into it. This new, so-called salvation, which in fact brings the wish of death exhausts me so much that I loathe it.'

Later Father admitted he was sometimes unkind to his family. He wrote to my mother in 1885:

'I have realised how wrong I have been and I say this not merely to placate you. When I realised this I emptied my heart of all its bitterness and re-established in it my love for you and Serejha and now all is well and it will be well, no matter what happens in the outside world.'

In his diary he wrote in the same vein:

'I sat upstairs with Serejha and I was so happy—there was none of my former irritation for him, on the contrary only love. When I re-read my diaries of last year I was so disgusted with myself for all the unkind things I wrote about Sonia and Serejha. I love and treasure Sonia more and more. I understand Serejha and have no other feelings for him but love.'

In the years that followed the relations between my parents varied; sometimes they improved and at other times grew sharper, but they were never really at peace with one another in spite of the great love between them. They established a certain *modus vivendi* to which Tania and Masha, my sisters, both contributed. Tania, both Mother's and Father's favourite, a talented and enthusiastic girl, abandoned the hectic social life she had been leading (though she kept on friendly terms with everyone) and came round to my father's way of thinking. Masha had never enjoyed parties and entertainments; she loved the country, worked on the land and was devoted to my father. They both helped him with copying and with his immense correspondence.

Chapter 3

Jassnaia Poliana

In the autumn of 1884 my brother Ilya and I went to Moscow to study. In September I got the following letter from Father:

' Hulloa, Serejha! How are you? I'm not worried about you in the sense that something may happen to you, but I am so afraid you'll do something wrong. And the older you get the worse it is. Don't take offence at what I have to say. You'll feel the same yourself when you have children of your own. It's a great pity that Markovnikov behaved like that to you. I thought you have been merely breaking crockery in a friendly way, now it appears that the general did not approve of that.* How are the Olsufievs? It's a pity that you lost your nerve about the apples. You seem to have left the whole thing in the air†. We are all well, and living at peace with one another. Tomorrow we, that is

*This is what had happened. I had been working on experiments on heavy oils and had been given a copper bolthead to use for it. Instead of using a hammer to crush the natrium I used the lid of the bolthead and the lid got damaged. The General (that was Professor Markovnikov's nickname in the lab.) flew into a temper and demanded that I should buy a new bolthead. My finances did not allow me to do so, and so I gave the lid to be repaired. When the Professor heard what I had done, he said to me: ' As a punishment and to teach you to be careful I want you to prepare me some cyanide of arsenic.' This preparation is so poisonous and self-inflammable that I was afraid to attempt it and refused.

†I was to receive the apple crop of that year in Moscow from Jassnaia and to sell it on the spot. But the cases arrived damaged, many apples were stolen and I had to bring them to the shed in the Khamovnik house. I wrote to Jassnaia asking to be relieved of the task of selling them.

Tania, Masha and Miss Lane and myself are going to Pirogovo in a dog-cart. The weather is not merely fine, this year the countryside is unusual in its beauty. I saw wood, I read, but do nothing and this mental idleness weighs on me. Mother is not well, but in good spirits. I cannot contemplate Moscow without horror nor you without pity. And the younger you are, the more do I feel that. Aunt Tania was delighted to see you at the station. She loves all you children and you in particular.'

An old revolutionary friend of mine had been arrested and sentenced to be deported to Siberia for three years. In the meantime he was in the Moscow prison, where the warders were decent men and looked after political prisoners extremely well, fulfilling all their demands but begging them never to mention this tolerant treatment for fear of reprisals. The governor of the prison at the time was also a liberal-minded man and I went along to ask him to give me the permission to visit my friend. He did so, adding with a laugh: ' Look out, or I'll tell your Mamma that you frequent political prisoners! ' I replied that she was well aware of it and that Papa would have gone himself had he been in Moscow. When Father came to Moscow he did, in fact, go to see my friend and many of the scenes he saw there he was to describe in *Resurrection*. I remember how indignant he was that one of the prisoners who had married in a Kiev prison, was only allowed to see his wife in public though she had come to Moscow in order to follow him to Siberia. He also told how he saw a couple dancing gaily on the landing of the prison stairs before going to Siberia together, they were so delighted to be leaving the hateful prison.

When my university days came to an end, I felt rather lost and did not know what to start on next. I could have gone on with science—and I afterwards regretted that I had not done so—or I might have got myself a job in public affairs or perhaps taken over the running of the country estates, which was what my mother wanted me to do. In my indecision I turned to my father. It was at the very height of his quarrels with my mother. He was irritable and answered: ' Work is easy to find: there are many useful jobs to be done. Sweeping the streets is a useful employment, for instance.' His words stung me and probably this contributed considerably to my growing estrangement from Father's ideas. I couldn't accept that my four-years study at the university could be cast aside as useless. Unfortunately indeed I did little to keep abreast with developments in the natural sciences but through them I had acquired a steady foundation of knowledge and a practical outlook on life.

At my mother's request I began to look after both the Samara and Jassnaia Poliana estates. It was a very considerable undertaking. My father did not like the idea at all, and was prepared to do nothing to start me off on the right path. He refused to agree that certain precautionary security measures should be taken. I was inexperienced; my mother was set against all improvements in what was an extremely primitive way of farming, and all this made it almost impossible to achieve any results at all. I discovered the bailiff we had in Samara had himself gone completely to seed. The land was by now entirely leased to peasants and his job was merely to collect the money. He was a pale, gaunt man, with listless eyes, wearing slippers and a torn woollen vest. He came to meet me when I arrived unexpectedly to look round the estate. He had no interests left in anything, he read nothing. I brought him Father's two new stories, but he did not even bother to read them, a bad sign indeed, as previously he had been one of Father's most fervent admirers. His wife was the same. Our conversation was strictly limited to agricultural subjects, but at the end he remarked rather pathetically that the moral, upright life led to nothing but misery. I did not agree with him and his own life was not exactly a demonstration of this theory; I was glad to get away from the hopelessness of it all. I was young and virile and, for me, life was something to enjoy and suffering really did not come inevitably into it. Later on my mother wrote to him explaining that she was not satisfied with the way he was running her affairs and that perhaps it would be better if he were to find other employment. ' You are a good man and I am sure will be glad to withdraw from a false situation,' she added.

I wrote begging him not to be in a hurry to leave, that we might work out a compromise when next I came to visit him. For, after all, at one time I had learnt a lot from him. But when I went to the farm in the autumn I found him in an even more pitiful state and he was very ill. In the end, however, it was all for the best.

He became a tutor in a private house in Moscow and after that the head of a commercial college in Nijhni-Novgorod. He came to visit us often and my parents were always delighted to see him.

In the summers of 1885 and 1886, at Father's instigation, the young people of Jassnaia took to hay-making. My mother joined in it as well. We used to do it for the sick and incapacitated peasants of Jassnaia who couldn't do it for themselves. We had a fine time singing songs and drinking vodka. One day having had a drop too much one of the younger peasants had a scuffle with his father and broke his arm. Another time when he was in the fields haymaking, Father knocked his foot against a cart and cut it badly. He pulled off the scab far too early, and it became infected, and he began to run a high temperature. Mother summoned the best doctor from Moscow, who worked wonders, and the fever went down, but Father had to stay in bed for quite some time. I think he must have been quite dangerously ill.

One of the entertainments in Jassnaia Poliana was the ' pillar-box '. It was an ordinary wooden case with a slit in it; it had a key and hung upon the stairs. Anybody who wanted to would drop in piece of paper with descriptions of amusing incidents, or character sketches of any of the various inhabitants of Jassnaia, etc. It is difficult now to tell who were the authors, and indeed many of the sketches were written collectively. Here are a few examples that come to hand:

> ' No. 1, Lev Nikolaevich. Of sanguine temperament. Is to be ranked with the " quiet " ones. The patient is suffering from a mania called by German psychiatrists weltverbesserungs-wahn, the mania of world improvement. The core of the sickness is the patient's belief that his message can alter other people's lives. General symptoms: discontent with the existing order, criticism of everyone except himself, an irritable verbosity, disregarding his audience. Switches often from anger to tearful sentimentality. Individual symptoms: occupations with unsuitable and superfluous labours, like making shoes, cutting grass, etc. Cure: total indifference on the part of his audience to his speeches, and occupations of a character that would absorb the patient's energy.'

The author of this was Tolstoy himself, but he wrote not what he himself thought of himself, but what he thought others

97

thought about him. He could not believe that he criticised everyone but himself; in every word of his one sees that he blamed himself before anyone else. And of course he could never have borne those around him to be indifferent to his words.

The next question was: *What makes him contented and what makes him discontented?*

' In fact Tolstoy is discontented with himself and with the entire human race. He dreams that improvement will come from all sides. He is always contented with servants, and continually discontented with his children, and as to his destiny, this not even those closest to him would know. Discontent with himself has made him tolerant, gentle and understanding. But leaving feelings aside, let us analyse the expression of the face: the corners of the mouth are pulled down, the lips compressed. The eyes, oh, heavens! the blood runs cold at the very thought of those eyes. They fix you with an icy severity and even their colour changes, it turns to glass. You cannot avoid the stern, silent reproach; what a miserable specimen you are, they say, what a worthless pitiable, spineless creature; you'll never begin to understand. the meaning of life. Go out and dig the fields; they add. And indeed you begin to feel pitiable, weak, petty. You feel ashamed and embarrassed and turn away from those eyes and then suddenly know relief, freedom from a yoke. Why have I deserved this? What have I done, you ask yourself? Just how is his life so much better than mine, is it then so much more exalted than my life? And you turn back boldly, armed with fresh courage, to face the silent reproach. But no. The force of glass, truth and cold is too strong. And again you shrink, shamefully, devastated, crushed under the burden of your own worthlessness.

' *Occupations?* Tolstoy feels himself to be a prophet. He lives by the conviction that he has solved the problem of living. For him Moscow is a living death; he finds there nothing but desolation. He would like to be thought an ascete, a missionary, and at heart he is a kind and passionate man. His is an overpowering personality, but he means no harm. His ideal is to live in poverty, peace and companionship, to burn all that he once adored and to adore everything that he had once burned. It is Hell for him to be surrounded with luxury and malice and idleness. He writes books and gathers crowds around the porch. When he plays cards, he does not believe in imposing penalties for revoking, etc. He plays decent croquet, with great confidence.*

' *Countess Tolstoy, No.* 2, is also in the " quiet " department, but has to be isolated now and then. The patient suffers from the mania of petulance and haste. The core of her sickness is that she believes that everybody is making demands on her and that she has no time to meet it all . . .

' *Symptoms:* she is continually trying to solve problems that have never been set, always answering questions that have never been asked, justifying charges that have never been made, trying to satisfy demands that have never been presented.

Cure: hard work. *Diet:* abstention from giddy society life.

' Only partly contented with herself she feels the same about her children and about the world at large. Satisfied with fate. When dissatisfied with herself, two wrinkles form upon her brow, and her eyes dart here and there, almost in anger, and then it is time to withdraw and leave her to herself for you might be in trouble. But when she is at peace with herself, then it's another story, then rush to her, reader. It would be hard to find a sweeter, kinder woman; her eyes are gentle and her movements soft. Where now are the wrinkles on the brow? Her eyes light up and a serene and kindly smile never leaves her lips. And when Aunt Tania comes from the annexe, she says to her: " Tanichka, sit with me a little, I never see you, I just sit here all the morning sewing for the children." When Tania recognises that voice, she'd not only sit down, there's nothing in the world she would not do for her.

' *Occupations:* underwear, mushrooms and children. She lives by the conviction that she is the wife of a famous man and that it is her duty to waste her energy on trifles, like the picking of wild strawberries for instance. She dies when the boys are ill or when Ilya gambles. Seventh heaven for her would be to have 150 babies that never grow any older.

*The author of this must have been his sister-in-law.

Hell for her is vulgarity, her children's illnesses and having to take important decisions or steps in life.

' She produces: turmoil, dinners, luncheons, big and small children, dresses to fit the future and sick peasant women at the door.

' When she plays cards, she is too afraid of having to pay a fine. She would play better if she were not so afraid of losing.'

' *Sergei Lvovich (the author), No.* 7. The patient is suffering from the mania of " universitarian liberalism ". Belongs to the category of the somewhat violent. *General Symptoms:* a desire to know what other people know and what he shouldn't know and a reluctance to know what he ought to know. *Individual symptoms:* pride, irritability, self-confidence.

' Illness still in process of investigation.

' *Cure:* intensive work, a job, a love-affair or both. *Diet:* less confidence in knowledge and more concentration on the knowledge acquired.

' He takes himself and life quite serenely. There are occasions when he is too satisfied with himself; for instance while reading his childhood diary he pursed up his lips and his eyes acquired such a naïve expression when he read the lines: " *Monsieur, monsieur, j'ai attrapé un rat, il était dans la souricière, disait la ménagère,*" that not only he himself, but the whole world would have been satisfied with him.

' He lives in the belief that he will one day lead a different life. He dies at the thought that Alina, his cousin, has gone. When he plays cards, and loses, especially with a poor partner, he is inclined to blame his partner.'

All the events mentioned in the pillar-box were every-day, insignificant events; the coming and going of guests, picnics, how a chicken got stuck in a bowl full of jam and flew out of the window with the bowl stuck to him, how the young ate up all the raspberries and gooseberries and the grown-ups were furious with them, etc.

There were funny incidents like the bustle which one of our ladies dropped on her way to the bath-house. And the story of the tailor Feinermann who very unsuccessfully cut a pair of trousers for Tolstoy.

Father enjoyed the pillar-box game and apart from the character sketches he wrote a number of notes for it. There was one
called ' Russian Chronicles of the Year 2083 ' in which he writes
about two mad families—ours and the Kusminskis—and all
the sane ones: the families of the Jassnaia peasants. One day he
set an ambiguous question which he dropped into the pillar-box;
' Why do Aliona, Piotr, Ustiusha and others have to cook, bake,
sweep, serve, carry out, while the masters eat, drink, mess about
and waste their time and then sit down to eat again? ' Another
of his notes:

> ' On July 7th 13 chickens were eaten in the two houses;
> on July 8th a lamb in one house, a joint in the other. July
> 9th, 6 hens and 2 chickens, July 10th, 11th, 12th, 30 pounds
> of roast beef, 40 pounds of soup meat, 2 hens, 7 chickens and
> a calf weighing 70 pounds. This is certainly no vegetarian
> society. Long live meat, veal, beef, mutton, game and
> poultry.
> ' The routine of the house in Jassnaia: 10–11 a.m. coffee
> in the house, 11–12, tea on the croquet lawn, 12–1 lunch,
> 1–2 tea again on the croquet lawn, 2–3 work, 3–5 bathing,
> 5–7 dinner, 7–8 croquet and boating, 8–9 small tea, 9–10
> high tea, 10–11 supper, 11–12 sleep. And they say we work
> too little; why, if we go on like this we'll soon be tubercular,
> all of us.'

There were many other subjects besides events at Jassnaia that
made their way into the pillar-box, like notes on Baroness
Krüdener or the Turkish war, and so on.

Chapter 4

Father and Son

In July 1888 I went to visit a university friend, who took me to see a neighbour of his, the famous Professor Mendeleev, and the greatest chemist of our day. He was a man of immense intelligence, charm and determination, who had great faith in his convictions of the moment and did not like anyone to contradict his bold paradoxes, in which he reminded me rather of my father. He regretted deeply that my father wrote against science and all my attempts to explain that it was not really against science but against the privileges of scientists were in vain.

At that time he was interested in the progress of industry in Russia. Quite recently the university of Edinburgh had made him doctor *honoris causa* and he told us how he had lectured in Edinburgh in Russian, dressed in the mediaeval toga and hat. His lecture was listened to with veneration though no one understood a word and it had had to be translated later.* He then proceeded to expand his theory on the necessity of industrial development in Russia, particularly in the Don region: ' Russia must become an industrial country, rather than an agricultural one, for during the six winter months, there is nothing for an agriculturist to do in Russia. The Don region has a particularly great industrial future—it will become the Russian Manchester or Sheffield. Nothing must stand in the way of industrial expansion . . . For instance women are not allowed to work in the mines. This is wrong, for it is easier for women to bend their spines than it is for men: and there is every reason for them to become miners.'

Swayed by all he had said we decided to explore the Donetz

*A few years later I found in the library of a women's college in Cambridge a translation of Mendeleev's *Foundations of Chemistry* which was being used as a text book.

basin, but though it was a fascinating and instructive journey, we disappointed Professor Mendeleev by not writing about it.

He was a convinced protectionist and used to say that it was all very well for the British to encourage free trade, for their industry was well organised. For us it was a matter of beginning from the very beginning and educating the workmen.

He read Father's essay *On Life*, and protested against my father's hostility to the positivist outlook when all we needed was a reply to the question: how to live? His argument was that, after all, we eat every day, but that should not prevent us from investigating from a scientific point of view the problems of nourishment. In what way, he asked, were exact sciences incompatible with Count Tolstoy's views?

In 1889 I went to Petersburg where I must admit that I ' sowed my wild oats ' on a rather lavish scale. I first worked in the Peasants' Bank and then found a niche for myself in the Ministry of the Interior where I was able to attend the International Penitentiary Congress which took place at that time. I was very interested in penal reform and I had hoped to learn at the Congress what was being done in this field in western Europe compared with the miserable prison system in Russia. But in fact I learnt very little because as soon as it became known that I spoke several foreign languages, I was delegated to duties at the Prison Exhibition. It consisted solely of diagrams and some of the prisoners' handiwork and certainly there was nothing on show of the wretched prisons themselves, the crowded conditions in them and the horrors of deportation to Siberia. The aim of the exhibition was simply to prove that the prisons were not as bad as they were painted, but this aim was not achieved, and besides, very few foreigners were there to see it.

It was there that I got to know the chief Prison Inspector in the Far East, Kamorski. One day he offered to give me a lift in his carriage and during the drive he said to me:

' Do you know who my coachman is? He's a convict from Sakhalin, a murderer who killed an entire family.'

' And how is it he is allowed to live in Petersburg? '

Kamorski smiled at my naïvety and said:

' He is an excellent coachman and is devoted to me. So I brought him here.'

Father told a friend about my being at the Congress:

' Serejha deliberated for a long time as to what new night club he should go to and the result was—the Prison Congress.'

This was repeated to me and though in fact there was a certain amount of truth in what he said I complained in a letter to my sister that my father treated everything I did with great irony. To which my father replied in 1890:

' Don't think, Serejha, that I treat you with " irony ", as you wrote to Tania. I was only joking when I spoke about the Congress. I try to remember and indeed I do remember my own youth and I hope, and I'm almost certain, that you are being and always have been less foolish than I was, even taking into account the different times and circumstances we have lived in. If there was one thing that upset me in you (it used to upset me, it doesn't any more) it was that you, so reasonable and, I should say, so practical in acquiring scientific and practical knowledge, so capable of making use of what had been discovered before you, and not inclined to go off at a tangent and invent logarithms and other wild theories of your own when there are perfectly good ones in existence, and so aware of where to search for knowledge, that, in spite of all this, when it comes to the most important of all sciences, the understanding of good and evil and of how one ought to live then you want to experience everything for yourself and learn the hard way and are not prepared to listen to the voice of experience; you seem determined to disregard everything that has been proved over and over again more indisputably and clearly than any geometrical theorem.

' For example, you have discovered that one must find an occupation and you try to find one; but you're not sure what it should be: the bank, the prisons, the land or local government. But there are all sorts of other things: why not music, literature, industry, travel, etc.? It is clear that the assumption that one should be occupied has no meaning or importance unless it is decided what the occupation should be. And people who had long deliberated on that question have long ago decided it. One must have something to do—*au risque de te déplaire*, I must repeat what you imagine you have long since proved to be wrong—one must have something to do in our privileged position, first and foremost in order to climb down from the necks of the people on which we now sit: before trying to do something in your opinion useful for these people, you must stop pestering them with demands for the satisfaction of your whims, and learn to see to your own needs. Once that is done there will be no problem as to what to do next and life will be serene and peaceful. An exception is only possible when you have a definite calling. But it is not for him who has such a calling to determine its exceptional character; it is other people who, in that case, will demand that the man devotes himself to that useful and satisfactory calling.

'Please, my boy, don't make this into an argument. I'm not writing this for the sake of argument, but in the hope that it may be of some help to you. Try to take all that I am saying in the same serious way as one might tackle an algebraic problem, that is accepting that x (in this case your situation) may be a positive or a negative factor or nothing at all. Not merely accepting beforehand that x is a positive factor and therefore inventing the other factors that would make a positive factor out of x.

'The trouble is that we, the descendants and heirs of tyranny and oppression wish to find, before changing our ways and admitting their criminality, some occupation through which we can atone for all our past and future sins. One must accept our position once and for all, and that is not a hard thing to do. And having understood it, it becomes obvious that before thinking of the good you can spread among the people, you must stop participating in their oppression, through land ownership, bureaucracy, hard-bargaining, etc. In the end it comes down to this: to accept the least possible service from other people and to work as much as possible yourself. This rule, though you must have had enough of it by now, is such a basic one that it can be applied to even the complicated, tangled circumstances in which we find ourselves today. No matter what the situation, this principle must be our guide, and we must try to live by it. It is not a question to be determined superficially, it is an attitude of mind that decides not, where should I work, or live, but what am I? What is the essence of my life? What is my relationship with the people? What are my rights and what are my obligations towards them? And so goodbye. I embrace you.

'Read this letter with the same love that I put into it.'

I replied at once to this letter:

'I was so glad to get your letter. I am always tortured by your silence, for then I begin to imagine that you can find no good at all in me. Your opinion, however harsh it may be, is something I deeply cherish. The last thing I would do is to argue. What is there to argue against? I am agreed that one should give as much as one can, working for others and taking less oneself. Except that you seem to believe that one should start with the latter, that is, with taking less . . . But I know that if someone really works, he needs to take very little to satisfy his essential needs. I believe in fact that the two parts of the rule are indivisible: usually the man who gives a lot, takes little, and *vice versa* . . . For myself I know that I lead an idle and a bad life: I take a lot and give nothing. But every cloud has a silver lining and recently, when I have been indulging in low pleasures, I have found myself perfectly conscious of just what I was doing and found I was no longer attempting to justify my actions as I did in the past. Perhaps you will ask: how is it that I am so aware of the evils of my life and yet don't attempt to change it? I have thought about this a great deal and can only reply sincerely that I am too fond of my petty little passions and not fond enough of what I know to be good.'

Impressed by my letter, Father wrote to me:

'I opened your letter with fear but in the middle of it began to cry with joy and am now crying as I write to you. God help you.

L. T.'

This short letter of Father's showed me that he did not repudiate me altogether and that I was very dear to him, not because of my life or my ideas, but simply because I was his son. And I too had tears in my eyes when I read his letter. But I must confess it had little influence upon my subsequent behaviour.

In May 1890 the newspaper *New Times* published a report of the Head of the Synod in which there was a statement that made me very angry. It said that the elder sons of Count Tolstoy were doing their best to control his financial recklessness. My brothers Ilya and Leo wrote to me saying that we ought to publish a denial of this slander, so I wrote the following letter to the editor, asking him to publish it:

' Sir,

The *New Times* of May 6th published an extract from the report of the Head of the Synod concerning the dissemination in the Kochakov parish of the ideas and moral convictions of Count L. Tolstoy, and in it we read among other things that " Count Tolstoy was no longer able to distribute money to the peasants to the same extent that he had done in the past, because his elder sons had begun to control both his reckless habits and the attempts of the peasants to set themselves up as masters of his estate." Having noted that our father considers as effective only that help which is given by personal effort and that this precludes spendthrift habits and leaving out all the rest of the report, we, the elder sons of Count L. Tolstoy, consider it our duty to declare publicly that not only would we never allow ourselves to control any financial recklessness on the part of our father, since we have no right to do so, but that we would consider it impertinent and disrespectful to interfere in any of his actions. We hope that all papers that published the report of the Synod will also publish this letter. Signed: the three eldest sons of Count. L. Tolstoy:

SERGEI, ILYA and LEO TOLSTOY.'

The editor replied:

' Count Sergei Lvovich,

I have forwarded your letter to the Head of the Synod as I did not consider it would be correct for me to refute an official document. I learn that the Head of the Synod has nothing against the publication of your letter. I am glad that he has been objective in this matter.'

Our letter was published on May 27th.

1890-97

In September 1890 I accepted a position in local government and in June 1891 the whole family gathered in Jassnaia—to discuss Father's decision to divide his estates between us, that is into nine parts, between my mother and the eight children. The plan was that Jassnaia was to be divided into two parts—one part to go to my mother, the other to Ivan, the youngest child. The other estates—each share amounting to 55,000 roubles—were to be divided between the seven remaining children. Masha, who was very much of my father's convictions, refused her share which was given to Mother. I offered to buy it from my mother, hoping to raise the money on a mortgage and from the sale of forest land. Afterwards, when Masha was married to Prince Obolensky she asked for her share to be returned and I paid it back in instalments.

The agreement was signed on July 7th, 1892. Father did not approve at all of my work in local government and I was well aware of it, though he never talked about it and went on treating me with great affection. He wrote me the following letter in December 1891, from the village where he was organising canteens to feed the peasants in the famine areas:

> ' I haven't forgotten you; on the contrary I keep thinking about you and wondering how you are getting on. Write to me. We are all well, except your mother, who is kind, wise and active as usual but her health leaves much to be desired . . . Such a lot would like to say . . . but there is no time. I kiss you.
>
> L. TOLSTOY

> ' Write and tell me what the situation of the peasants is in your part of the country.'

In 1893 I wrote a story ' The Case of Prinkin ' in which I described how the peasant, Jacob Prinkin, was condemned to be flogged for stealing sticks from a landowner's hedge and how this sentence was executed. I described the flogging in the words of an eye-witness.

My sister Masha wrote to me:

' Dear Serejha,

You probably know that we read your story and approve of it highly. Father wants to have it published in Moscow if you have nothing to say against it. He found a few small mistakes, as for instance, when you say that the sticks had to be broken before being pushed into the stove, etc., and with your permission he will make a few corrections. He also said that the flogging provokes a feeling of horror at the physical pain, but not at the humiliation . . . and that that is a pity . . . He also felt that the story would produce a shattering impression on the reader and that it is a " useful work " . . . '

Father added to the letter:

' Masha has written with a truly feminine sense of proportion. It is all true. Was glad to see you, though it was too short. I embrace you all.

In July 1895 I married a friend of my sister Tania—Marie Rachinsky, the daughter of the Director of the Agricultural Academy. My father wrote to a friend about my marriage:

' There is news in our family. Serejha is marrying Marie Rachinsky. The marriage will take place on July 9th. I am happy and at the same time frightened and also sorry for them . . . People who marry like that seem to me like people who fall before they stumble. I married like that, too. Don't do the same. If you fall—there's nothing to do about it. But if you didn't stumble, why do you have to fall? '

Later he wrote to another friend:

' Today Serejha came to see us with his fiancée. They seem to love each other very much, but I'm always afraid for people who love each other when they marry, just as one is afraid for a woman about to give birth to a child, only in this case there are more unhappy than happy births.'

Soon after our marriage my wife and I went abroad for six months, and on our return we went to live in Moscow where I started on a musical career. In the autumn my wife went to stay with her father and from there wrote to me that she was pregnant and did not want to return to me. It is hard to say what caused the break between us. In 1897 our son Sergei was born. Soon after that she fell ill with lung tuberculosis and three years later she died.

Chapter 5

The Dukhobors

In 1898 we celebrated my father's seventieth birthday at Jassnaia. At that time he was much concerned with the migration to Canada of the Dukhobors,* who were being persecuted by the Government.

At that time V. Chertkov and the Quakers were organising the affairs of the Dukhobors in England. It turned out that through the efforts of Prince Kropotkin and a friend of his, a professor in Toronto, the Government of Canada had agreed in principle to accept the Dukhobors, but insisted that the majority of them should not move before next spring and that only one hundred families should proceed there in the autumn. Father on hearing that I was on good terms with Chertkov, asked me to go to England and discuss the publication in English of *Resurrection* and *Father Sergius*, the profits of which he had decided to give towards the emigration of the Dukhobors. He wanted to know who could do the translation and if he could get an advance on the publication.

I went to England via Berlin and Flushing on September 1st. Chertkov lived in Essex, in a small place called Purley. It was a two hours' train journey and about five miles by coach on top of that.

In Chertkov's house, besides his wife and son Vladimir, lived a Miss Pickard, an elderly Quaker spinster and the Ukrainian,

*The Dukhobors are a religious sect started in 1785. They acknowledge no earthly ruler since all men are equal, and believe military service to be sinful. They were first permitted to establish themselves near the Sea of Azov, then banished to the Caucasus in 1840. Through Tolstoy's intervention they were allowed to emigrate in 1899 to Canada (about half their number, 7,000, did so). They interpret Scripture in a spiritual and figurative sense.

Anna Morcosova, who had come as a servant and had now become a member of the family. She was always busy, gay and witty. She had learnt to speak a little English. There had recently been a competition for laundresses in London, with fifteen women, including Anna, taking part in it. They had had to wash and iron some towels and Anna had been the winner, and in spite of being a foreigner had received first prize—a china tea-set.

On September 12th Chertkov introduced me to Prince Kropotkin. We met in a Quakers' hotel in London, where Chertkov usually stayed. Kropotkin also lived outside London, but came often to town.

The 'dangerous anarchist' turned out to be an elderly man of middle height, with a greying beard, alert and active, with a slightly hasty manner, dressed modestly, and wearing spectacles. He looked rather like a kindly professor. I felt at once as though I had known him all my life. His simple, trusting attitude towards people, his faultless manners, which came from a true considera-tion for other people—all this made him a very attractive person-ality. The whole plan of the Dukhobors' emigration to Canada had been his work. On September 11th he showed us the British Museum. Unfortunately it was a Sunday and some of the rooms were closed. One could not have had a better guide and I re-marked how much I admired his versatility. He replied that he had to have a good working knowledge of science as he had been in charge of the scientific section of the *Fortnightly Review* for several years now.

Our party attracted a great deal of attention because of the Dukhobors in their wide trousers, dark blue jackets, high boots and astrakhan caps. As we were going from one building to another we passed a tall man in a top hat who seemed to stare at us rather closely. Kropotkin asked: ' Did you notice the man in the top hat? He is a spy; I have seen him often. He keeps an eye on anyone who has anything to do with me. You had better keep away from me if you want to avoid trouble when you return to Russia.'

Kropotkin told me about the death of the revolutionary Stepniak who had killed the Chief of Police Mesentzev. He had been a close friend of Kropotkin and Kropotkin told me that he had had no remorse at all about his terrorist activities. He lived in a London suburb and went to work every day, by a short cut along the railway line, on a path that was so narrow that there was no room to escape if a train was coming. Usually he went this way when he knew no train was due. But one day he made a mistake or else a train passed at the wrong time. On this occasion he was caught at the dangerous part of the line and unable to cross to safety, he was run down and killed. I asked Kropotkin what his own attitude was towards the recent murder of the old Austrian Empress. He replied that in this particular case he was sad that a harmless old lady had lost her life but hard as it was for him, he could not avoid accepting responsibility even for this murder, for in principle he was an advocate of terrorism.

I read his book: *The Conquest of Bread* which was banned in Russia and I searched in it for an answer to the problem I had pondered over for years; was a man's moral and mental develop- ment influenced by his way of life, his environment? If the old way of living was completely changed and private ownership done away with, would human relationships really improve? Or would the same thing happen all over again, as it does when you start dissolving crystals? When the solution boils over the crystals form exactly the same cubes and rhombs as they did before. I asked him what reason he had for believing that things would ever be better. People would be exactly the same, after all. His reply was that people were in fact better than the lives they were forced to live . . . The patterns of their lives had been formed over the years, often by inertia, and now they were unpractical and out- of-date. He envied me because I was returning to Russia, and doubted if he himself would ever see it again . . .

But times changed and after the October Revolution Kropot- kin did return to Russia. I saw him several times . . . Once it was on his birthday and he was having a musical party, for he was a great lover of music. Father did not know him personally, but sympathised with his anarchistic ideas, though he was against their achievement through violence. Kropotkin's book *Fields, Factories and Workshops* interested him very much, and particularly what he had to say of the tremendous possibilities of intensive farming. Father found that Kropotkin's facts were a denial of the Malthus theory: agriculture, market-gardening and fruit-growing can feed a great number of people, and the more people, the more working hands; less land is needed for producing food-stuffs if it is intensively tilled. Father added that of course if man were to become vegetarian there would be even less need of land, and meadows or foodstuffs for cattle would be things of the past.

To return to my visit to England. There was a meeting one evening at which one of the Dukhobors told us the story of the burnings of arms by Dukhobors which took place in Tiflis in June 1895. They brought all their guns, daggers, revolvers, two cartfuls of coal, twenty carts of fuel and petrol. During the burning they prayed and sang psalms till two o'clock in the morning. Some of the weapons were loaded and exploded into the earth. The governor, Shervashidze, sent messengers, ordering them to come and see him. They replied that they would come when they had finished praying. A quarter of an hour before the religious service was over the cossacks arrived with whips and began to flog. They flogged the people so mercilessly that you could not see the grass for blood. The cossacks' leader could not disperse them, and they formed circles holding hands, to protect their womenfolk within the circle. Finally the cossacks hounded them all the way to the governor. They would not take off their caps to him, and the cossacks knocked the caps off their heads, while the governor himself helped to flog them and shake them.

This story affected the audience very deeply.

Before leaving for Paris I received the following letter from Father:

' Thank you, dear Serejha, for your readiness to serve the cause of the Dukhobors and—I know it—mine as well. I appreciate it greatly and think of you with joy. Even if you do not achieve all you want to achieve, your journey will I'm sure have been very useful. I pray that all will go well with you and somehow I feel that it will. In any case, here is a practical matter I would like you to attend to: to find out from London and Paris publishers what they will give for the two stories, and on what terms, how much a word or a letter and how much in advance. Goodbye, everything is well here at the moment.

L.T.'

On October 1st I went to Paris. On the cross-channel steamer, a strange-looking man sat down beside me, and I immediately took him to be a Russian informer. When he saw me take out a cigarette in the dark, he very politely struck a match, lighting up my face, and began to question me in Russian with a Jewish accent: ' You're from real Russia? On your way to Paris? You'll stay there for some time? ' I wondered, though I could not be sure, if he were the same man in the top hat that we had seen with Kropotkin at the British Museum.

After a few unsuccessful approaches to French publishers who all pointed out the difficulties of publishing Russian works when there was no literary convention between Russia and France, I went to the *Revue des Deux Mondes*, to see the editor, Brunetière. To get access to him was as difficult as getting an audience with a Russian minister. He told me that if Tolstoy's stories were suitable to read in a family circle, he would pay one thousand francs a page for them. When I said that this money was to be devoted to the emigration of Dukhobors, he replied that this was no business of his. I found a translator in the person of Theodore Viseva, a Pole with a Russian wife, who had translated Goncharov's *A Simple Story* and *On Art* by L. Tolstoy. Thus I had a translator, but as yet no publisher, so I decided to return to Russia.

On October 11th I arrived in Jassnaia and told my father exactly what the situation was with the Dukhobors and I told him of my frustrated attempts to find a French publisher. My relations with my father had been strained for some time, but now they were very good again, for indeed the Dukhobor affair had brought us together. He writes in his diary: ' Serejha is very close to me both in action and in feeling. And I deliberately avoid arguing with him.' He was at that time busy working on *Resurrection*. He asked a friend of mine, Zurikov, a barrister, to come to Jassnaia and make corrections on the legal procedure in the book. This is what Zurikov wrote in his diary:

> ' Started reading the manuscript of *Resurrection*. The old man kept coming up and watching me read; then he asked me to make my corrections directly on the manuscript, for there are some grave errors in legal procedure, which I had to alter. I had to change the description of the clothes of the prisoner. Also the description of the Easter service, for some of the wording of the church songs was incorrect. Have promised to come back and read the third part. I feel frightened and a bit humble at being asked to alter a text written

by Tolstoy himself, though he urges me to be quite frank about it and is most kind and friendly. He has told me a great many stories, we have argued, and he pours out the most brilliant ideas one after the other, dazzling like lightning.'

On November 1st Zurikov returned and rewrote the whole of the tenth chapter which contains the speech for the prosecution. In the morning he read it to Tolstoy who approved of it, and then sent it first to be copied, then typed and from there to the printers.

At the end of October, Sulerjitsky arrived unexpectedly at Jassnaia, deported by the police from the Caucasus where he had been trying to commission a second ship for the Dukhobors.

Father sized up the situation at a glance and decided to act without delay. He advised Sulerjitsky to return to the Caucasus and he suggested that I should go with him. The responsibility of allowing us to assist the Dukhobors lay with the 'Commander-in-Chief' of the Caucasus, Prince Golitzin. Father hoped that Golitzin would at least give me permission to go ahead. And though he disliked the idea of approaching the authorities he gave me the following letter:

'Confident as I am that the Government would wish to avoid the inevitable and consequences of the Dukhobors being prevented or delayed on their journey to Canada, consequences maybe involving great expense, illness or even death, and confident that the refusal to allow Suler-jitsky to continue his work on it is a mere misunderstanding, I humbly request that you should see fit to allow him to carry on with his task, aided by my son, Count Sergei Tolstoy, who will hand you this letter. He intends to assist Sulerjitsky in the expedition of the second consignment and will himself direct the third consignment, also of two thousand men. In the hope of your favourable decision I am, etc. Your obedient servant.

L. TOLSTOY

November 8th 1898.'

I made quick plans to go. I thought I should be staying in

116

the Caucasus only till the departure of the Dukhobors, but it turned out that a guide was needed for the *émigrés* going on the second boat and I decided to accompany them.

We proceeded to the Caucasus with Sulerjitsky, who was most apprehensive of the police, but we complied with all the police regulations and at first all went well. Then I went to see my friend Miliutin, the editor of a local paper, to ask him to help us with the local authorities. He was not very encouraging. He agreed that the Dukhobors had in fact been badly treated but he held that they rather enjoyed posing as martyrs and that the authorities could hardly avoid persecuting them since they were continually refusing to obey the laws. He placed most of the blame on the administrators for not knowing the local dialects and having to rely on interpreters. He had written many articles on the subject but Alexander III was displeased with what he had written and marked in the margin: ' Let the Georgians and the Armenians learn to speak Russian and not the Russians the local dialects.' By this time the police had again started making inquiries about Sulerjitsky, so I decided to go and see Golitzin myself, with my father's letter. He received me very affably, read the letter, promised to do what he could to help with the emigration of the Dukhobors and to allow Sulerjitsky and myself to carry on organising it. He advised however that Sulerjitsky had better go to Batum, leave with the first party of Dukhobors and not return to Tiflis afterwards. He spoke of my father's influence on the Dukhobors and considered that he was behind the whole movement. I tried in vain to dissuade him. We telegraphed the result of my visit to my father and left for Batum. On the way we stopped in a Dukhobor camp where we were welcomed with great effusion particularly Sulerjitsky, whom they looked on as their saviour. A crowd of them gathered in our hut all calling each other by their first names, even children their parents. There was a centenarian among them, a former Sebastopol soldier who was all ready to go and ' have a look at Canadia '. On December 2nd we received a letter from Father dated November 19th:

' Dear Serejha and Leonid,

I have had no news from you since your telegram. Am anxious to know about your work and about you, personally, Serejha. Was your journey perhaps premature? Have you got a lot to do? If not, are you quite content anyway and happy? What about Golitzin? There is nothing new here concerning your work that you don't already know . . .'

On December 6th, Sulerjitsky became very depressed and apathetic which was unusual for him. Suddenly we saw the sky was red—obviously there was a fire in the town. Sulerjistky loved putting out fires and rushed to the spot, tremendously excited; seizing a hose he was about to plunge into the flames. Knowing that the next day he had a lot of hard work in front of him—organising the embarkation of two thousand people, I took a quick decision, and tearing the hose out of his hand I ordered him rather sharply back to the hotel. He was very surprised but did what he was told.

December 8th was a warm sunny day. The Empress Maria Feodorovna was passing through Batum in her yacht. Prince Golitzin went to meet her and I saw him afterwards and spoke to about him more Dukhobors passports. This time he was more than a little impatient and shouted at me that all this business was on my father's conscience, ' a lot of silly nonsense ' was what he called it.

On the 9th embarkation began and it went on all that night. The Dukhobors were polite, very orderly, and I never heard a coarse word from them. In the morning their passports were examined by the police, there was a whistle, the anchor was pulled up and they were off, singing their monotonous, plaintive psalms to the heavens. A rocket was sent up from the boat as is the British navy's custom when an emigration ship sails. Suler-jitsky, a sailor himself, climbed the mast and waved goodbye from the top. All this was very moving, but I felt sad and rather frightened about the future of these two thousand people. They had a month's journey ahead of them—cold and illness, lack of bread and hot food, bad water, seasickness, and all that to contend with in small, dark, badly-ventilated cabins. There would surely be some deaths on the journey. It seemed sad that they were forced to go simply because of the stupid behaviour of some individual in authority and one could not help wondering whether they would be happy when they arrived at their journey's end.

Two days later a woman doctor and her friend arrived to accompany the party of Dukhobors who were leaving on December 14th. They brought me a letter from my father, telling me how energetic and unsparing the doctor was, and how she had worked for Chertkov during the famine and the outbreak of cholera. He told me I could trust them both implicitly. Then the ship *Lake Super.or* arrived, which was to take us to Canada. I went up on deck, made myself known to the Captain. The *Lake Superior* was a better ship than the previous one, more modern and larger. But it still was not adequate for such a great number of passengers.

Embarkation began. The Dukhobors swarmed like bees on the pier, with all their bundles. Then started the examination of their passports which was a complete muddle, though in fact it was much more severe than it had been with the first party. And indeed, owing to this lack of proper organisation, one young man, of military age, was able to pass himself off as a woman, using the passport of a girl, who had died a short time ago and of whose death the authorities had not been informed. It went on almost the whole day and then the gangway was lifted about four o'clock. It was a clear, sunny afternoon. This time no rocket was sent up from the ship, for the port authorities had been displeased by this gesture on the previous ship. We were off on our journey of 5,350 miles from Batum to Halifax and it passed comparatively without incident, except for three deaths. When we arrived in Halifax we had to remain in quarantine and all had to be vaccinated against smallpox. When all this was over, I sent Father a telegram saying we had arrived safely.

I left Canada at the end of March, and was seen off by a crowd of grateful Dukhobors who sang songs and presented me with a dozen handkerchiefs which they had embroidered themselves. I travelled via Toronto and Montreal, stopped to admire the Niagara Falls, and stayed three days in New York, where I saw Ernest Crosby, a disciple of my father's and several other of his followers. I returned to Moscow on April 4th 1899 and was very happy to find my mother in very much better spirits than when I had last seen her.

Chapter 6

Tolstoy in Illness

My youngest brother Vania died at the age of seven in 1895. He was a very gifted child, warm and sensitive. With his death my mother seemed to lose interest in life and the hysteria latent in her character revealed itself with great force.

My two sisters, Tatiana and Maria, married within the next five years and left home. His daughters were Father's favourites and he suffered deeply from their absence, though he tried to fight this sense of loss. He was going through a difficult period . . . the emigration of the Dukhobors, his quarrels with Mother, the intense work on *Resurrection*, his excommunication from the church, the beginning of a liberal movement . . . all these things moved him deeply. And always he suffered agonies over the apparent incongruity between his life and his convictions. I say ' apparent ', because he had already changed his way of life a great deal, indeed he could hardly go much further if he went on living in Jassnaia. He tidied his room himself, worked in the fields, was a strict vegetarian and except for riding, allowed himself no pleasures that demanded service from others. He could, of course, have left Jassnaia and devoted himself entirely to physical work. But with his age and his deep creative impulse it would have been impossible. Wherever he lived people would try to organise his life so that he would be able to write. His health also left a lot to be desired. He had pains in the liver, his temperature fluctuated continually and his pulse was uneven. The doctors advised him to go to a warmer climate. A friend, Countess Panina, offered him her house in Gaspra, twelve miles from Yalta. He accepted this and on September 5th, 1901, he and Mother left for the Crimea. I was struck by the stern expression on his face when he got into the carriage to drive to the station.

In Gaspra my father soon began to recover, but the walk from the sea to Countess Panina's house was quite an ordeal, as the house was on a steep hill, and the result was that he strained his heart. When he was in the Crimea he met both Chekov and Gorki. He had a high opinion of Chekov's stories, but did not admire his plays and said: 'Your plays, Anton Pavlovich, are even worse than those of Shakespeare.' He had no liking at all for Shakespeare, as is well known, and he criticised his work mercilessly. Chekov listened to him, but with a certain scepticism; indeed, their views were very different. Father tried often to draw him into an argument, but Chekov was very careful to avoid committing himself. It seemed to me that Father wanted to get really close to him and to try and exert his influence over him, but he came up against a sort of passive resistance all the time and there was always a barrier between them.

'Chekov is not a religious man,' my father said.

Maxim Gorki lived nearby. After the adulation he had been subjected to in Moscow, which he had disliked intensely, he enjoyed being in Gaspra, where he was surrounded by simple friendliness and he was not worshipped as a literary lion. He was a modest man and told us a lot about his life; but on the whole he spoke little. He used to play rounders with the children with great enthusiasm.

Father admired his writing on the working class, but used to say: 'Gorki has found a gold mine in literature, the have-nots; he understands them and writes well about them, but on the other hand he knows little about people of a different milieu and when he describes them has to make it up as he goes along.'

The Grand Duke Nicholas Mikhailovich used to come over often from Ai-Todoz. Black-haired, bald, tall, dressed in the uniform of the Chevalier guards he used to walk rapidly and straight to Father's room where they sat and talked on all sorts of subjects, one of them being the legend about Father Fedor Kusmich who was supposed to have been the Emperor Alexander I. The Grand Duke had examined carefully all the existing material, but was convinced that the man was not Alexander I. Father was also of this opinion. His story: *Posthumous diary of Father Fedor Kusmich* is fiction, and Father never attributed any historical truth to it.

Soon Father's health began to deteriorate. The weather was bad. My mother was longing to get back to Moscow. The

atmosphere in the house was heavy. There is a note of my sister
Tania referring to these days:

'Papa not well, a slight temperature. But in a good mood
and writing. Masha has been copying his article on religion
and Lisa Obolensky another article on religious tolerance.
Gorki came this morning, a gentle, kind, sensitive man. He
is like a child, eager about everything and about art in
particular. He argued with Papa today about Skitaletz,*
whom Papa attacked and whom he defended. As he left,
he said, in the doorway: " Ah, I feel that Leo Nikolaevich
must be right! " The argument was about a story written
by Skitaletz which Papa had just read.'

There was a consultation of all the best doctors who worked
out a treatment for Father. But the next day Father had a sharp
attack of asthma, his temperature soared up and the doctors discovered he had congestion of the lungs. The situation became
grave, the doctors did their best and Father, in spite of his
scepticism towards medicine, was forced to obey them. The
family and friends took turns sitting at his bedside . . . Chekov,
when he learned about his illness, telephoned constantly for
news. He would have liked to help, but was ill himself. Very soon
Father grew so weak that he could not turn over on his side without help. He lay on his back, his body slipped downwards, so
that his feet reached the end of the bed and he had to bend his
knees. Somebody would pull him up from time to time, but it
needed a great deal of strength. It seemed impossible that a man
who had reached such a state of debility could remain alive. I
asked the doctor whether Father's state of health was hopeless.
Being the eldest son I had to know. The doctor replied that no
doctor pronounced a condition as hopeless, but that pneumonia
when it affects old people is called *pneumonia terminalis*.

Father's mind often wandered because of his high temperature,
but when fully conscious he was completely lucid and dictated
corrections to his article on freedom of speech. Here are some of
his remarks in the course of his illness:

He once asked one of the local doctors whether all old people
were looked after as he was. He was perturbed at the idea that he
was given such a lot of care and was only reassured when he was

*Revolutionary writer.

told that the same treatment was given to everyone in the hospital and that the patients were looked after either by the nurses or by their relatives. He kept repeating a sentence he had read in some novel: 'To die means to join the majority.' And he remembered the words of an old peasant: 'One should die in the summer—it's easier to dig a grave.' He said to my sister Tania: 'It isn't easy at all to die; it's very hard to shed the outward shell which is the body.' One day he said: 'The whole of diamonds does not increase in proportion to the increase of the number of carats, but in proportion to the square of the number of carats. Thus the wisdom of the old does not increase in proportion to time, but in proportion to the square of time. And one should hasten to share it, and give it to the world.' I remember his saying: 'Let my relatives ask me, when I am dying, whether I consider my faith to be the true faith. If I am unable to answer in so many words, I will either nod, or shake my head.'

At one moment he decided he was going to die and we all went in turn to kiss him goodbye. But for some reason I was certain that he would recover. The crisis came and it was a time of great anxiety. 'I keep balancing on a tightrope,' said Father. He had continual camphor injections, and his pulse was hardly perceptible. The owners of the house arrived in order to be on the spot in case of his death and also to protect him from the ardent followers of the church. We were afraid that the police would seal and confiscate Father's manuscripts and that a priest would come, without being asked, to the dying man to give him the last sacrament and then publicise the fact that Tolstoy had returned to the church. Father kept asking to be buried near the place where he died and the owners of the house very kindly offered a place for his grave in the garden, on a small hill.

In spite of his weakness and quite a lot of pain, Father kept his mind constantly on his work and continued to dictate. At the end of December he wrote to the Emperor appealing to him to 'stop the persecution that prevents the people from expressing their needs and desires,' and to cancel the 'exceptional laws that place the working class in the situation of pariahs,' to grant 'freedom of transport, education and religious practices,' and to abolish private property on the pattern of Henry George. The letter in its final version was sent on January 16th through the Grand Duke Nicholas Mikhailovich. The latter telegraphed on the

28th that it had been passed on. On February 18th, two days after the crisis, he dictated an introduction to his two memoranda: *To the Soldier* and *To the Officer*, in which he spoke of the inevitability of a revolution. ' There are only two solutions,' he said, ' the first, the hardest one, is a bloody revolution, and the second— the admission by the government of its duty not to hinder the natural law of progress, not to fight to retain the *status quo*, or, as it is in our case, not to return to the dark ages. Having assessed the direction in which mankind must naturally go one must lead one's peoples along that path. Because revolution is inevitable, I am writing these memoranda, hoping that the thoughts contained in them may moderate the civil war towards which governments are leading their people.'

When the Petersburg doctor returned, it was he who expressed for the first time a hope of recovery. On February 5th my mother received in a letter from the Petersburg Metropolitan Antony a request to influence her husband in the matter of his reconciliation with the church. Father, when he heard of it, said: ' There can be no talk of a reconciliation. I am dying without any bitter, hostile feelings. What is the church? How can one become reconciled with something indefinite?' So my mother left the Metropolitan's appeal unanswered.

On February 20th Father felt better and said to the doctor: ' Evidently life must go on '; to which my mother said: ' Does it bore you?' Suddenly he brightened up and replied: ' Bore me? Not at all. I'm glad.' After that his recovery proceeded in fits and starts, though he did not quite believe in it himself. On February 28th he said: ' A protracted illness has its good side. It gives you time to prepare for death.'

About that time I visited Chekov in his remote little villa. He was alone, and welcomed me but he was very silent. A tame heron walked about the yard and there were flowers everywhere. A small dog, Kashtanka, wagged her tail in greeting. ' I was given this dog for my story, *Kashtanka*,' he said. ' But it was not I who called her that.' I asked him what he thought of my father's state of health, and if he thought Father would recover. He replied: ' Yes, he may recover, but he is old, very old . . . ' It was very clear that at the back of his mind he was thinking: ' He will not last long.' I often remember that talk with Chekov. Father lived another eight years, Chekov not quite three.

Father began to recover his appetite, and spent his days basking in the spring sun, and receiving visitors, one of whom was Gorki. We were all very happy, for we felt we had all contributed towards keeping him alive. He was in fine spirits again. One day, the doctor was examining his chest with a stethoscope. He had just come from Moscow where he had heard a famous opera singer and Father asked him: 'Who do you prefer listening to—her or me?'

The doctor said aptly:

'I like each in their own way, Lev Nikolaevich.'

'Make sure that next time you hear Olenina, you won't say to her: " Just give a little cough! " '

This new, serene atmosphere, together with the beautiful sunny surroundings seemed also to cure me of the neurasthenia I had been suffering from for several years.

On March 10th I wrote down the following conversation with my father. I asked him how he was feeling.

'I'm much better; I feel in fact I am coming back to life . . . '

'Are you glad?'

'Yes, I am, but it's an effort . . . I think I can still perhaps be of some use to others. Without that I wouldn't want to live. I thought a lot about life and death when I was ill. Thoughts about death are only necessary while you go on living. We are restricted by the limits of life and cannot transgress them. All we can say is: Thy will be done.'

In March Dr. Nikitin came to Yalta and was to remain Father's doctor until his death. Chekov came to see Father on the 31st, and Mother left for Jassnaia on April 22nd. However, our happiness was not to last. At the end of April Father contracted typhoid; true, it was a mild form of typhoid, but in his state of weakness the illness was very serious. Only at the end of May did he begin again to recover, but we put off our return to Jassnaia till the end of June, travelling to Yalta by carriage and then by ship to Sebastopol. From the ship he went to the station where a special train compartment had been reserved for him. As he waited on a bench in the garden in front of the station he was accosted by a lady who said that no one had any right to sit there as it belonged to the stationmaster. Tolstoy meekly obeyed and left. You can imagine the lady's feelings when she learnt a few minutes later that it was the great Tolstoy himself whom she had thrown out of the garden, the great man she had always wanted to meet. But by now all access to him was out and she had to content herself with a bunch of flowers and her humble apologies.

His illness in the Crimea was a turning-point in my father's life. He remained in Jassnaia and never returned to Moscow. He lived there in the two rooms downstairs, and he stayed in them until that fatal day on October 28th, 1910, when he left Jassnaia for ever.

His whole nature changed after that illness. He was less stern, less discontented with himself and with his life, less critical of his family; more tolerant altogether. The thought which he was to express in the last year of his life: 'No one is guilty in this world,' had began taking root in his mind. The real culprits were the conditions, the surroundings—so he wrote in a story at that time.

The last time I saw Chekov was in 1904, at the beginning of the Russo-Japanese war. He had just arrived from the Crimea. When I went to see him, I found him looking very ill; he coughed and kept leaving the room to spit into a glass spittoon. His wife, Olga Knipper, was there, too. I remarked that perhaps he needed a warmer climate, but she said that he liked being in Moscow. Yes, possibly he found living in Yalta boring, but it was clear that he would never survive for long in the Moscow climate. Very soon after that meeting he went to Badenweiler, where he died.

Father felt Chekov's death acutely. He re-read his stories and divided them into categories according to what he considered to be their merit. He wrote an introduction to *The Darling* and placed Chekov himself in the category of great writers.

Autumn

1905

THE first big railway strike started in October of that year. The atmosphere in Jassnaia was anxious; we were cut off from the world without post, railway or telegraph. There were rumours that there was fighting in the streets in Moscow and that a provisional government had been declared in many towns. I had to go to Moscow and went to Tula to try and hire horses, as many other people were doing at the time. The high road was crowded with vehicles all taking passengers to Moscow. When we reached the outskirts of Moscow I was amazed to see a passenger train rush by. I asked the watchman at the level crossing whether the strike was over and with a beaming face he announced that yes, the manifesto of October 17th, granting all the freedoms, had come out and jubilant processions were in full swing. I hurried to the station and took the first train to Moscow. When I arrived it was almost midnight. The streets were empty. I drove to my club, where the atmosphere was festive, somebody was playing the *Marseillaise*, everybody was expressing unfamiliar, bold views, toasting the fighters for freedom. Life seemed to have entered a new phase. But not for long. Very soon the festive spirit gave way to suspicions, to lack of confidence in the promises given.It ended in what was called the armed revolt, a movement organised mainly by young students and workmen as a reply to arbitrary reactionary measures. Students spent their last pennies equipping themselves with revolvers. The days that followed were filled with horror, shooting and chaos and terror on both sides.

Part IV

THE LAST DAYS

Chapter 1

The Will

A CURIOUS and most unpleasant 'incident' took place in my private life the year 1910 which prevented me from spending more time with my parents; had I been able to be more with them just then—who knows, things might have turned out differently. One of my new neighbours was a passionate rider to hounds and though I had no liking for the man and disagreed with his profoundly reactionary ideas, I gave him permission to hunt wolves in my forest. Then my brother Michel, also a great sportsman, asked me to allow him to hunt in my forest, too, which I did, thus necessarily cancelling the permission given to the neighbour. The whole thing ended in insulting letters and clashes between the two men. One day I learnt from the forest guard that Mr. S. was, in spite of all, hunting in my forest. I drove there immediately and drove Mr. S. and his men out. He made off as soon as he saw me without waiting to give any explanation. When I next met him at a fair, I refused to accept the hand he stretched out to me. A few minutes later I was challenged to a duel by his two seconds. I had no intention of fighting a duel with him, but had to engage two seconds to enter into negotiations for ending the matter peacefully and they succeeded finally in doing so only after many fruitless attempts, two long anxious months later. I tried to keep the whole thing from my father who would have been deeply upset by it. He had his own share of trouble just then. My mother, ever since the death of her beloved youngest son, Ivan, in 1895, and after a serious operation in 1906, had become increasingly nervous and unbalanced; my father had put her in charge of all his affairs in Jassnaia, but she knew very little about the business and ran the estate in a very haphazard fashion. The estate needed guarding, appeals to the authorities against pilfering and other illegal practices had constantly to be made and every time this meant intense suffering for my father. The culprits would seek protection from him and he would grant it. All this made life in Jassnaia abnormal and difficult for both of them. There was also the matter of copyright which he had given her for all his works up to 1881, leaving all the others free of copyright. It was not surprising that she insisted on keeping to her rights as her children came often to her for financial help and she always had to give it to them. Father, on the other hand, acted on the basis that he had been one kind of man up to 1881 when that man had died leaving his property to his family and a new man was born who had different ideas about the whole thing. This new man hoped that one day his family would think as he did and he therefore remained with them. This is what he wrote in a letter which he never sent to a woman whose name remains unknown except for the initials: ' E. Sh.' I still believe that things would not have reached the tragic climax were it not for the matter of Father's will. Before he made a formal will, his desires and intentions were expressed in his personal diary. He wrote in it: ' I ask that my heirs should relinquish the copyright on my ten volumes and *The Alphabet*. But I only *ask* them to do so, I don't *demand*. If you do it—all the better. But if you don't—it's your affair, it means you are not ready for it. The fact that my works were sold during the last ten years was the greatest pain I suffered in life.' He requested in the same diary that all his papers should be examined by his wife, V. Chertkoff and N. Strakhoff. When the latter died, he asked V. Chertkoff to examine his papers *with his wife* after his death and decide as they thought fit. He also asked: ' Though it may be nonsense, that no rites should be performed at the burial of my body. I want a wooden coffin to be taken to the 'place of the green stick.'* In the formal will he repeated the same clauses, but did not mention his wife as participator in the examination of his papers. The notes in the diary did not legally bind his heirs, only morally. But they could not be destroyed or hidden. In 1895 there were three copies: one was in the hands of my sister Masha, one in Chertkov's, and one in mine. It was

*' The greatest secret of all; how to live so that men would know no unhappiness, never quarrel or be angry, this secret so my brother Nicholas told us, was written on the green stick and the stick buried in the valley, by the high road, where I would like to be buried in memory of Nicholas.'

different with the formal will. This was legally compulsory for the heirs but it could be destroyed. Chertkov was the one who insisted most on the formal will for he knew that in the absence of it his role as protector of Tolstoy's works would be nil.* He was afraid after the will was drawn that my mother might force Father to destroy it and therefore he kept it hidden. This was the main cause of the rift between my parents which led to my mother refusing to see Chertkov in the house.† She resented, too, of course, that his diaries of the last few years were in Chertkov's keeping, for she herself had had access to them all until then. My father was in principle against making a formal will, but nevertheless he drew up the final one himself in June, 1910. My mother's condition worsened every day and so did the hostility between her and Chertkov. In his letters to his Bulgarian friend Dosser he exaggerated, putting all the blame on my mother, abusing her, talking of the ' shadow of this crazy woman, mad with egotism, wrath and greed ' which hovered over his relations with Tolstoy. He wrote that so far as he was concerned my father was a saint to go on living in Jassnaia at all, and that he was proving by his fortitude that it was possible for a human being to carry in his heart a truly indestructible love. To exercise this fortitude he needed a merciless, cruel warder like Countess Tolstoy, with whom all his life was bound. And he referred to various notes from Father's diary which proved his point. Then he sent the letter to my father, who was deeply upset to find that someone had been reading his diary. Mother suspected the existence of the will and lived in the shadow of that suspicion. She kept asking Father and Father would always reply evasively. My brother Andrei also asked him and father told him that he was not bound to answer him at all. Meanwhile Chertkov was busy guarding the secret, repeating, at the same time, to Tolstoy that his wife was insane. The proof of my father's duality in this matter is that he now kept a small diary. The big one was typed out by Chertkov almost at once. Everybody read it. The little one, the ' diary for myself ' Father let no one read. In it he noted: ' A letter full of reproaches from Chertkov. They are tearing me to pieces . . . Chertkov has involved me in a struggle which is distasteful to me.'

*Though the initiative did not come from him.
†Chertkov admitted it himself. He said ' The will is the focus of all the complications that led to his departure.'

I do not approve of Father's will because, having provoked animosity among all the people closest to him, it poisoned the last year of his life, and because in indirectly appealing to authority it was a contradiction of all his convictions. In a letter to Chertkov he said: ' I don't believe that the widespread distribution of my works will counter-balance the suspicion of them which must be provoked by the inconsistency of my behaviour.'* But for us, my mother and brothers and sisters, it was of great use from a moral point of view. It placed all the responsibility for the literary inheritance on Chertkov and freed us, the family, from all possible reproaches. Had there been no formal will, some of us might have tried to draw material privilege from his writings, in spite of his wishes which he clearly expressed in the diaries. Those who might had succumbed to such temptations would have suffered agonies of remorse and public opinion would have made mince-meat of us and been quite relentless towards us all. As it was, no one could say that his will was not carried out, as we, my brothers and I, signed the power of attorney.

In the first part of 1910 things went better, and there was a certain degree of peace in Jassnaia. My father rose at eight, tidied his rooms, went for a walk and after breakfast began to work. He lunched alone about two o'clock, then rode and on his return, rested, then dined with us about six, read and talked or played whist or chess or listened to music. He had tea at ten and about midnight went to bed. Chertkov did not live in the neighbourhood for a whole year from March 1909 to July 1910 as the local authorities had prohibited his living in the department of Tula because of his spreading of ' Tolstoy's heresies '. But this ban was withdrawn and he used to come daily until my mother forbade him in the house. My family at that time lived in Moscow, but I had to go to Nikolskoe at various times of the year and usually stopped on the way at Jassnaia. My father at that time treated me with great coldness. He wrote in his diary: ' Unkind feelings towards Serejha, which I try to fight. But very kind feelings towards Sonia . . . ' On June 5th he notes: ' Same feelings towards Serejha, but I control myself. Unbearable self-confidence. How easily people lose love because of self-confidence! ' I can't

*Chertkov's main reason for insisting on removing the copyright from Tolstoy's works was their consequent widespread distribution.

remember what caused this feeling in my father; perhaps my disagreement with his views or maybe his discontent with my way of life. He was eighty-two years old at the time and all he needed was rest instead of constant strife. He began to feel that the basic reason for his remaining with the family was losing its meaning. The dream about a new life was reborn and came out in many of his works, too; in the story of the Dekabrist who follows the deported, in *Father Sergius, The Young Tsar, The Notes on Fedor Kusmich* and others.

But on October 3rd, after his usual ride, he returned, trembling with cold his limbs quite stiff. He lay down to rest, without taking off his boots. He slept, so that we sat down to supper without waiting for him. Mother, after pouring out the soup, went to see how he was and returned saying he was sitting up in bed, but looked strange and as though his mind was wandering. He began to have convulsions. My mother was overcome with remorse. She was convinced that this was the result of her constant nagging, of her attitude to Chertkov. He recovered quite soon and I am certain that the collapse was originally caused by his falling asleep in his tight boots that affected his circulation. When he woke up on October 4th he was very weak and asked for his small diary. I gave it to him, having removed it from his pocket when he had collapsed, and I added: ' I didn't read it.' It made me very happy to hear him say: ' Well, it would have been all right if *you* had read it.'

On October 5th Mother agreed to let Chertkov come and go at Jassnaia again. I had a serious talk with her, and after that things took a better turn. But not for long. We were all very miserable. When I left the house it was like going into the fresh air out of a stuffy room. My sister Tatiana wrote to Mother on October 13th:

' Dear Mamma,
     I can see from your letter that you're not happy. From afar your troubles seem absurd, one could laugh at them if one didn't love and pity you. Papa likes Chertkov—what's wrong in that? Thank God that he has a friend in his old age, someone who is ready to give his life for the spreading of Father's ideas. Don't fight against him, it will bring nothing but harm . . . '

The situation became so tense that a solution seemed inevitable.

On October 26th Father wrote in his private diary: ' Find life more and more unbearable. Conscience won't allow me to leave. I must be patient and work on the soul within her.'

On October 28th came the last stroke that compelled him to leave. He notes in his diary:

' Slept till 3 a.m. Woke and heard as before some noise in the next room . . . a light through the chink in the door to my study . . . rustling . . . It is S. searching for something, reading. The night before she begged me not to lock my doors. Both her doors are open, she can hear my every movement. All my movements, every word, day and night, must be known to her, under her constant vigilance. More steps, more careful shutting of doors, and she is gone. I feel uncontrollable indignation, repulsion. Tried to sleep, but can't, and after an hour lit a candle and sat up. The door opens. S. comes in and asks how I am, why I have a light. My indignation rises, I choke from it, and my pulse is racing. Suddenly I make the final decision to leave.'

And he went . . . On October 28th I got a wire in Moscow: ' Come immediately '. Not knowing about Father's departure I wondered what had happened. I told my brother Ilya about it and we left for Jassnaia. On the way we learnt that Father had left for an unknown destination. At home I learnt that he had left in the night, that Dushan Makovitsky had taken tickets to Gorbachev, and that Mother had thrown herself in the pond and been dragged out, that she now refused to eat. We read the letter Father wrote to Mother just before he left:

' My departure will upset you; I regret it but try to understand and believe that I couldn't do otherwise. I can't go on living in the luxury I have indulged in until now and am doing what old men usually do at my age, leaving the worldly life to spend their last days in peace and solitude. Don't come after me even if you learn where I am. Your arrival will only make matters worse for us both and will not alter my decision. Thank you for your honest life with me for forty-eight years and I beg you to forgive me all the wrongs I have done you just as in my heart I forgive all the wrongs you have done me. I beg you to resign yourself to this new situation and bear me no ill-feeling.'

Mother came out into the hall to meet us, her hair dishevelled, and wearing a dressing-gown. I was appalled by the change in her face; suddenly it was old, shrivelled, and trembling, her eyes could not keep still. This was a new face to me. She talked incessantly, wept, and repeated that she would certainly put an end to her life and if they insisted on fishing her out of the pond, well, she would starve herself to death. I told her, rather harshly, that such behaviour would have an adverse effect on Father, she had to control her nerves and calm down, and then Father would return. She said: ' No, no, you don't know him, the only way to influence him is to provoke his pity.' I knew myself that she was right and though I protested it was only faintly. The painful situation was that we had to watch Mother all the time, as she threatened to commit suicide and though she might well have been simulating and play-acting, she was quite capable of harming herself by sheer miscalculation. We decided, all of us, anyway, to prevent her from following Father and from searching for him, and to get a psychiatrist and nurses to look after her. We recognised this was harsh, but there was nothing else we could do. It was obvious that the police would soon find Father—for how could Tolstoy manage to conceal himself? It would all be rather like a game: who would find him first?

The next day my brothers and sister arrived, except Leo who was abroad, and we decided that we would all write to Father, that is all of us except Michael. I wrote him the following:

' . . . I am writing because I am sure you would like to have the opinion of your children. I believe that Mamma is in a nervous condition and often irresponsible, that you had to part (perhaps you should have done so long ago) however hard it may be for you both. I also think that even if something happened to her, which I don't expect, you mustn't reproach yourself. The situation was insoluble and you chose the right way out. Forgive me for writing so frankly. Serejha.'

Tatiana wrote:

' . . . Dear, darling Papa, you have always suffered from too much advice, so I'm not giving you any. Like all of us you act as you think best and as you can. I'll never be the one to judge you. I can only say of Mamma that she is pathetic and miserable. She cannot learn to live in any other way. And she will never really change. She needs fear and authority. We will all try to subdue her and I think it will be for her good. Forgive me. Goodbye, my friend. Your Tania.'

Ilya wrote:

'. . . . Dear Papa.

I must write frankly to you and I'm sure it's what you want. We are not criticising your action. There are many reasons for it and even if we knew them all, which we don't, we would not be in a position to judge. We must, before all things, try and calm Mother. She has eaten nothing for two days and is so wretched that we cannot talk to her without tears. Some of it is as it always is play-acting, perhaps, often pure sentimentality, but on the whole so sincere that there is no doubt her life is in danger. We fear both suicide and a slow death from a broken heart. I know how hard life has been for you here. But you always considered it your cross and so did all who loved you. I am sorry that you could not bear it to the end. After all you are eighty-two and Mamma sixty-seven. Your lives are over now but one must die decently. I cannot bear to think what would have happened if Mamma had not been pulled out of the pond or anything like that. Forgive me if I'm harsh, but I love you and I understand you and want to help. I cannot ask you to return; I know you can't do that, but for Mamma's peace of mind don't abandon her, write to her, give her a chance to improve her nervous condition and after that—well, may God help us. If you write to me, you'll make me happy.'

Andrej's letter was written in the same spirit, pointing out the dangers of Mother's condition, the impossibility of either of us being constantly with her and telling Father that in his opinion he ought to have resigned himself to the situation.

We got his reply from Shamardino:

' Thank you, my dear, true friends, Serejha and Tania, for your sympathy in my grief and your letters. Your letter, Serejha, made me particularly happy, it was short, clear and what is more—kind. I live in fear and cannot free myself of responsibility, but I had not the strength to act differently. I wrote to you through Chertkov—he'll let you see the letter. I'm writing to her, to Mamma .She'll show you the letter, too. I wrote to her after much thought, as best as I could.

' We are going now, I don't know where yet. Chertkov will let you know.

' Goodbye, my children, and forgive me for all the pain I'm causing you. You particularly, my darling Tanechka.

' Well, that's all. I'm in a hurry to go, in fear that Mamma would find me. To see her now would be terrible. Goodbye. L.T.'

Father's letter to Mother:

' To see you or to think of returning to you is now quite impossible. It would do you a lot of harm as everybody tells me, and for me it would be terrible for everything would be so much worse now with your irritability, your excitability, your nervous condition. I can only advise you to resign yourself to these facts and the main things—try and improve your health.

' If you—I don't even say love, but just don't hate me, you must try and understand. If you do so you won't blame me, but will try and help me to find the peace that I need to go on living. Your condition now, your attempt at suicide, show your loss of control over yourself, which makes my return impossible. You alone can save all the people you love from all this pain. Try not to wish only the one thing you want for yourself—my return, but to bring peace to yourself, humble your soul and you will find what you want . . . I am not telling you where I am going because I consider separation necessary for both of us. Don't think I'm going because I don't love you. I love you with all my heart but cannot act in any other way. I know your letter is sincere but you are not in any condition to carry out your own wishes. And it is not a matter of fulfilling *my* wishes or demands, it is important that you should regain your balance . . . While that is not right—my life with you is impossible. It would mean— to give up living and I don't feel I have the right to do that.

Goodbye, dear Sonia, may God help you. Life is not a joke, we have no right to relinquish it, nor measure it by the length of time. Maybe the months we have still to live are more important than all the past years and they must be lived well.'

He also wrote to my wife,* asking her to help a widow with six children and giving her name.

His last letter was dictated from Astapovo:

' Dear Serejha and Tania.
    I know you will not be offended at my not asking you to come here; it would be too painful for your Mother and your brothers if I had done so. I asked Chertkov to come but then his position is an exceptional one. He has devoted his life to the cause to which I have devoted mine for the last forty years. I may be mistaken but I believe that cause to be vital for all mankind, including yourselves . . . I also wanted to add, Serejha, a word of advice to you and to beg you to think about the meaning of life. The Darwinist theories, the theories of evolution and of the struggle for survival which you are steeped in will never help you find life's meaning and will be no use as a guide to your way of living; this is a sad prospect. Think about this; I write these things because of my love for you. Goodbye, try to help your mother whom I love sincerely and deeply.
        Signed in his own hand.   Your loving father,
                                                Leo Tolstoy.'

Father ascribed these viewpoints to me remembering our arguments in the past. By 1910 my outlook had altered considerably, but still I avoided arguing with him. Though we did not differ so much in our outlook, I could never accept his criticism of the function of pure reason, of scientific thinking. I believe that there is no domain which man's reason cannot delve in; it can solve matters concerning people's relationship, sociology, law, history, economics, everything.

On the 27th I left for Moscow to look for a psychiatrist to take over to Jassnaia and a Professor Rastegaev and two nurses left

*S. Tolstoy has married again, this time Countess Marie Zubov.

the following day. I met Michael Novikov in Moscow, who told me about his last conversation with Father. Father had told him that he wanted to go and live in a hut, without servants, with no sort of luxury. Novikov had replied that it would be artificial for him at his age to change his way of living but Father insisted he could no longer bear the terrible rift between himself and his wife.

Then Novikov told him: ' We peasants can only laugh at that, Lev Nikolaevich. A woman can be taught anything.' And he explained how his own brother had taken the whip to his wife who drank and she had stopped drinking pretty quickly after that.

I was on my way to Nikolskoe where I wanted to put the finishing touches to work I had on hand before devoting my time to Mother. I somehow did not believe that for Father there was any imminent danger. But on the train I got a wire from my wife: ' Situation grave in Astapovo. Bring Dr. Nikitin immediately. Wishes you and Tatiana to be informed; dreads the arrival of others.'

I changed my route and went to Astapovo at once, arriving on November 2nd.

Chapter 2

Astapovo

FATHER had been accommodated, as is known, with the people who had arrived with him, in the house of the station-master. When I arrived I found everybody round a table in the first room, while Father was lying in the adjoining one. Dushan Makovitsky told us that their plans had been so hazy that they had not really decided where they were going at all, mainly in order to cover up their tracks, like an ostrich hiding its head in the sand. There had been talk of the Caucasus and even of Bulgaria; Father had hoped that he would be allowed to cross the frontier without a passport.

The situation was grave, but not without hope. The doctors had diagnosed inflammation of both lungs, particularly the left one. His temperature was high, but his pulse quite strong. Father asked the doctors whether he could get up in two or three days and when they said that he would not be able to move before a fortnight, he turned to the wall in silence.

We all wondered whether I should go to his room. He still believed that we none of us knew where he was and we were afraid it might upset him. But finally I decided to go in. He was half-conscious. A paraffin lamp burnt in a corner on a table littered with medicine bottles.

Dushan Makovitsky said: 'Lev Nikolaevich, here is Sergei Lvovich.' Father opened his eyes and looked at me with anxious surprise. I kissed his hand (which was unusual between us). He asked me:

'Serejha? How did you find us? How did you know?'

I invented on the spot that I had asked the conductor on the train if he knew where he was, and that he had told me. It was partly the truth. I had asked the conductor where Father was but only after receiving the telegram saying that he was in Astapovo. The conductor confirmed this. Father asked:

'But how did the conductor know who you were?'

I replied that many conductors on that line knew me.

Then he closed his eyes and did not speak. Judging by his voice I did not think his condition was too bad.

The next day I was told that my father kept repeating:

'Clever chap, Serejha! How quickly he found us! I'm glad he came, I like him. And he kissed my hand.' And there were tears in his eyes.

About midnight the train arrived with Mother, her doctor and the nurses, and the rest of the family. No one went to see Father that night.

On November 3rd, in the morning, Tania went to see Father. She wrote to her husband:

'Father called me because they brought him his little pillow and when he asked how it came to be there, Dushan could not tell a lie and said that I had brought it. . . . He wasn't told about Mother's arrival or that his other sons were there. He began by saying in a weak, breathless voice: "How smart you are, how well you look." I said I always knew he had no taste and we both laughed. Then he asked about Mamma. I feared that most of all because I didn't want to tell him she was here and I hadn't the courage to tell a direct lie. Luckily he put the question so that I didn't have to.

"With whom is she?"

"With Andre and Misha."

"Misha, too?"

"Yes. They all agree that she shouldn't see you until you ask for her."

"And Andre?"

"Yes, Andre too. They are very kind, the boys, and they are trying very hard to see she doesn't get too excited."

"Tell me what she is doing."

"Papa, perhaps you had better not talk too much, it isn't good for you."

Then he interrupted me firmly, but still in a tearful, breathless voice:

"No, no, tell me all, this is the most important thing of all for me." He asked whether the doctor she had was a good one. I told him she had a very good nurse who was well used to such patients.

" Does she like her? "

" Yes."

" Does she eat? "

" Yes, she is eating now and tries to keep well in the hope of seeing you."

" Did she get my letter? .'

" Yes."

" What did she think of it? "

" She was particularly reassured by the fragment from your letter to Chertkov, saying you would come back if she recovered her calm."

" You received my letters, you and Serejha ?"

" Yes, Papa, but I'm sorry you didn't write to the other brothers, they have been so good about everything."

" But I meant all of you, I said: ' My Children ' . . . "

I spent the day in the train with Mother. We had all decided that we would first follow Papa's wishes, then the doctor's orders, then our own decisions. Mother reluctantly agreed with us, and kept repeating that of course she did not wish to be the cause of Father's death. But we were afraid she would nonetheless go to see him, and therefore kept an eye on her. My brothers decided to stay away from Father too as otherwise it would have been impossible to keep Mother away at all.

In fact, we took it in turns to guard his door.'

When I walked in, Father was asleep, or rather in a semi-conscious condition. When he came to, he asked me, hurriedly:

' Are you going today, Serejha? '

I said no, not yet.

' You must go, you really must.'

I believe he hoped that he would recover soon and wanted me to leave so that I should not prevent his further journey—though he was really not conscious at the time. Towards the evening he was exhausted, upset at the idea that everybody knew where he was, upset by his conversation with Tania. He insisted on having the papers read to him, and wrote in his small diary. Chertkov read him some of his letters.

On November 4th when there was no one but myself and Chertkov in the room, he said: ' I may be dying . . . but perhaps . . . . anyhow, I'll try . . . ' Then Chertkov left and I stayed a long time alone with him. I was able to realise that he was conscious of dying. He lay with his eyes closed, murmuring now and then whatever came into his mind, just as he often did when he was well and thinking of something upsetting. He said: ' Things aren't too good, are they? . . . ' Then suddenly: ' How wonderful! ' Then he opened his eyes and looking upwards, said loudly: ' Masha! Masha! '

A shiver ran down my back. I realised that he was thinking of my sister Masha who had died, also from pneumonia, in 1906. I left him then and returned again at five o'clock. When he was given something to drink, he said: ' Not now, let me be . . . leave me alone . . . ' Death was constantly in his thoughts. On that day he dictated the following telegram: ' Tell my sons not to let their mother come, my heart is so weak that seeing her would mean death, though my health is better.' The telegram was read out to Mother in Astapovo, in the train where she was living.

On November 5th I was sitting with Father, and Tania came in. He kept repeating: ' How is it you don't understand? Why don't you want to understand . . . It's so simple . . . Why don't you want to do it? ' His thoughts seemed to torment him, and he was terribly frustrated not to be able to explain to us what it was he wanted us to understand and what it was he wanted us to do.

In the evening he fumbled with his sheet—believed by superstitious people to be a sure sign of nearing death, ' tidying up ' as it is called. Or perhaps he was moving his hand on his sheet as if he were writing.

Tania told me that during the morning of the 6th he said: ' It is the end, and there is nothing to it . . . ' Then he sat up and said: ' I advise you to remember one thing: there are hundreds of people in the world beside Tolstoy—but you concentrate only on him.'

During these days I lived between my father's room, the train where Mother was staying and the station where we had to have our meals. It was painful to see my mother's grief. She knew, though she may not have admitted it to herself, that she had driven Father away from home and that this illness was the result of it; she knew that he did not want to see her, and realised her own helplessness and the irrevocability of what had happened haunted her.

At the station there were crowds of newspaper men, who drank vodka and asked questions. There were policemen, too, and spies, and Father Varsonofij, who had been secretly urged to give Tolstoy communion. Before Dr. Rastegaev left us I asked him to give me a diagnosis of my mother's illness. This is what he wrote:

' . . . I did not examine Countess Tolstoy on my arrival because I had decided to concentrate on her nervous condition. She is quite normal in her reactions to outward events and her orientation in time and space is also perfectly normal. She is perfectly conscious of her actions even when excited. The main trouble is that she is determined to make herself and her own interests the centre of all attention. Her memory is good, she can remember details of the present and the past with great accuracy. In the sphere of judgment there are some disorders. They are expressed mainly in a total lack of self-criticism. In her desire to prove herself right she turns away from the truth and even from reality. She is quite capable of endangering her own life in her determination to achieve what she wants though realising the danger. Her whole behaviour is highly emotional. Her judgments are inconsequent and incoherent. When excited she is so uncontrolled that she may easily overstep the limits of normal behaviour. All this leads me go diagnose Countess Tolstoy's illness as acute hysteria which may reach at times mental derangement. I have indicated to you my advice as far as treatment is concerned.'

On November 3rd I wired my wife in Moscow, asking her to buy a good bed and mattress, which she did and sent to Astapovo. We moved Father on to it at once.

On November 6th I wrote to her:

' Mother is under constant observation by the nurse whom she seems to like. She is more calm, but just as self-centred. She talks incessantly, worst of all, she has all the newspaper correspondents at the station listening to her avidly and we

live in constant terror of what she might say. This is, of
course, the source of all the filthy gossip in the newspapers.
Sometimes she allows herself to be persuaded by us. We
don't allow her to see Father and will not do so until he
asks for her and the doctors allow it. They think it would
be dangerous now. We have told her this and she realises
fortunately that to see him now would be to kill him.'

About one p.m. I went into Father's room. His breathing
was very rapid. He was having camphor injections and oxygen.
But his face was drawn, and his colour blue. I thought that this
must be the end. But he rallied a little after the injections. I
returned again about ten p.m. He was restless and moaning,
trying to get up. At one moment he said: ' I'm afraid I'm dying.'
Then he coughed and made a face of disgust. Then he murmured:
' I'll go somewhere where no one will interfere . . . Leave me in
peace.' I was terribly shocked when he suddenly sat up and said
loudly: ' Escape, I must escape! ' Soon after that he saw me
though I was standing in the dark (there was only one candle in
the room) and he called out: ' Scrcjha! ' I rushed to the bed and
knelt to hear better what he said. He uttered a whole sentence but
I could not understand a word. Dushan told me later that he
distinguished a few words which he wrote down at once: ' Truth
. . . I love all . . . all of them . . . ' I kissed his hand and moved
away.

Towards midnight he grew restless again, his breathing was
stertorous, heavy, the rattle in the throat grew louder, he hic-
coughed . . . My brothers came in. I felt quite numb . . . About
two a.m. my mother was called. She stood at the foot of the bed,
watching him, then came close quite calmly, kissed him on the
forehead, knelt down and began to whisper: ' Forgive me ' and
something else which I didn't hear.

About three a.m. he started to moan. But his pulse was hardly
perceptible and he didn't recover consciousness. Dushan offered
him some water, and he opened his eyes and drank.

Somebody brought the candle close to his eyes, he frowned and
turned away. His pulse grew worse. The doctors gave him more
water. Dushan murmured: ' Moisten your lips, Lev Nicolaevich.'
He swallowed some water. It was now five a.m. After that life
showed only in the breathing which became more and more

shallow, less and less loud. It suddenly stopped. The doctors said: ' The first stop.' Then came the second . . . a few sighs, another stop and the last rattle . . . About ten minutes before his death Mother came up to the bed once again and knelt down, whispering.

After the last sigh silence fell. It was broken by one of the doctors saying: ' A quarter to six! ' Dushan came up to him first and closed his eyes. I only remember that everybody left and the doctor, Dushan and I remained to undress him, wash him and put on his grey blouse again. His body seemed to me strong and young for its age. He had been ill for such a short time that he had not time to grow thin. His expression was calm and concentrated.

Chapter 3

The Last Journey

November 7th went by in a continual bustle. The doors of the house were open and more than a thousand people came to pay Tolstoy their last respects.

Mother sat all day at the head of the bed, her head shaking. It was painful to watch her. The painter Pasternak made a drawing of him, the sculptor Mercurov made a cast. Photographers were busy and someone drew the outline of his shadow on the wall. I was asked if his skull could be opened, but after consultation with the family we refused it, knowing how Father hated scientific experiments of that kind. A medical student gave him an injection of formalin.

On November 8th we four brothers carried the coffin out of the house and into the train, decorated with fir-tree branches and wreaths. The whole family went in another carriage and in a third one the newspaper correspondents. We arrived at seven a.m. at Jassnaia, by which time we had already been inundated with telegrams of sympathy. A great crowd had assembled at the station. We carried the coffin out again, and then the peasants of Jassnaia took our places and the funeral procession, with funereal songs, moved along the road which Father had so often taken. It was a still, misty day; snow lay here and there, and there was a slight frost. I think the crowd numbered from three to four thousand people. As we moved along I was told that Chertkov had arranged that the coffin should not be brought into the house and that it should be left unopened only for a few moments' halt in front of the entrance. I protested against that and so did Mother and my brothers, knowing that many people would like to see Father once more. I hurried ahead. Our old servant and I pulled out the frame of the door that led into Father's favourite study, and there we put the coffin. The procession by the coffin went on from 11 a.m. to 2.30 p.m. A policeman came and stood by the coffin. I asked him to go away and when he didn't do as I asked I told him sharply that we, the kith and kin of Count Tolstoy, were in charge here and that we desired him to go. And then he went. Maria Alexandrovna Schmidt, his closest friend, was the last one to say goodbye to him before the family and then finally the coffin was closed.

He was buried, as he had wanted, in the place in the wood which he had indicated. Everybody knelt down, only a solitary policeman remained on his feet. Somebody shouted: ' On your knees, policeman! '

There were no speeches at the graveside. My mother was silent and controlled. I hoped she would cry, but she did not shed a tear. Chertkov was not there.

A dark, autumn night set in and gradually everybody drifted away.

Tolstoy's burial was the first public burial without a church ritual, which was what he had wanted.

Among the three thousand telegrams that we received was the one from the workmen deputies of the Third Duma,* saying: ' The social-democratic fraction of the Duma, in the name of the proletariat, expresses its grief at the loss of the great artistic genius, the unconquerable and implacable fighter against official-dom, the enemy of all servitude, who raised his voice against capital punishment, and was the friend of all the downtrodden.'

Among the various letters and telegrams were some rather curious ones. I received one from the peasants on my estate: ' We pray for the absolution of the sins of our drunken priest who has not been able to conduct a funeral service for your father and we offer you all our sympathy.' We had another from a priest asking us to grant him a priest's attire in which to pray for the peace of Tolstoy's soul, and he actually added his measurements.

Mother fell ill and had to keep to her bed for about a fortnight. Her sister came to try to console her. She was crushed with grief, but no longer mentioned suicide. Gradually she began to return to her usual occupations—correcting proofs, busying herself in the house, etc. But her state of mind was desperate, as seen from the notes in her diary.

*The Russian Parliament of November 1st 1907–June 9th 1912.

148

' *Nov. 12th–25th.*   Illness.

Nov. 25th   Terrible insomnia.

Nov. 26th   Neuralgia day and night.

Nov. 27th   Got up, but neuralgia raging.

Nov. 28th   Easier when people about. Terrified of solitude. No future.

Nov. 29th   I suffer agonies of remorse.

Nov. 30th   What has life to offer me?

Dec. 7th   There is no end to my despair.

Dec. 8th   My sister left. I cried desperately. Nobody cares for me.

Dec. 11th   Have put away my husband's things, to protect them from moths. How terrible life can be.

Dec. 13th   I have not slept at all. These dreadful nights with my soul steeped in darkness.

Dec. 16th   Went to the grave with all the peasants from Jassnaia. I suffer terribly, but was moved by the sight of their love for him. And they are all so kind to me.'

Chapter 4

Mother's Death

On October 25th, 1919 I received a note in Moscow from Jassnaia saying that Mother had fallen ill and that her life was in danger. It was difficult at the time to get a ticket from Moscow to Jassnaia at once, for it usually took several days and I had to leave immediately. So I decided to apply for help to the secretary of the Soviet of People's Commissars* whom I had met with Chertkov in England in 1898 when he was an *émigré*.

I went to see him in the Kremlin. He was very kind and promised to go at once and ask Lenin for a pass. I waited in his study and twenty minutes later he came back with the necessary paper.

PERMIT TO TRAVEL

Owing to the grave illness of Sofia Andreena Tolstoy, widow of Lev Nikolaevich Tolstoy, her son Sergei Lvovich is allowed to leave Moscow urgently for Jassnaia Poliana. All railway and military authorities are asked to assist him on this journey and he is permitted to travel on all types of transport.

R.S.S.S.R.	President of Council of
Council of	People's Commissars
People's Commissars	
Kremlin, Moscow	V. ULIANOV.
Oct. 26th, 1919	(LENIN)
No. 3306	

I left at 10 p.m. having telephoned to say I was arriving. Horses were sent to meet me. My mother was very ill. Her mouth had fallen in, her nose grown sharper. She recognised me, though her mind was wandering. She had a high temperature. She kept

*V. P. Bonch-Brujevich.

asking: 'When are we going? Where is your aunt Tania?' (her sister). And repeated: 'I'm ashamed,' and she meant ashamed to be ill.

She had caught cold washing her window with cold water.

She said to me: 'One ought to go without grieving, like the peasants do.' She was a meek, obedient patient and did not get irritable or angry.

On the 29th she was better and not only recognised me, but when told that I had brought her some wine, wished to drink my health. She had her old face again, with wrinkles. In my absence Tania asked whether she wanted a priest. She replied: 'I'm not yet as bad as that, let's wait until tomorrow.' And added: 'You must bury me as a Christian.'

Half conscious, she moved her hands as if she were sewing, threading a needle. I remembered that Father had moved his hands on the sheet as if writing.

On the 30th she took a turn for the worse. I came to say goodnight to her and asked if she knew me. She said: 'Of course, I know all my children.' I kissed her hands and she leant across to kiss me on the forehead.

The doctor said the illness was progressing normally but owing to her age there was only a ten per cent chance of recovery.

On the 31st Mother was unconscious. Her temperature had gone down. She called for me in the evening and said 'goodbye!' I replied: 'Goodnight.' At about 10 p.m. she murmured words in French, called Masha who was dead and her dead housekeeper and then again my brothers Leo and Misha who were still alive.

Nov. 1st   Mother unconscious, moaning. The doctors have nothing new to report.

Nov. 2nd   I told her that Dr. Nikitin had arrived from Moscow and that she would soon be better.
'I'm very weak,' she said.
In the evening I said again: 'Goodnight.' She didn't reply.

Nov. 3rd   She hasn't recovered consciousness, moans, talks incoherently. The doctors say she has emphysema of the lung. No hope.

Nov. 4th   We sat the whole night in the room next to hers. Her sister Tania was with her. About 4 a.m. I heard a rattle . . . and then nothing. We called two servants who prepared the body and laid it on the table. We sent for the nuns to watch and pray. Before leaving the room I glanced at my mother's face—beautiful, calm, but the face of a stranger.

Mother had always wanted to be buried beside Father. But we doubted whether that would be the right thing. There might have been awkward, insulting questions. She said shortly before her illness: 'If you don't bury me next to your father, bury me next to the children in the graveyard.' These words served us as a pretext rather than a reason for burying her there.

Tania said she had talked to her on October 27th. Her bed had been moved and this made her restless as she did not see the photograph of her son Ivan. Tania showed her where it was and asked whether she often thought of him. 'Yes, often,' she replied. 'And of Papa?' asked Tania. 'All the time,' she said. 'I live with him, torment myself that I was not good enough for him. But I was faithful to him, in body and in spirit. I married at eighteen . . . never loved anyone but him. I can tell you now before dying: I never shook any man's hand in a way that could not have been done in public.' Tania told me that and I wrote it down.

Nov. 5th   It is cold, very cold. The snow is falling. I went to the cemetery to choose the place. Decided to bury her next to Masha.

Nov. 6th   We carried the coffin up to the church. The cook's wife sobbed loudly, remembering Mother's many kindnesses.

The grave was a large one. We found in it three skulls, some bones and brass buttons, belonging to an officer of the time of Alexander I. A child was being buried near by, beside Mother's coffin stood a tiny one with the small sweet waxen face of a child of five. All her life Mother had had to do with children and here she was, being buried beside a child.

Nov. 13th   We found a moving letter from Mother written on July 14th of the same year, inscribed: 'To be read after my death.'
'The circle of my life is obviously closing in. I am gradually dying and I want to say to you all—goodbye and forgive me.'

Part V

THE PEOPLE AROUND TOLSTOY

Chapter 1

Father's Brother

I KNEW my father's brother, Sergei, rather well and liked him. He was a very handsome man, witty, proud and sincere, without pretence or hypocrisy. He never concealed anything about himself nor wanted to appear something that he was not. Father used to say of him that his soul was open like the mechanism of a glass clock—you could see quite clearly all his feelings and thoughts. He said that he always wondered at his brother's frank egotism but had never understood him. Sergei Nikolaievich was the prototype of Volodia in *Childhood, Boyhood and Youth*. He was a better pupil at school than his brother Leo, got a degree in philosophy, then joined a crack regiment for a short time. He was very social, much more so than his brother who was shy, awkward and self-conscious. He could easily have made a success in some career, but had no ambition except to do what he liked and not have to think about the consequences. He took the line of least resistance in life. He played for a while at being a squire, was a keen sportsman and hunted wolves. There was a path on his estate, hedged with two rows of wolves' teeth—all the wolves he had killed himself. When he was very young, he enjoyed listening to *Tsigane* gypsy songs and fell in love with an attractive gypsy. Gypsies are usually excessively puritanical and it is not easy to have a ' liaison ' with them. But the girl was in love, he carried her away to his estate and lived with her for eighteen years, without marrying her, and only did so quite late in life, perhaps for the first time putting duty before pleasure. But it was never a happy relationship and threw a shadow over his whole life. He read only newspapers, or French and English novels. This is how he learnt English; he read the first volume of an English novel in translation, then lost the second volume. My father had both volumes in English and told him to read the second one with a dictionary, which he did, and from then on read steadily in English. He could not, however, learn to speak it properly.

His daughters, when they reached the marriageable age, were highly influenced by Father's teachings, particularly those expressed in *The Kreutzer Sonata,* on the subject of chastity. But chastity did not seem to satisfy them completely. One day one of them said: ' *Nous sommes un nid de vielles filles et nos enfants seront aussi un nid de vielles filles. Comme c'est triste!* ' We all laughed on hearing this pronouncement and teased her: how on earth were spinsters going to have any children?

They did not remain spinsters, however. One of them had a baby by a Bashkir doctor who had come to administer a treatment of mare's milk to her. He died early and this affair gave my father the theme for his last story, *What did I see in my dream?*

Another daughter lived with a local peasant. Only one of them married a neighbour and this marriage was a success.

Uncle died of face cancer, a slow and painful death, growing quite blind. Father went to stay with him for a time before his death. My uncle's wife was very eager for him to take the last sacrament but was afraid to ask him herself. Father undertook the task and strangely enough Uncle agreed to take communion, though he had been indifferent to religion all his life.

Chapter 2

Father's Sister

My father's only sister, Maria, was the prototype of Luba in *Boyhood*. She first learnt about it when Turgenev read to her an extract from a story by an unknown author, signed L.T. in one of the thick periodicals. She was amazed to listen to a story about a family so like her own and could not understand who could have known such intimate details about her brothers and herself. She never thought it was her brother Leo, having not read *Childhood* which had appeared in the periodical before. Her brother Nicholas wrote to my father: ' Masha is very enthusiastic about Turgenev. I would so love to meet him. Masha says he is simple in manner, plays tiddley-winks with her, and cards, but Masha is not a worldly person and she could be mistaken about such a clever man as Turgenev. People now are so sly, you have to break many a crust with them before you know them.'

Turgenev wrote to his friends that when he first met Aunt Masha he almost fell in love with her and in fact they were always friends and he even dedicated his story *Faust* to her.

She married a neighbour—a cynic and a rogue, from whom she was obliged later to separate. Turgenev wrote to Madame Viardot about it, saying: ' She had to leave her husband, a sort of rural Henry the Eighth, and a very repulsive man.'

Her brothers, for some obscure reason, disapproved of her platonic friendship with Turgenev and Father even wrote: ' Turgenev behaves badly towards Masha. A scoundrel.' Later she travelled a lot, went to Hyères and Algiers and settled down in Switzerland, coming back only for short spells to Russia. In Switzerland she fell in love with a Swede by whom she had a daughter and at that time asked her brothers to start divorce proceedings against her husband. But Father wrote to her urging her to come back to Russia, which she finally did. Her husband soon died and she lived for a time in Jassnaia, though my mother never approved of it. Aunt Masha was always restless and never seemed to settle down anywhere. One day I met her unexpectedly at a station in Russia with a pretty eighteen-year-old girl. Aunt Masha, very embarrassed, introduced her as ' my ward.' It was in fact her daughter by the Swede. She was then living with her mother.

She was of a religious nature, and believed in superstitions and miracles. But she was also musical, talented, and a good witty story-teller. I remember one of her ' repartees ' when a group of trippers came up to her in the garden in Jassnaia asking her to show them my father. To protect her brother she said to them: ' No, the Lion (Leo) is not being shown today, only the monkeys.'

She was capricious and irritable and her solitary lot exasperated her. At one time she gave much of her time to music, and raved about Anton Rubinstein. Then she became friends with a religious doctor of homeopathy who had a great influence on her. She became more and more religious-minded. She went to live in a convent, the Shamardino Convent near Moscow, before finally taking the veil. At the beginning of her conversion to orthodoxy she and my father argued very hotly about it, but soon each understood that the other would never change. And there was also in Aunt Masha a wonderful fusion of naïve faith, coupled with an understanding for the ethical principles that my father believed in. When he wrote his article *I cannot remain silent*, about the death penalty she strongly supported him, from a religious point of view.

It was more difficult for her to come to Jassnaia after she had taken the veil. But she did come now and then. One day Father asked her why she did not stay longer and she replied: ' To do that I should have to have the blessing of Father Joseph.'

' How many nuns are there in your Convent? ' asked Father.

' Six hundred.'

' And none of you six hundred fools can live on your own brains! '

Aunt Masha remembered these words and she sent Father a pillow she had embroidered with the words in silk: ' From one of the Shamardin fools !'

She mellowed as time went on, and grew less capricious. She said it was because of the influence of a girl in the Convent who looked after her and whenever she lost her temper with her would say: 'Forgive me, Mother Maria.'

I went to see her in 1911 and told her of Father's last years before his death. She was sad that he had left Shamardino without saying goodbye to her. She wrote a moving letter to my mother after Father's death saying that he had been a remarkable man and no wonder therefore that his death had been remarkable too. She knew very little of what had happened between them, knew only that something had been wrong, that he had wanted solitude and also that Chertkov was much to blame. How could she not love her, Sonia, when her dear Leo had loved her so much. She hoped to be able to visit her brother's grave but complained of feeling old and weak.

She died of pneumonia in the spring of 1912. She had no fear of death and died peacefully. Shortly before her death she wrote two letters, one to Charles Salomon, a friend of our family, and one to my sister Tatiana. I will quote some fragments from them: To Salomon.

'I don't think my brother was seeking refuge or consolation for his grief when he decided to leave the house. His grief was too complicated. He merely wanted to live a quiet, spiritual life . . . The more he soared to heaven, the more she became *terre à terre* . . . He wanted to live in the Convent " if your nuns will let me " he said. I don't believe he wanted to return to the church but I had hoped he would develop a sense of humility which was not far from him in his last days. Now he has gone and why— no one will know . . . '

To my sister she wrote how much she wanted to see us all and my mother again. ' Between her and Leo there were two enemies at work, one seen, one unseen, I know that. They loved each other so much, after all. How could they then so hate one another? '

Chapter 3

Turgenev in Jassnaia Poliana

TURGENEV and Tolstoy, the story of their mutual relations, the clash of two different points of view, two different characters— what a rewarding subject for historical and literary research! However, that is not my task. I wish only to tell about Turgenev's visits to Jassnaia Poliana, of which I was an eye-witness.

In 1856 Leo Tolstoy, a young writer who had already won recognition owing to his *Childhood, Adolescence,* and his war stories, joined a group of Petersburg authors as a full member. Turgenev played first fiddle in this group and, of course, he interested Tolstoy more than anybody else. Soon, in fact very soon, a friendship sprang up between them. As a man, Turgenev was bewitching. He was already famous as the author of *A Sportsman's Sketches* which had greatly influenced my father, of *Rudin, A Nest of Gentlefolk,* etc. Turgenev was one of the first to appreciate my father's talent and he was ten years older than Tolstoy. No wonder that the younger man came under his spell. However, this did not last long; gradually my father began to free himself from Turgenev's influence and to stand on his own feet.

Endless arguments on matters of principle ensued. Turgenev liked to lead the conversation; my father was not always tolerant of other people's opinions. Their relations deteriorated and, finally, broke off in a quarrel. This was not accidental. It had been brewing for a long time and was the outcome of the great differences in their character and outlook.

During five years, between 1856 and 1861, they met frequently in St. Petersburg, in the country and abroad. Their relationship could be described as close, but something hindered real friendship. Turgenev used to say that at times as abyss would open between them; it would appear to close and would become a hardly noticeable chink; then it would open up again.

159

As early as 1856 Turgenev writes to Tolstoy: ' I shall never cease to like you and value your friendship, though—probably through my fault—each of us will feel embarrassed in the other's presence for quite some time to come. Where does this embarrassment come from . . . I think you recognise it yourself. You are the only man with whom I have ever had a misunderstanding . . . '

During his stay in Paris in 1857 my father constantly met Turgenev; they went visiting together, frequented theatres, exhibitions, concerts. In my father's diary the statement that ' Turgenev is boring and heavy going ' stands next to such remarks as ' Turgenev is charming ' . . . ' chatted gaily with Turgenev '. On leaving Paris for Switzerland he notes in his diary: ' Called on Turgenev. Both times after having said goodbye and left him I wept, I do not know why. I am very fond of him. He has made, and is still making, another man of me.'

However, the ' abyss ' which separated them widened with the years; Turgenev's indifference to religious and moral questions went against my father's grain. He needed straight, vigorous replies to the questions which were tormenting him. Already, at that time partly consciously, though fumblingly, he was seeking in religion and ethics answers to questions on the aim and the meaning of life. Turgenev used to say to him: ' This is unimportant. You have been given a great talent, make use of it.' In 1857 Turgenev wrote to my father:

> ' You write that you are very pleased at not having followed my advice and become exclusively a man of letters. I will not argue—perhaps you are right, but I, sinner that I am, cannot, much as I rack my brain, make out what you actually are if not a man of letters? An officer? A land-owner? A philosopher? The founder of a new religious teaching? A civil servant? A businessman? Please help me out of my difficulty and tell me which of these surmises is correct. I am not joking. Truly, I would so much like to see you speeding ahead at last under full sail.'

As can be seen from this letter as well as from some others, Turgenev wanted Tolstoy to devote himself almost exclusively to literature; he treated all his other occupations such as farming, schools, and, particularly, philosophy, with contempt. He could not understand that, if Tolstoy wrote as he did, it was only because he had an inner world of his own, his own ideas which urged him to write in this way and in no other. Turgenev's indifference to his most treasured thoughts and feelings offended Tolstoy. On the other hand it is possible that Turgenev was annoyed that the young writer whom he had protected and influenced was now standing on his own feet and even criticised his novels *Rudin*, *Nest of Gentlefolk* and *Smoke*. These dissensions and mutual strictures eventually led to a quarrel, almost a duel. This happened in 1861.

Relations were interrupted for seventeen years. However, the two men continued to take an interest in one another. Having heard that Tolstoy had sold his *Cossacks* to Katkov to pay a gambling debt, Turgenev writes: ' I hope to God that in this way at least Tolstoy will return to his real work.' On the appearance of *Polikushka* he writes: ' What a master! What a master! '

War and Peace he both praised and criticised; he thought that its weakest points were those which sent the public into raptures —the historical and psychological aspects.

My father in his turn kept up his interest in Turgenev and his writing. I remember his remark on Turgenev: ' Why does Turgenev worship the young and flatter them? What is there to worship in them? Young people must be taught, not worshipped!'

When we were still children, my father advised us to read *A Sportsman's Sketches*. I remember how he once said of *The Singers* that Turgenev had communicated astonishingly well the impression produced by singing, but that in this case the author had crossed into the province of another art—music. He considered *First Love* to be the best of Turgenev's short stories as he had described in it his own experience. He thought less well of Turgenev's novels than of his stories, I only remember that he praised the beginning of *Asya* and *The Torrents of Spring*.

However, even after the break, Tolstoy was still interested in Turgenev's opinion of his works. Thus he wrote to Fet on the publication of *War and Peace*: ' Your opinion is valuable to me as well as that of a man whom I like less and less since I have grown up—and that man is Turgenev.'

1877 was a year of crisis in my father's life. It was then that the complete change in his outlook described by him in *A Confession* took place. This was preceded by his torments at the realisation of the futility of life and his fear of death. A new religious approach to life required an examination of himself and of his relations with other people. I do not think that my father had any personal enemies, but the hostility between himself and Turgenev weighed heavily upon him. It was then that he wrote to Turgenev the following conciliatory letter:

'Ivan Sergeyevich.

'While re-examining my feelings towards you some time ago I suddenly discovered with surprise and delight that I felt no hostility whatsoever towards you any longer. I hope to God that the same has happened to you. To tell you the truth, knowing how kind you are, I am almost certain that your unfriendly feelings towards me disappeared before mine towards you.

'If this is so, please let us shake hands and please forgive me in your heart of hearts for any offence I have committed in your eyes.

'It is so natural for me to remember only your goodness because there was so much of it in your relations towards me. I remember that it is to you I owe my literary fame, and I remember how you once liked both my writings and myself. Perhaps you, too, will recall some such memories of me because there was a time when I was sincerely fond of you.

'If you can forgive me I sincerely offer you all the friendship of which I am capable. At our age there is only one blessing—loving relations between people, and I shall be very glad if they could be established between us.
April 6th, 1878.   COUNT L. TOLSTOY.'

Turgenev replied on May 8/20, 1878 from Paris:

'Dear Lev Nikolayevich.

'I have only just received your letter which you sent *poste restante*. It has deeply touched me and has afforded me much joy. It will give me a great deal of pleasure to resume our former friendship and to shake the hand you are offering me. You are quite right in assuming that I have no hostile feelings towards you; if they ever existed, they vanished a very long time ago and there has remained only the memory of you as a man to whom I was sincerely attached, and of a writer whose first steps I was to welcome earlier than others did, and whose new works always awakened my liveliest interest. I am heartily glad that our former misunderstandings have ceased to exist. I hope to visit the Orel province this summer and then we shall certainly meet. Until then I send you my best wishes and once more shake your hand.

IVAN TURGENEV.'

In August 1878 Turgenev was in Moscow and wrote to Tolstoy: 'I shall be staying in Tula where I have some business. I myself would very much like to see you, and I also have a message for you. So what would you prefer—will you go to Tula or shall I come to see you at Jassnaia Poliana?'

A few days later Turgenev wired that he would drive from Tula to Jassnaia Poliana. Tolstoy himself went to Tula to meet him, taking with him his young brother-in-law, a student of the Law School, Stepan Bers. No notes have remained describing the meeting of the two writers after an interval of seventeen years and what they talked about during the one and a half hour drive in a carriage from Tula to Jassnaia Poliana. It can be presumed that the meeting was a friendly one and that both avoided unpleasant subjects of conversation.

In the summer of 1878 a large number of people were living, as usual, at Jassnaia Poliana. The big house was occupied by our family which consisted, besides our parents, of four brothers and two sisters. I, the eldest, was fifteen, my sister Tatiana thirteen, Ilya twelve. At that time we had a French tutor, M. Montels, an ex-Communard of 1871 who was hiding in Russia under the name of Nief, an English governess, and V. I. Alekseyev. The annexe of the house was inhabited by the Kusminski family. Moreover, there was a constant flow of guests. At that time Baroness Mengden and her daughter were staying as well as Stepan Bers. And then in 1878 Turgenev came to Jassnaia.

Naturally we all awaited Ivan Sergeyevich with the greatest excitement. I knew that Turgenev was very tall, but he exceeded my expectations. To me he seemed to be a giant—a giant with kind eyes, a reddish face and with what seemed to me to be flabby leg muscles; thick, well-groomed white hair with a yellowish tinge, and a beard of a similar colour. Compared to him my father appeared short (though he was above average height) and younger than he actually was. True, Turgenev was sixty and my father fifty. But Turgenev's hair was white while my father's was dark without any grey streaks in it. In their relationship also one could feel that Turgenev was the older of the two. It seemed to me at that time that my father's attitude to him was reserved, courteous and tinged with respect, whilst the latter, in spite of his exuberance, treated my father with a certain caution.

Turgenev had brought with him beautiful travelling accessories; an expensive leather suitcase, an elegant dressing-case, two ivory-backed brushes, etc. I remember his velvet coat with matching waistcoat, silk tie, also, I think, a soft silk shirt and a pair of beautiful gold watches. He used to take much pleasure in showing these watches, saying that they were chronometers, that in general he liked good watches, and that he always saw to it that they kept exactly the right time. He also had in his pocket an exquisite snuff-box filled with snuff. He told us that he had given up smoking because two very nice girls had refused to kiss him when he smoked: ' and now,' he added, ' my Parisian ladies do not even allow me to enjoy snuff .' He wore soft shoes with very wide toes because of his gout.

Turgenev had long talks with my father in the study or during their walks. Probably, the main subject of these conversations was literature. They also discussed poetry and Father said: ' When a writer writes poetry his choice of expressions is restricted by rhyme and rhythm. Anyone wishing to express his ideas clearly cannot do so in verse.'

I do not remember Turgenev's reply but I know that my father agreed with him that rhyme does sometimes endow an expression with a special charm as, for example, in much of Pushkin's poetry.

However, my father made the reservation that he had a great admiration and weakness for Pushkin. In this, as well as in a weakness for Fet's and Tiutchev's poetry, he agreed with Turgenev. Turgenev, who followed closely what was going on in literature, recommended two new writers to my father—a Russian, Vsevolod Garshin, and a Frenchman, Maupassant. Later my father fully appreciated both, though at first he was repelled by the subject of *La Maison Tellier*; having, however, read

Une Vie, he recognised in Maupassant a first-class writer. It was then, too, that Turgenev recommended to my father a woman writer, I think Mme. Stechkin. About her my father remarked: 'Turgenev is always fussing about some woman novelist.'

In the company of others Turgenev always led the conversation and held everybody's attention. He was an inimitable story-teller and we listened to him spellbound. He told us how, having been put under arrest for an article on Gogol, he tried to cajole his guard, a robust N.C.O.; or he imitated a hen in a coop by placing one hand under the other; or he would show us how his gun-dog pointed. He would describe his villa at Bougival, speaking of the Viardots and himself as ' we '; or, how he acted the part of a wood elf at Baden–Baden in amateur theatricals at the Viardots' house and how everybody gazed at him in bewilderment.

He also told us how once, at a masked ball, he and the poet A. K. Tolstoy met a graceful and attractive mask who talked very intelligently to them. They both tried to persuade her to unmask, but it was only several days later that they discovered who she was, when she invited them to her house. ' And what did I see then,' Turgenev said, 'but the face of a Finnish soldier in a skirt.'

This masked lady later married A. K. Tolstoy. One of his best poems was inspired by this first meeting with his future wife. I believe that Turgenev must have exaggerated her lack of beauty. I met A. K. Tolstoy's widow later—she was not at all ugly and she was certainly a very intelligent woman.

Somebody asked Ivan Sergeyevich whether the way of life in Russia seemed strange to him after such a long absence from the country. He replied that at first many things had amazed him, but that he soon got accustomed to everything Russian, as it belonged to his native land.

In spite of his sixty years Turgenev was vigorous and active. He took long walks with my father and our group of young people, was interested in farming, in the forest and apple tree plantations and admired the beauty spots in the garden and in the woods.

At that time one of us had built a kind of primitive see-saw near the house consisting of a plank balanced on a cross-beam. Passing by it, my father and Turgenev succumbed to temptation and, standing on either end of the plank, began to throw each other up and down amidst general laughter.

On one evening Turgenev read us one of his stories, *The Dog*. He read with great expression, in a simple and lively way without any affectation. However, the story itself did not make a great impression on any of us, including my father.

On another evening Turgenev played chess with me, and, as far as I remember, with my father and Urussov. He was a good player, far better than my father.

Giving me a rook, he won one game and lost another. He told us that one day, playing the decisive game in an international chess tournament against a Pole, he had the opportunity—owing to an error on the part of his opponent—of making the winning move, an uncovered check. The public waited in agitation to see whether he would make the move. After a moment's thought Turgenev acted as expected and the Pole had to surrender. He moved his bishops particularly skilfully. ' Chess players call me " *le chevalier du fou* ",' he said (the knight of the bishop).

Talking of chess he was reminded of a phrase, very fashionable at that time with the French: ' Whatever you say to a Frenchman,' he said, ' he always replies: " *Vieux jeu* ".'

In spite of all his love for France Turgenev did not particularly admire the French. He pointed to their shortcomings—their great patriotic conceit and their bourgeois, calculating minds. He said that French people had begun to speak bad French, the coarse Paris jargon.

He himself frequently switched from Russian to French. And how well he spoke it! It was well known that the French themselves admired his accent and his turn of speech.

Speaking of French women Turgenev said: ' How much better educated Russian women and girls are than the French! When you arrive in the midst of a Russian family it is like leaving a dark room and entering a lighted one.'

On the day of his departure Turgenev took leave of everybody very cordially. He said to my father: ' You have done very well, my friend, in marrying your wife.' He promised to look in at Jassnaia Poliana in the autumn.

Fresh from the impression of this visit my mother noted: ' Turgenev is very grey, very quiet, he has enchanted us all by his eloquence and the picturesque way in which he expounds the simplest as well as the loftiest subjects. He described the statue of Christ by Antokolski in such a way that we could see it before us and then told us a story about his favourite dog, Pegasus, with the same skill. A weakness, almost a childish, naïve weakness of character, is now noticeable in Turgenev. At the same time he is soft-hearted and kind.'

On his return to Spasskoye, Turgenev wrote to my father on August 14th:

'I cannot but repeat to you what a pleasant, good impression I have carried away from Jassnaia Poliana and how glad I am that our misunderstandings have vanished without a trace: as if they had never been. I felt very clearly that the years which have aged us have not been spent in vain, that you and I have both become better characters than we were sixteen years ago—and I was very pleased to realise this. It goes without saying that on my way back I shall most certainly look in on you . . . '

My father's reply was also cordial and several days later (August 25th) Turgenev once more wrote to Tolstoy:

'I am very pleased to hear that everybody at Jassnaia Poliana has looked upon me with a friendly eye . . . And there is no doubt that between us there exists the link of which you speak—and I am glad of it, though I cannot undertake to disentangle all the threads of which it is composed. Art alone is not enough. The main thing is that it does exist.'

Turgenev's second visit to Jassnaia Poliana, on September 2nd, lasted three days. Soon after that he went abroad. In his letter to Fet he says: 'I was very happy to have come together again with Tolstoy and I spent three pleasant days with him. His entire family is very likeable and his wife is charming. He himself has become more subdued and mature. His name is acquiring European fame. We, Russians, have long known that he has no rival!'

My father did not speak of Turgenev with the same enthusiasm. In a letter to Fet of September 5th, 1878, he wrote: 'Turgenev came to see us on his way back. He is just the same as he was, and we both know the degree of intimacy which it is possible for us to achieve.'

In his next letter Turgenev seemed to confirm that neither of them ought indeed to overstep the bounds of a certain degree of intimacy. One of his letters (November 15th, 1878) made an unpleasant impression upon my father:

'I am glad that your physical health is good and I hope that the "mental disarray" you speak of has gone as well. I, too, am familiar with it; sometimes it appeared in the guise of an inner ferment before the beginning of work. I presume that this is what happened to you. Though you beg me not to speak of your writing, I cannot help but tell you that I have never laughed, even "a little" at your expense; some of your writings I liked very much, others I disliked, some, as for instance *The Cossacks*, gave me great pleasure and filled me with wonder. But what reason should there be for laughter? I presume that you have long ago got rid of such "reactions".'

My father made a brief comment on this letter when he wrote to Fet on November 22nd: 'Yesterday I received a letter from Turgenev; do you know, I have decided to keep away from him for fear of sinning . . . Such a provocative, quarrelsome person.'

A shadow had once again fallen between my father and Turgenev, but this was the last time it happened. After that the good relations between them were never interrupted. Turgenev, like an old nurse, as he himself described it, took the greatest pains to spread Tolstoy's writings abroad. Their correspondence was resumed. On the occasion of a libel printed in the *Moskovskiye Vedomosti* by Katkov, my father expressed to Turgenev his warmest sympathy and Turgenev, always grateful for kindness and sympathy, replied on December 2nd, 1879: 'I was very touched by the sympathy expressed to me by you on the occasion of the article in the *Moskovskiye Vedomosti* and for my part I am almost glad that it appeared because it moved you to write such kind and friendly words to me.'

However, Turgenev kept to his opinion and regarded Tolstoy exclusively as a man of letters. In 1879 he writes to Polonski: 'Leo Tolstoy, as a man of great talent, will scramble out of the bog into which he has landed and it will be for the good of literature, but Fet-Shenshin has become so swamped in the slime

168

of philosophy that all he can do is blow bubbles and these are not too fragrant.'

In January 1880 Turgenev sent my father a flattering comment made by Flaubert on *War and Peace*. In the spring of the same year he came to Russia and once again visited Jassnaia Poliana. This time he had undertaken the difficult task of persuading Tolstoy to participate in the festivities on the unveiling of a monument to Pushkin. He arrived in Jassnaia Poliana on May 2nd. It was spring—' the birches were covered in green down—the nightingale was singing in the silent night . . . ' and the day before various song birds had been singing and chirping in the garden. Turgenev had a good knowledge of birds and distinguished them by their song. ' This is a bunting,' he would say, ' this one is a kind of finch and that's a starling ' and so on. My father admitted that he did not know birds as well as that.

The flight of the snipe was in full swing; Turgenev, my father and my brother Ilya and I with our guns, accompanied by my mother and my sister Tatiana, went off to take up our stands for the flight. We drove in a kind of shooting-brake to the crownforest Zaseka beyond the Voronka river. Having arrived at the river we crossed to the other side balancing on a tree trunk. I remember the enormous picturesque figure of I. S. Turgenev in a brown coat and wide-brimmed hat as he walked cautiously along the log to the other bank.

My father placed him in the clearing he considered the best, for the snipe were sure to fly over it, and took up his own position not far away. My mother who was talking to Turgenev remained beside him. She asked him why he never wrote anything any more. Turgenev replied that he was already finished as a writer.

' Can anybody overhear us ? ' he continued. ' No ? Well in that case I shall tell you. I can no longer write. Before, every time I began to write I would shake in a fever of love. Now this is gone. I am old and can neither love nor write any more.'

Suddenly during this conversation a shot rang out and Tolstoy's voice was heard sending his dog to retrieve the bird.

' It has started,' said Turgenev. ' Lev Nikolayevich has already bagged one. He's lucky, he has always been lucky in life.' And in fact many more snipe flew over my father than over Turgenev, probably simply because Turgenev frightened them away by talking. At last Turgenev heard the grunt and whistle of a snipe approaching him, the bird appeared above the trees and he fired.

'Is it a kill?' my father called out from his post. 'It fell like a stone,' Turgenev replied.

However, though the dog and all of us looked for the bird we could not find it in the darkness. And—strangely enough—this upset both my father and Turgenev. But next day my brother Ilya found the bird; the dog had been unable to do so because it was hanging in a tree.

Before Turgenev's departure my mother went to call him and my father to dinner. They were sitting in a hut my father had built himself in a grove near the house, to be able to work in solitude.

Turgenev was trying to persuade him to take part in the Push-kin festivities. My father resolutely refused. He did not like speaking in public and, in general, avoided all celebrations and solemn occasions, even if they were in honour of Pushkin.

Turgenev had not expected this and left disappointed.

During 1880 and 1881 the friendly correspondence between the two writers went on. Turgenev continued as before to spread Tolstoy's works abroad, but was still contemptuous about his philosophy.

'I am very sorry for Tolstoy,' he wrote to A. I. Urussov on December 1st, 1880, having heard of Tolstoy's depression, 'but *chacun à sa manière de tuer ses puces.*'

In June 1881 he invited Tolstoy to his house at Spasskoye. On July 4th, 1881, he wrote to my father: 'I am looking forward to your early visit and am made happy by what you say of your feeling towards me. It is particularly good because it is mutual.'

My father wrote in his diary about that visit:

> 'July 9th and 10th. At Turgenev's. Dear Polonski quietly busy with his painting and his writing, uncritical and, poor man, so calm. Turgenev fears the name of God though he acknowledges him. But he, too, is naïvely calm in his life of luxury and idleness.'

At the end of August 1881 Turgenev came to Jassnaia Poliana for the last time. On August 22nd—my mother's birthday—many guests were assembled, among them my uncle Sergei Tolstoy and Prince Urussov. In spite of the fact that Urussov was Vice-Governor of the Tula province at that time he might have been described as a follower of my father's ideas. My father at that period was occupied with research on the gospels and had initiated Urussov into his work. Urussov had accepted Father's interpretation of the first words of the Gospel of St. John: ' The beginning of everything was the understanding of life ' and liked to talk on this subject. And so, one evening round the tea-table, Urussov began to prove to Turgenev that the beginning of everything was the understanding of life. I do not remember Turgenev's objections but, apparently, he was not interested in the subject and was trying to switch over to another one. Urussov, however, obstinately continued to expound his thesis and gesticulated violently, not noticing that he was moving towards the edge of his chair. Suddenly the chair slid from under him and he fell under the table, the palm of his hand outstretched before him. Not in the least embarrassed, he continued from under the table the sentence he had begun. Turgenev could no longer contain himself and burst out laughing—a little too loudly perhaps. ' *Il m'assomme, ce Troubetzkoy,*' he shouted in a falsetto voice between his laughter, confusing the names and calling Urussov 'Troubetzkoy'.

Everybody began to laugh except Urussov and my father. The latter only smiled, he did not like Turgenev's slightly contemptuous attitude towards Urussov nor towards the questions he had raised. After this the conversation on the understanding of life was not resumed.

I believe that it was on that occasion that, as we were thirteen at table, the conversation turned to the fear of death. Turgenev considered that the fear of death was a natural reaction. He admitted that he was afraid of death and frankly declared that he never came to Russia when there was cholera in the country. My father and Urussov both said that he who fears death cannot live. Death is as inevitable as night or winter. We prepare for the night or for winter; in the same way we must prepare for death; only then will it not be intimidating. Turgenev continued: ' *Qui craint la mort leve la main.*' He was the first to raise his hand, but nobody else followed his example. He said ' *A ce qu'il parait je suis le seul.*' Then my father also raised his hand. I do not think it was done out of politeness but because he was reminded of the distressing days of Arsamass—those terrible moments when the fear of death overcame him.

It was on one of the evenings during Turgenev's visit that the conversation took on such a purely Turgenev turn that it might have been an episode from one of his stories. I do not remember who raised the question as to which were the happiest moments of one's life, nor for what reason. I think it was Turgenev who then suggested that everyone should tell the story of the happiest moment he had experienced in his life. Everybody started trying to remember. My uncle Sergei whispered something that seemed to flatter her into the ear of Tanya Kusminski with whom he had long ago had an affair. She blushed and said: 'You are an impossible man, Sergei Nikolayevich!' Urussov said something to the effect that the happiest moment of his life would have been to hear of the triumph of goodwill on earth. We, of course, turned to Turgenev: 'Tell us which was the happiest moment in *your* life!' He replied: 'Of course the happiest moment in life is connected with a woman's love. It is when you gaze into her eyes, into the eyes of the woman you love, and realise that she also loves you.' He was silent for a short while and then added: 'This has happened to me once in the course of my life—perhaps twice.'

Recalling now these words of Turgenev I understand the jeering comment made on his novels by his unfriendly critic N. Strakhov: 'In almost all of Turgenev's novels a young man wants to marry a girl and never manages to do it.' This is almost correct: Turgenev's heroes fall in love with youthful passion but do not marry. Strakhov, however, had intended to be abusive, instead of which he praised him.

Turgenev is not the bard of physical love but of that pure, self-sacrificing love which can restrict itself to gazes and insinuations but which—as Maupassant puts it—is often stronger than death. This is how he understood love and therefore there was no need to marry off his heroes. He himself was until his old age the young man who loves deeply and unselfishly, but who cannot and will not marry. His mother used to say about him that he was a man of one love, that he could love only one woman.

On this, his last visit, Turgenev was infected by the mood of wild gaiety which reigned among the young members of our group. One evening somebody started a quadrille. Turgenev was asked whether the old *contredanse* was still danced in France or whether it had been replaced by the unseemly can-can.

'The old can-can,' Turgenev said, 'is not at all that indecent dance which is performed in *cafés-chantants*. The old can-can is a proper and graceful dance. There was a time when I could dance it. Perhaps I might even dance it now.' He asked my cousin Masha Kusminski, a twelve-year-old girl, to be his partner; pushing his thumbs in the armholes of his waistcoat he proceeded with great ease to dance the old can-can according to all the rules, bending and straightening out his legs. The dance ended by his falling down, but he picked himself up with the agility of a young man. Everybody, including himself, burst out laughing, but we were all somehow embarrassed for him.

On that day my father noted in his diary: 'Turgenev—can-can. Very sad.'

This was Turgenev's last visit to Jassnaia Poliana. I have to add only a few fragmentary memories of conversations I had heard that time.

I remember one on the force of imagination. Turgenev said that, lying on his side he could, by exercising his imagination, bring himself to experience insufferable pain from the pressure of a cushion or a mattress on his hip. I remember, too, how he told us that once, in Paris, he had attended a lecture on pornography and that during the lecture experiments had been conducted on the people present.

He talked a lot about a group of French writers who were close to him: Flaubert, Zola, Daudet, the Goncourts, and Maupassant. He did not approve of the intentional realism of Zola's style and language and did not think that the Goncourts were talented. He put Flaubert and Maupassant high above the others. By the way, this is what he said about the writer known by the name of Jules Verne: 'I spent a whole evening with him. It would be hard to find a more boring and uninteresting man. Moreover he has never travelled.'

Turgenev thought very highly of Shakespeare. I remember how he tried to impress upon my father his own conviction of the greatness of Shakespeare. He pointed out the truly dramatic situations in which Shakespeare placed his heroes. 'Truly dramatic situations,'—these were approximately the words he used—'do not arise when virtuous people struggle against wicked ones as in melodramas, or when people suffer from external disasters like the plague or earthquakes. Dramatic situations arise when suffering inevitably springs from the characters of people and from their passions. We find precisely these situations in Shakespeare's dramas.'

At one point the conversation turned to Dostoyevski. It was common knowledge that Turgenev did not like Dostoyevski. As far as I remember he used to say something like the following about him:

' Do you know what an inverted commonplace is? When a man is in love his heart beats quickly, if he is angry his face is flushed, etc. These are all commonplaces. With Dostoyevski, however, everything happens the other way round. For instance, a man meets a lion. What does he do? Naturally he pales and tries to run away or to hide. This would be so in every straightforward story, like one by Jules Verne, for instance. But Dostoyevski will say exactly the opposite: ' the man flushes scarlet and remains glued to the spot." This is an inverted commonplace. It is a cheap way of acquiring the reputation of originality. Moreover, Dostoyevski's heroes—on every second page—are either delirious, in hysterics or in a fever. This does not happen in real life.'

After 1881 Turgenev no longer came to Russia. He fell ill with the painful disease which brought him to his grave.

His relations with Tolstoy became more and more friendly. In his letter of March 29th, 1882, after hearing that Grigorovich had resumed his former relations with Tolstoy and saying that he was glad about this, Turgenev writes: ' Leo Tolstoy is an oddity, but undoubtedly a genius and a very kind man.'

In another letter (April 9th) he says that he was glad to have had good news of Tolstoy. ' Convey my greetings to him and to his family,' Turgenev writes.

Turgenev replied as follows to a letter of sympathy written by my father: ' Dear Tolstoy, I cannot tell you how touched I am by your letter. I embrace you for each one of your words.'

However, even in this letter Turgenev could not refrain from expressing the wish that Tolstoy should return to his creative activity: ' You must go on living for a long time,' he writes, ' and that not only because life itself is a good thing whatever one says but because you must finish the work to which you have been called and for which, besides you, we have no other master. I remember your half-promises given last year and do not want to believe that they will not be kept! I cannot write much—but you understand me.'

In his next letter of May 14th Turgenev wrote: 'I have heard that your article (this was *A Confession*) has been burnt on censor's orders. But, perhaps, you have kept a copy of it. If so, would you be so kind as to send it to me here? . . . I am not asking you whether you have returned to your literary work, as I know that such a question is not much to your taste.'

After this Tolstoy sent Turgenev *A Confession* asking him to read this book without anger and to try and understand his point of view.

Having read *A Confession* Turgenev wrote to Tolstoy: 'I had begun a long letter to you in reply to your *Confession* but have not and will not finish it precisely to avoid becoming argumentative.'

Turgenev, of course, could not agree with the merciless condemnation, expressed in *Confession*, of the 'opinions' which reigned at the close of the fifties among the Petersburg men of letters, opinions which were primarily those of Turgenev himself. However, he was not offended.

One can see from Turgenev's last letter before his death, which could be called his last poem in prose, how close Tolstoy was to his heart as a Russian writer. Here is this letter of June 27th, 1883:

' My very dear Lev Nikolayevich.

' I have not written to you for a long time as I was and am, to put it frankly, on my deathbed. I cannot recover—it is no use even thinking about it. I am writing to you only to tell you how glad I am to have been your contemporary and to express my sincere, my last request. My friend, return to your literary work. This is a gift that came to you from the source whence everything comes. Ah, how happy I would be if I believed that my request would move you! As for me, I am a finished man—the doctors do not even know what to call my disease, *névralgie stomacale goûteuse*. No walking, no sleeping, oh, well, it is boring even to repeat all this. My friend, great writer of our Russian land, hearken to my prayer! Let me know if you receive this bit of paper and allow me to embrace you once more very very warmly, you, your wife, and all yours . . . I cannot write any more . . . I am tired.'

This letter contains love for his country, love for literature and a friendly appeal. Tolstoy did not forsake his literary activities—this was proved by the works that followed.

I think that my father understood Turgenev well. Having realised that Turgenev was not a religious man, he ceased to demand from him what he could not give—a religious approach to life. But this did not prevent him from appreciating Turgenev very highly as an artist and being a friend to him as a man.

My father did not reply to Turgenev's last letter, perhaps because he received it too late—at that time he was in the Samara province, whereas the letter had been addressed to Tula; perhaps because it was difficult for him to reply. And on August 22nd Ivan Sergeyevich was no more.

During Turgenev's illness my father was full of the warmest sympathy for him and when he died he felt his loss deeply. Notwithstanding his dislikes of public appearances, he then decided to read a paper on Turgenev at the Society of Lovers of Russian Literature.

I remember how warmly my father spoke of Turgenev in those days; how he re-read all his works and wished to remember kindly his elder fellow-writer and point out his significance in literature. It is common knowledge that the authorities prevented him from doing this. However, his conscience could rest in peace. In the last years of Turgenev's life he had done everything possible to erase the memory of the dark shadow that had at one time fallen between them.

Chapter 4

Sergey Ivanovitch Taneyev

I DO not know for certain when and how our family's acquaintance with Sergey Ivanovich Taneyev originated. It was probably through my sister Tatiana who knew some friends of his that we met Taneyev.

Taneyev kept a diary from December 1894 until 1909. This diary can be used as a source of good factual material for his biography and the history of musical life in Moscow during these years, but only as factual material. In the foreward to his new diary which he began in 1911 and later continued, Taneyev wrote: ' Thus, in my diaries, I have restricted myself to facts . . . I avoided mentioning my feelings because each time earlier letters of mine fell into my hands, letters containing lyrical passages, I began to feel embarrassed . . . I found it unpleasant to imagine myself being stirred by feelings I did not experience any longer.' Taneyev did not enter only important events in his diary, but minor details as well; when he got up in the morning, what he wrote or played, who had visited him, where he had been, what he had bought, who was his doctor and what treatment he had ordered, etc. Unfortunately, part of his diary for 1895 was written in Esperanto which is incomprehensible to many. A truthful and tidy person, he wrote precisely and in detail. His entries during his visits at Jassnaia Poliana are more interesting as material for a biography of Tolstoy than as a picture of himself. He wrote down conscientiously and fairly accurately what Tolstoy said, but made few entries concerning his attitude to Tolstoy's opinions and his own replies and objections to what Tolstoy said.

During the first half of the nineties, Taneyev began to visit us in our Moscow house on *Khamovnicheskiy pereulok* (now Lev Tolstoy Street) and in the spring of 1895 my mother invited him to spend the summer in Jassnaia Poliana. He would not agree to live there as a visitor without paying and insisted that she fix a charge for his rooms and food. She mentioned a nominal sum; he, however, as a conscientious person, considered that it was too low. They bargained and in the end still settled on the small sum of 125 roubles for the whole summer.

Taneyev spent the following periods at Jassnaia Poliana: in 1895 from June 3rd to August 29th; in 1896 from May 19th to August 1st and a few days in September. After that he came only for short visits—in June 1897 for two days and in July of the same year (from 5th–13th), in August 1898, in June 1899 and, after a long interval, in February 1906 and in February 1908.

When my parents lived in Moscow (until 1902) he often came there; he also visited my mother when she used to come to Moscow after 1902.

In 1895 and 1896 he settled with his old nurse Pelageya in the annexe at Jassnaia Poliana and brought his upright piano. Sergey Ivanovich would get up at seven or eight, Pelageya would prepare his tea and breakfast, after which he would sit down to work. He either wrote his *Invertible Counterpoint and Canon* and his compositions or practised on his piano and worked with his pupil Yusha Pomerantsev, who lived with him for a time. At about noon he would go out for a walk and a bathe in the river, a mile away from the house. He then went to dinner. At that time dinner in Jassnaia Poliana was at two, we drank tea at five and had our supper at nine. He would spend the time between dinner and supper in various ways: at his piano, going for walks, playing tennis, or studying Italian with my sisters. He readily took part in the young people's amusements: tennis, cycling, playing games, bathing; but he was heavy and clumsy and would soon get exhausted. It took him a long time to learn how to ride a bicycle; this explains why later on, in 1899, he fell off his bicycle and seriously injured his leg.

In the evenings he came to supper and tea with the rest of us in the drawing-room or on the terrace. My father liked him, they talked and played chess and my father listened to him playing the piano. During these games of chess somebody would read aloud from different books, mostly those recommended by Lev Nikolayevich. Most frequently their conversations touched upon the meaning of art, which occupied my father at that time.

Taneyev's entry in his diary about a conversation which took place on August 9th, 1895, between him, Tolstoy and Strakhov, then on a visit to Jassnaia Poliana, is illuminating. Here are extracts from this entry:

' Lev Nikolayevich said that " he still could not decide what art really was, and what place it should have in a man's life." Strakhov gave the following definition of art: " Art is a means for the expression of a person's feelings and moods, not in an abstract but in a concrete and graphic manner . . . " Tolstoy said that he would like to see a definition of art which would draw a border-line between artistic and inartistic works. I said that it was hardly possible to expect a definition of such a border-line in the same way as it was impossible to draw a border-line between animals and plants, though no one would hesitate to differentiate between a plant and an animal. Tolstoy said that there was a feature distinguishing an animal from a plant, for instance, the ability to move. I replied to this that there were animals deprived of this ability and that there were plants which could move. Tolstoy said that questions concerning the development and history of art did not interest him as much as the question of art from the moral point of view. He said: " I would like to know whether art is necessary in a man's life. If this is so, then why do the majority of people live apart from art? Is art worth the sacrifices spent on it? Is it necessary to go on torturing tens of thousands of people in factories, take away the last mite from people tilling the soil, so as to make it possible for girl-students at a conservatoire to play the piano for eight hours a day, to build theatres for the performance of Wagner's operas, compel hair-dressers who consider themselves artists also to work for singers, etc.? Can it be considered as normal that works of art should be only accessible to a small number of rich people and that a special training is required to understand them?".'

Taneyev did not write down what his own reaction was to these words of Tolstoy's; apparently he did not agree with him but probably kept silent.

During a conversation with Stassov some of Taneyev's views on musical form are brought to light.

' I went to the Tolstoy's. My conversation with Stassov was very entertaining. He said that the eyes of Madonnas should be pierced, that Raphael was gifted but wasted his talent on trifles, that he placed Beethoven higher than any other composer but that, unfortunately, he wrote compositions that had a shape and obeyed stupid laws, as, for instance, when he ended his composition in the same key in which he had started it, wrote symphonies in four parts, etc. I replied that the form of a symphony was the same as that of a sonata or a quartet, that there were sonatas consisting of two parts (the E minor) and quartets consisting of five or more, that a form for fantasias had existed long ago and that Beethoven deviated from established forms when he considered it necessary to do so. It was very difficult to put a word in whilst Stassov was speaking. I said to him: " Let us elect Lev Nikolayevich chairman ". He agreed. Tolstoy tapped his glass and said that it was my turn to speak. Stassov immediately began to speak very loudly. I began to laugh and so did Tolstoy and Sofia Andreyevna. Tolstoy said that he agreed with most of what Stassov had said, that one should not conform to established forms, that form like clothing must sometimes burst at the seams. To justify existing forms I explained the working out of a form for the allegro of a sonata and said that this was not done arbitrarily. Some artists create by obeying their inner feelings, but it turns out in the end that willy-nilly they have to join the existing trend and participate in the working out of musical language.

' On March 29th . . . at the end of breakfast we continued our conversation of the previous day. Tolstoy expounded a thought with which both I and Sergey Lvovich disagreed; he said that if a work of art is liked by some and disliked by others it means that it is worthless, because a real work of art must be appreciated by everybody, just as all people agree that fresh air is better than a poisonous one, that man needs food and that good deeds are praiseworthy.'

In Jassnaia Poliana Sergey Ivanovich played the piano nearly every evening. I remember him playing Mozart's rondo in A flat, Beethoven's sonatas, in A flat major with the funeral march, A flat major Op. 110, and in E minor: the *quasi fantasia and appassionata*, small pieces by Schubert, Schumann, Chopin and Mendelssohn, the overture from *Der Freischütz* in Liszt's arrangement, the duet from *Romeo and Juliet* by Tchaikovsky, Arensky's *Basso Ostinato* and *Romance,* parts from his opera *Orestea*, and others. Naturally he mostly played what Tolstoy liked, or the pieces that he wanted him to hear, including his own compositions or those by Wagner or Tchaikovsky. However, my father did not very much like Tchaikovsky. Sometimes Sergey Ivanovich even practised specially the pieces my father praised. Thus, for instance, my father once praised Schumann's nocturne No. 4 which he had heard me play. Taneyev, who had not played this piece before, practised and played not only this one but all four nocturnes. He played, of course, always from memory, played simply and without affectation; his phrasing was clear and impressive; he played at the right tempo, not carried away by speed as many pianists are and showed strength where it was needed.

His aim was to convey correctly the intentions of the composer. His performance of Beethoven and Bach, never dry or pedantic, was particularly fine and accurate. I remember his magnificent and energetic interpretation of the overture to *Der Freischütz* in Liszt's arrangement. However, he was not always so successful: Chopin, with the exception of the polonaises (A flat major and F sharp minor) lacked colour in his execution.

On the whole his touch was rather heavy; he liked to bring out the lower and middle notes and it sometimes seemed to me that his left hand struck the keys more strongly than the right one. He was always serious about his playing and never performed negligently: he was entirely submerged in the music. I remember his eyes during his playing, thoughtful, concentrated and with an inward look. When he was asked to execute a piece he had not played for a long time he would say: 'I shall play this for you tomorrow,' and the next day in the afternoon he would practice the piece in his annexe so as to play it properly at night to his audience.

One afternoon I looked in on him and found him playing Schubert's *Moment Musical* in A flat major in preparation for the evening. He said: 'I am just wondering whether to stress the third beat of a bar, rather than the first one?' so punctiliously did he consider his phrasing.

My father enjoyed listening to Sergey Ivanovich's music, thanked him for playing and expressed his opinion on the pieces performed; he praised Mozart, Schubert and Chopin, abused Wagner, criticised Beethoven but enjoyed him at the same time. He did not like Taneyev's compositions but did not tell him this.

Sergey Ivanovich enjoyed playing chess but he was not a good player. At Jassnaia Poliana he played nearly every day with

Tolstoy. My father was somewhat better than he, but played carelessly and took risks, thereby frequently losing the game. On June 6th, 1896, Taneyev noted that he had lost five games at a stretch after which Tolstoy gave him a knight. Without the knight, however, Tolstoy began to lose and soon the handicap was removed and the knight back in his position. They had agreed to play matches; the winner of the first five games was regarded as having won the match. They arranged that if Sergey Ivanovich lost the match he was to play pieces chosen by Tolstoy and if Tolstoy lost, he was to read aloud something from his own works.

During his stay with us Taneyev wrote three pieces specially for Jassnaia Poliana, namely a serenade, a barcarolle (*Venice at Night*) and variations on Triquet's song in *Eugene Onegin*, apart from his serious compositions—a quartet, a symphony—and his scoring of Tchaikovsky's quartet, etc.

The three pieces had a part for a mandoline played at that time by my sister Tatiana.

In my reminiscences of Taneyev I cannot but mention his relationship to my mother. On February 23rd, 1895, her youngest and most beloved son, seven-year-old Vanechka, died, and the hysteria to which she had been prone earlier became more acute. Music had a soothing effect on her nerves and distracted her from her grief, and she tranferred to Taneyev the effect of the music he played to her. This explains her unhealthy infatuation with his person and his music. She used every available opportunity to see him and listen to his music. Such an extreme infatuation in a woman between fifty and sixty years of age for a man who had no particular feelings for her cannot be described as normal. She herself was conscious of this. I can speak of this passion of my mother's without concealing anything, as there is nothing to conceal. She herself spoke of it to her daughter Tatiana several days before her death. Neither I nor my sisters and brothers ever doubted that my mother spoke the truth and that in the relationship between her and Taneyev there had never been a ' handshake which could not have taken place openly '; but this infatuation of hers pained us, particularly, because it upset my father.

For a long time Taneyev was not aware of Sofia Andreyevna's abnormal partiality for him and, probably, assumed that she was attracted only by the pianist and the composer. I do not know when he realised the truth but he could no longer remain in doubt about it when in 1904 he received from her an ' absurd letter ' as he called it in his diary; this letter has not been found, for he probably destroyed it. A certain idea of it can be gained from the following letters which demonstrate his good manners, restraint and reserve. He wrote:

' Esteemed Sofia Andreyevna,
   Kindly excuse me for failing to call on you today. The reason for this is that I have not yet replied to your letter sent to me after Nikish's concert and have not given you the explanations which you so insistently demanded. As I have not yet expressed my opinion on the questions raised by you, I do not consider it proper or right to be your guest. This had not occurred to me at the concert last night, but on my return home it became quite clear to me. To justify my delay I can say that as soon as I received your letter I began to put down my explanations in writing, but, having heard from you that you do not wish the letter to be addressed either to your address in Moscow or to Jassnaia Poliana I then refrained from continuing. At present I definitely cannot resume my letter for lack of time. I beg you once more to accept my apologies and my assurances of profound respect, and my readiness to be of service to you.

S. TANEYEV.'

Two days later, on November 17th, 1904, Taneyev wrote:

' Esteemed Sofia Andreyevna,
   If it had been only a matter of explaining why I left the hall during the interval and why, during the next part, I gave up my seat to somebody else, it would be easy for me to reply by, say, pointing out that everybody present at a concert can enjoy the unrestricted right of giving up his seat as well as leaving the hall in the interval. However, the questions raised by you in your letter involve such a number of facts, relationships and misunderstandings as to make me incompetent to act as you wish and give you simple explanations, verbal or in writing. I feel it would be a real task which

183

would require time to weigh and to think over every expression and every word. At present, however, for various reasons—including material ones—I cannot interrupt the work I am engaged upon for several days. Therefore I again beg you to excuse me and to accept the assurance of profound respect from your sincerely devoted,

S. TANEYEV.'

Apparently Sergey Ivanovich never wrote the letter which required time, but after this episode he began to see less of Sofia Andreyevna. However, he paid two more visits to Jassnaia Poliana; I think that he was urged to do so by his desire to see Tolstoy.

Taneyev's attitude to Tolstoy had always been one of profound respect and great liking.

This was noticeable in spite of his reserve. Tolstoy's influence on him was expressed among other things by his drawing up of a synopsis of an article on art and his taking part in producing a vegetarian calendar.

In August 1898 he wrote to Sofia Andreyevna on the occasion of Tolstoy's seventieth birthday:

' I beg you to convey to Lev Nikolayevich my warmest greetings. I am grateful to him for much that I have acquired from his works and from my personal contacts with him. There is no need to be a follower of Lev Nikolayevich to experience the influence of his lucid, simple and vital ideas which, once they have penetrated your soul, remain there most persistently and sometimes cause no little disquiet to a man, by making demands on him which exceed his powers.'

What was Tolstoy's attitude to him? Tolstoy was always very polite to him, only sometimes it seemed to me that this politeness was forced; as we have seen he played chess with him, listened to his music and talked with him a great deal. He never blamed Taneyev for Sofia Andreyevna's infatuation and understood the abnormality of the situation. However, it upset him very much and it was only with the passage of time that he could treat

Sergey Ivanovich with equanimity.* Here are two of his remarks about Taneyev; the first is unjust in my view—it is an entry in his diary of May 28th, 1896, when Tolstoy suffered acutely from this unfortunate infatuation of Sofia Andreyevna: 'At home . . . Taneyev . . . annoys me by his moral complacency and—it seems funny to say it—aesthetic (genuine, not superficial) stupidity, as well as his *coq du village*† position in our house. It is a test for me: I am trying not to fail.' His second remark was made by him in June, 1904: 'I know two musicians who have had no schooling but who are nevertheless well educated people, with whom you can talk on any subject as they know everything—they are G. (Goldenveiser) and Sergey Ivanovich Taneyev.'

I now turn to what I remember of my own encounters and conversations with Taneyev. In 1895–96, when he lived in Jassnaia Poliana, I was there several times, talked to him, walked and bathed with him, played tennis and chess and listened to him at the piano. In Moscow I met him in our house, at concerts and at the Library for the Theory of Music, and several times visited him at his various homes.

During the second half of the nineties, I started studying composition and looked to Taneyev for advice, showing him my immature attempts. On March 3rd, 1895, he entered in his diary: ' Sergey Lvovich was here, brought me three songs which are not badly written.' I remember that he passed strict judgment on my

*In the *Izvestiya* of July 12th, 1939, a feuilleton by N. Rostov appeared, called ' New Texts on L. N. Tolstoy,' in which the author ' discovered' that the reason for Tolstoy leaving Jassnaia Poliana in 1910 was Sofia Andreyevna's infatuation for Taneyev. This is incorrect. True, in 1897, Lev Nikolayevich was tormented by this infatuation and wrote to Sofia Andreyevna that he intended to leave her. But at that time he did not carry out his intention. Later, from 1901 on, when his family no longer spent the winters in Moscow and finally settled in Jassnaia Poliana, Sofia Andreyevna saw Taneyev only during her infrequent trips to Moscow and Taneyev visited Jassnaia Poliana for a short time in February 1906 and February 1908. Sofia Andreyevna's infatuation cooled off. The complicated circumstances which moved Leo Nikolayevich in 1910 to leave Jassnaia have now been sufficiently clarified. Nothing has remained unsaid in all the literature on Tolstoy and there is no support in them for N. Rostov's ' discovery '.

†General favourite.

attempts but asked me about an unusual harmonic progression: 'Did you write this yourself? Did anybody show you this succession?'

I said that nobody had shown me anything; he was surprised that I had thought of it myself.

On March 12th, 1896, he made the following entry in his diary: 'Examined Sergey Lvovich on harmony.' I remember that he then said to me: 'Harmonise a chromatic scale.' It is well-known that a chromatic scale can be harmonised in different ways. I do not remember which harmonic series I played to him, but I remember that he did not approve of it.

Taneyev admitted that I had a certain gift for music and told my mother this, but he warned me: 'You want to compose right away. No, you must attend a course, study counterpoint and canon, master the C clef and write without playing.' He advised me to study musical dictation with Professor Morozov of the Conservatoire.

In 1899 Taneyev, knowing that I spoke English and that I was acquainted with the theory of music, suggested that I should translate from the English E. Prout's *Musical Form*, which I did. In the nineties I once showed Taneyev two pieces for the piano by Caesar Franck which had been sent to me from France: *Prelude, Choral and Fugue,* and *Prelude, Aria and Finale*. I was surprised that Taneyev did not know them. He glanced at the fugue and said, 'This man could truly write music.' Later he got to know the compositions of Caesar Franck whose style was close to his own, but I do not think that Franck had any influence on him.

Once I told Taneyev the following story. On one occasion Anton Rubinstein was invited to a musical evening. Taking off his coat in the hall he saw a score sticking out of the pocket of another overcoat. He took it out, glanced at it and put it back. During the evening the host asked Rubinstein to play. Rubinstein sat down at the piano and played the score he had just glanced at in the hall and had already memorised. This was a new piece which the well-known musician Kontskiy had brought with him with the intention of playing it at the party. Rubinstein's trick offended him deeply.

In reply to my story Taneyev said: 'This is not so difficult. I believe that I, too, could play a short piece, having merely looked at it. Give me a piece which I do not know.' I brought him a piece unknown to him—*Valse Caprice* by Chaminade. He glanced through the first page and in a few minutes played it without looking at the score and with only one insignificant inaccuracy.

Taneyev did not like Scriabin's music though the latter was his pupil. It was said that, having listened to *Prometheus* he said about the last chord of this piece: 'Now the music will begin'. It is well-known that *Prometheus* consists of discords except for the last chord which is a triad.

Once at a concert of Scriabin's music played by the composer I sat next to Taneyev. When Scriabin had finished playing his prelude in D major (from 24 Op. 11) Taneyev turned to me and said, 'How well he plays!' He was impartial and praised whatever in his opinion deserved praise.

In 1909 I was awarded the prize of the 'House of Song' for harmonising ten Scottish songs. These ten songs and another seven were published by the Russian Publishing House of Music. Taneyev was interested in my adaptation, came to see me in Moscow and he and I played these songs, I, the piano part and he, the voice part on a small harmonium. On the whole he approved of my work.

I do not remember when and how the famous singer M. N. Muromtseva produced the one-act play *The Little Haydn*. In this play the music theorist Porpora, with whom little Haydn lived as a servant, returned home one day to hear Haydn taking advantage of his absence to improvise on the harpsichord. Amazed by the boy's talent he began to teach him music from then on.

At this time Taneyev had taken in as a boarder his very gifted pupil Kolya Zhilaev. I said to him then:

'I hear, Sergey Ivanovich, that you have taken a little Haydn into your house.'

He replied: 'You wanted to hurt me by insinuating that I am not Haydn but Porpora. But you have not succeeded. I don't dream of being a Haydn, I dream of being precisely a Porpora.' He apparently valued his theoretical and pedagogical work higher than his compositions.

I was a member of the Society of the Theory of Music. During the first decade of the twentieth century the members of the society used to meet in the Conservatoire in a large sound-proofed room with book-cases round the walls and two grand pianos. In this room papers were read and musical works, particularly old ones, performed and rehearsed. Various musical problems were also discussed and conversations took place. One of the days of the week, I think it was Friday, was devoted to a social gathering of the members accompanied by tea-drinking; it had been decided not to play the piano after nine o'clock on those days. On one such day I came to the library and found Taneyev playing Bach's fugues for organ on the piano while the organ point was played on the other piano by the pianist Bogoslovski. Nine o'clock had struck long ago but Taneyev and Bogoslovski continued playing. Taneyev had, probably, forgotten the rule not to play after nine. The members present were very happy about this: the opportunity seldom arose of listening to the organ fugues by Bach, particularly so well executed. However, Taneyev's friend, V. Bulychev, thought otherwise. He was drinking tea and began deliberately to tap his glass with his spoon during the performance. Taneyev, having finished the fugue, asked him: 'Why, Vyacheslav Aleksandrovich, are you interfering with our playing?' Bulychev replied: 'Because it is past nine o'clock and we had all decided to have no music after nine.'

Taneyev did not reply but notwithstanding all the requests to continue firmly refused to do so. He was not hurt himself but many members of the society were offended on his behalf. An extraordinary meeting of the society was called at which a motion was tabled to reprimand Bulychev publicly for his action; Taneyev, however, insisted that the matter be closed.

In the winter of 1913–14 an interesting and gifted Indian musician—Inayat Khan—made his appearance in Moscow. He and three of his friends—also Indians—played and sang, first at the café-chantant Maxim and later at two or three concerts in the Polytechnic Museum.

The singing of the three Indians was accompanied on a *Vina* (a plucked instrument something between a guitar and a small harp) a stringed instrument something like a viola, and a small drum. These instruments sounded thin: they only doubled the tune on a monotonous organ point. Inayat Khan, therefore, decided to accompany his melodies with European harmony on the theme of the well-known ancient Indian poem *Sakuntala* by Kalidas. He composed a 'sketch' where the heroine was to be a dancer and the music was to consist of Indian melodies accompanied by an orchestra. He asked Taneyev to harmonise and orchestrate the tunes. Taneyev refused and suggested that Grechaninov do it. Grechaninov also refused; then Taneyev offered me the work. I tackled it gladly, but, not being sure of myself, particularly as regards orchestration, I asked V. I. Pol to co-operate with me. In the end seventeen of Inayat Khan's melodies were harmonised by the two of us. Pol also scored them for a small orchestra. Unfortunately Inayat Khan was unable to produce his ' sketch '. The piano version of his melodies in our adaptation was published and they were twice performed by an orchestra at the Sokolniki Circle.

I was in Jassnaia Poliana in February 1906 when Taneyev spent two days there. He played a great deal. A. B. Goldenveiser was also there; on two pianos they played Beethoven's concerto No. 4, Schumann's concerto and a suite by Arensky. They talked with Tolstoy mostly about the texts printed by him in the Reading Circle. It was then that Taneyev persuaded Tolstoy to play a waltz he was supposed to have composed. My father played it twice and Taneyev very quickly wrote it down; it was published in 1912 in the *Tolstoyan Yearly Review*.

In conclusion I would like to say a few words on my own impression of Taneyev. Sergey Ivanovich was a kind, intelligent, witty, modest, extremely conscientious—even pedantically truthful man, naïve in matters of everyday life. His kindness and selflessness were well-known to his pupils, whom he helped not only by his knowledge but also materially, though not a rich man himself. In his youth he had not received much general education of the kind acquired at school, as, at an early age, he had dedicated himself to music; he had always tried to improve his education: he read a great deal, was interested in philosophy, knew German and French, had learned Italian and at one time took up an international language, Esperanto, which he could not only read and write but even speak. His way of life was modest. He did not drink and neither played cards nor smoked. He did not like people to smoke in his presence. At his apartment he would send the smokers off to the kitchen and tell them to exhale their smoke into the ventilator. He was of a cheerful disposition—his laughter was infectious—and he enjoyed wit. Here is an example of his jokes. One day when he was busy with an urgent bit of work and did not wish to be disturbed he hung on his door the notice ' No entry '; the would-be caller, presuming that the door was closed for some particular reason, possibly repairs, went to the back door only to find another notice proclaiming that here, too, there was no entry.

Once Taneyev left the Conservatoire with the singer Litvin with whom he was going further; they called a sleigh and Litvin got in. As she was very stout she occupied the entire seat. Taneyev, himself a stoutish man, walked twice round the sleigh and, finding no room to sit, asked her: ' On which side are you sitting —the right or the left? '

I remember, too, some of his funny aphorisms, like: ' No good action goes unpunished ', ' Never do that which can be done for you by somebody else '.

Sergey Ivanovich's exceptional gift for music is well-known. He possessed perfect pitch. Once, at Jassnaia Poliana, we made the following experiment: six or seven notes were struck simultaneously on the piano, not in a certain order but quite haphazardly, and he was asked to name them. He did so without looking and made no mistake. It is known that he sometimes went to compose at monasteries where there were no musical instruments. He possessed a phenomenal memory, learned pieces easily by heart and remembered them for a long time. At one time he dreamed of learning by heart everything that existed in the way of outstanding piano music. He read scores with amazing speed, ease and precision.

He felt no embarrassment in expressing his sometimes very harsh views of contemporary composers and performers. In this respect he was justly called ' the Musical conscience of Moscow '. As regards different composers he had definite likes and dislikes. He liked the old ' polyphonists ', the classics, particularly Mozart and the Romantics; he appreciated Wagner and cherished with special piety the music of his master, Tchaikovsky, whom he never called otherwise than Petr Ilyich. He praised Arensky and Rachmaninov but he disapproved of the ' innovators ' because they disregarded the rules of harmony. He said that in the world of sound there exist immutable, eternal laws which cannot be broken with impunity. Some of these laws he expounded in his treatise *Invertible Counterpoint and Canon* in which he explains this rather specialised province of music.

Taneyev's compositions are not likely to appeal to the general public, though in some of his works he has reached considerable heights.

Chapter 5

Vladimir Grigoryevich Chertkov

VLADIMIR CHERTKOV, like Alcibiades, was rich and aristocratic. Tall, slim and handsome, with an aquiline nose, he looked, in youth, most effective in the uniform of the Horse Guards. The Chertkovs belonged to the highest Petersburg society, which provided aide-de-camps to the Tsar, adjutant-generals, governor-generals, and such like. The father of Vladimir Chertkov had been adjutant-general to Alexander II and Alexander III. His mother also belonged to an aristocratic family and was on close terms with the Empress Maria Fedorovna.

During his service in the Horse Guards, Vladimir, by his own admission, led a dissolute life, indulging in drink, gambling and dissipation. However, in time this life became repugnant to him and he and a few of his friends decided to turn to more un-selfish and more useful activities. He resigned from his regiment, and on the advice of his friend Pisarev, occupied himself with local government activities and charitable works. He founded a trade school, a surgery, a credit-and-savings company and other organisations on the Chertkov estate. This, however, gave him little satisfaction. At that time he was ardently and sincerely seeking some faith and activity to which he could surrender him-self entirely. A man with a strong will and very ambitious, he needed the kind of activity that would accord with his convictions and, at the same time, allow him to play an outstanding part. He had, however, not yet clarified his convictions.

Chertkov's mother was a follower of the evangelist teachings of Radstock. Vladimir considered himself to be a Christian but he was not entirely convinced in the orthodox faith. Radstockism, too, did not satisfy him. A disappointed man, at the cross-roads, still seeking a purpose for which to live and work, he met and made friends with my father who had earlier on also stood at the cross-roads, had also been tormented by doubts and had at last worked out a faith which he was trying to apply to life.

My father welcomed Vladimir with great warmth and soon a close friendship sprang up between them. My father treated him with touching tenderness. Many times he wrote about his affection for him; on April 6th 1884, after Chertkov had visited him, he wrote in his diary: ' He and I are amazingly as one.'

In the following lines I shall attempt to elucidate the reason for this exceptional feeling of my father's for Chertkov.

In the first place my father had been very lonely throughout his life. He had lost his parents at an early age. Consciously as well as unconsciously he was on the look-out for someone with whom he could be quite frank, of whom he could be fond and who would reciprocate the feeling. His elder brother, Nikolai responded in part to this need, but he was a brother, not the friend of whom he had dreamed, and when Nikolai died in 1860 my father felt his loneliness more acutely. He married in 1862. His wife, family and children smothered his longing for a time, but towards the end of the eighties family life no longer satisfied him; and it was at that time that his discord with his wife set in. The need for friendship arose more strongly than ever. It was at this moment that he and Chertkov came closer together. Their first meeting took place in October 1883.

The second reason for my father's and Chertkov's drawing close together was some traits in Chertkov's nature: his contempt of public opinion, his daring independence towards those in authority, his readiness to suffer for his convictions and, particularly, his perseverance in achieving his plans. My father paid no attention to the defects in his character.

Two sharply contrasting moods would alternate in Chertkov: the one—gloomy and irritable, the other—animated and restless. When influenced by the first he would be unpleasant, unkind, even rude; but when the second mood came over him, he was good-natured and would beg people to forget the harsh things he said to them in his black days.

The third reason for my father's friendship with Chertkov was the latter's break with high society in Petersburg. My father had mingled in it in the fifties. As a man who always expressed his thoughts freely and who favoured independence, he could not come to terms with a society which constantly kept an eye on the conductor's baton from the Tsar's palace. Chertkov, a notable representative of this society, had renounced it, thus sacrificing to his convictions all the privileges he might have enjoyed there. My father valued this sacrifice very highly.

In the eighties Chertkov was still on friendly terms with our family, including my mother, and we all, especially my sisters returned his feelings.

In 1884 my father planned to provide the working people with a serious range of popular literature and to replace inferior publications by good books, pamphlets and pictures at a low price. Until then ignorant publishers had issued hundreds of thousands of cheap books and pictures written by authors for a song and painted by artists of no education whatsoever; these publications were spread throughout Russia by hawkers. I remember my father asking us one day: 'Who is the most widely read author in Russia?' and he replied to the question himself: 'Kassirov'. None of those present had ever heard the name. Kassirov (the pen-name of Ivin) was the author of many popular stories of inferior quality like *The English Lord George, The Battle of the Russians against the Cabardinians, Yeruslan Lazarevich,* and others.

My father suggested that Chertkov should take over the management of this new publishing house. Chertkov undertook the task enthusiastically. My father was encouraged to write popular stories for the new undertaking. Chertkov was chief editor until 1893. From then on his activities acquired a different character. Under Tolstoy's influence be began to collect data on sectarians, plead for them and help them. In this sphere of activity one cannot but admire his boldness and his readiness to suffer for his convictions. The appeal for help for the Dukhobors entitled 'S.O.S.' was signed by Chertkov, Biryukov and Tregubov. Chertkov spread it with great courage and daring. It is common knowledge that all three of them were banished—Chertkov abroad and Biryukov and Tregubov to the Baltic provinces. Biryukov also went abroad later on. In Britain Chertkov began to publish Tolstoy's prohibited works and the periodical *Svobodnoye Slovo*.

It cannot be said that Chertkov and Tolstoy saw much of each other. Chertkov lived either in Petersburg, on his parents' estate, Lisinovka, or at his own farmstead, Rzhevsk. His visits to Moscow were only temporary ones, or he would stop there on his way to some other place. Only during the summers of 1894, 1895 and

1896 did he visit Jassnaia Poliana frequently, spending the summer months some five miles away from us in a village. From 1897 to 1907 he lived in Britain. However, they exchanged a vast number of letters. My father told Chertkov frankly about his work and his family affairs; and Chertkov wrote to Father as frankly about his own life, gave his opinion on Father's writings, proffered advice and even made ' suggested corrections '.

V. G. Chertkov, his relations with our family during the first ten years of the twentieth century, and the part he played in drawing up and executing my father's will, is dealt with in my section ' The Last Days '.

Chapter 6

Prince Sergey Semenovich Urussov

My father wrote to a friend on February 6th, 1906, ' There have been two people (besides Alexandra Tolstoy—she is the third) to whom I have written many letters which, as far as I can remember, might interest those who are interested in my personality. They are Strakhov and Prince S. S. Urussov.'

In one of his letters to Alexandra Tolstoy in March 1876, he says about Urussov: ' He is one of my Sebastopol friends and we are very fond of each other.'

Prince Sergey Urussov, son of the Senator, Prince Urussov (who died in 1857) and of a Danish beauty, daughter of the architect von Markschitz, was born on August 3rd 1827, and was, thus, a year older than my father.

He completed his education brilliantly at the First Petersburg Cadet Corps and served in the Horse Guards until 1852, when he retired with the rank of major, but just before the Crimean war he rejoined the service. He and my father became friends in the Crimea. In a letter to a friend of his, with whom he shared an interest in chess, he wrote from the village Kurtyer-fotz-Selo in the Crimea: ' I recommend to you an excellent writer and chess player, my pupil, Count Leo Nikolayevich Tolstoy.'

According to all eye-witness accounts and my father's own recollections, Urussov performed miracles of bravery during the war. He would come out of the trench in his uniform white jacket amidst a hail of shells and, because of his great height, he was a splendid target for enemy rifles. He was wounded in the chest by a bullet which was not extracted. The Poltava regiment in which he served lost its commander and all its senior officers and he, being a lieutenant colonel, found himself the senior in rank, and took over the regiment. My father always said that Urussov had remained alive only thanks to extraordinary good luck. He was awarded the Officers' Cross of St. George for valour and always wore it in the lapel of his frock-coat.

Urussov was an extraordinary character. He was over six feet tall, almost a giant. Notwithstanding his height he wore high-heeled boots. He was handsome and well-built. He was straight-forward by nature; resolute, impulsive, fearless, hot-tempered, proud, eccentric and extremely ambitious. My father particularly appreciated his sincerity and his independent mind: he called him ' *Selbstdenker* '—a man who could think for himself.

He was a mathematician and a first-class chess player. He had written and published at his own expense several volumes on higher mathematics, but they had no success. Mathematicians said that all the discoveries he believed to be his own, had already been known long ago and that the new theories he expounded were incorrect.

Urussov's name as a chess player was famous not only in Russia but also abroad; his matches were even published as guides to chess playing. He used to say that he had never met a better chess player than himself and if he did sometimes lose a game to the famous player Petrov, it was only because Petrov irritated him during the game: he would make a move and then begin to moan that it was the wrong one.

In society Urussov was always well behaved and courteous, particularly to ladies, and his unexpected judgments attracted attention. He had a fine voice, was very musical and used to sing—sometimes even his own compositions. In everyday life he was good-tempered and equable. He loved children and animals: he used to talk to dogs and maintain that they understood him. Only sometimes did he break out into fits of uncontrolled wrath. Ambition was an outstanding trait of his character. He could not forget, and was tormented by the fact, that his school-fellow Obruchev had graduated first from the Cadet Corps and he was only second, that Petrov still remained the best chess-player in Russia whilst he came only second, or that his works on mathematics were not appreciated. Urussov was so original in his speech and behaviour that he came to be regarded as a crank; some of his oddities sometimes made people wonder whether he was in his right mind. Thus, for instance, he used to say that he could calculate and predict the day certain people would die; that he had already calculated the day of Alexander

II's death and that he knew when my father would die but that he kept it secret. He wrote an article to prove that Paul I had not been assassinated but had died a natural death. He divided all people into those who were people in the strict sense of the word and those who were ' tailless apes '. Among women he made a distinction between ' the darling '—the loving woman, and the ' devil '—the seductress. He used to say that all great people were born in August, for instance, Napoleon, Goethe, Tolstoy and himself.

In his political opinions he was a monarchist but he despised the courtiers who debased themselves before the Tsar and the Imperial family. Having learnt that Alexander III, out driving somewhere, had put an officer on to the coachman's box, he was filled with indignation and said that in olden days such humiliation of an officer would have been unthinkable.

During the defence of Sebastopol one of the trenches changed hands several times, from the Russians to the Allies and back again. Urussov then went to the commander-in-chief and suggested that he should enter into negotiations with the enemy and propose that the trench be disposed of by a game of chess; he offered to play for the Russians. This suggestion was, of course, turned down.

After the end of the war something happened to Urussov which I would never have believed to be true, had I not heard about it from my father, Urussov's nephews, and himself. At the end of the Crimean campaign an inspector-general of German origin who had not taken part in the military operations, arrived to inspect the regiment commanded by Urussov. This general turned out to be an annoying prig and during the review he began to find fault with every small thing. Urussov was furious but kept his temper. When, however, the general struck one of the N.C.O.'s in the face for some trifling error—a man with whom Urussov had fought throughout the campaign and whom he particularly valued—he could not stand it any longer. He gave the unexpected command: ' Fix bayonets ', which means prepare for a bayonet attack. The front row of men immediately carried out the command and the general found himself faced with a line of bayonets pointed at him.

This command is usually immediately followed by the next one, ' charge! ' and the inspector-general was scared: what if that crazy Urussov gave the command and he were to be killed? He jumped back, got into his carriage and drove off. Later he lodged a complaint. But Urussov's action was so extraordinary that the complaint was shelved and the whole matter hushed up. According to military law Urussov ought to have been court martialled and, possibly, sentenced to death by the firing-squad. But who would execute a hero of Sebastopol? Soon after this Urussov was presented to Alexander II. He was received graciously but the Sovereign did not mention the incident though he knew of it. For some unknown reason Urussov took offence at this and resigned the service. On his retirement he was promoted a rank, as the custom was, and became a major-general. During the war of 1877 he applied for active service but was refused.

Urussov visited Jassnaia Poliana in the sixties and seventies. He was godfather to my brother Leo and my sister Masha and took his duties very seriously, calling his god-children ' my children '. From an early childhood I remember his majestic figure, his handsome face with the well-kept greying beard, his full voice and agitated speech and how, when excited, he would immediately start blinking with both eyes. Sometimes he played chess with my father, giving him a knight, or with me, giving me first the queen and then a rook; at that time I was still inexpert at the game. About 1878 he gave up playing chess entirely and presented me with all his books on the subject.

He was very susceptible to the weaker sex; in the summer of 1869, when he was staying in Jassnaia Poliana, this nearly led to a tragedy. My mother's sister, Aunt Tania Kusminski, had been very attractive in her youth and was a coquette. In 1869 she and father's sister, Aunt Masha Tolstoy, had the following conversation on the subject of Urussov:

' Though you are a well-known siren,' Aunt Masha said, ' you will never seduce this monk.'

' There is nothing easier,' aunt Tania said.

' I bet you won't get anywhere with him,' said Aunt Masha.

' We shall see,' said Aunt Tania.

Aunt Tania's vanity was pricked. She turned on all her feminine ruses and in three days Urussov was conquered. He followed her wherever she went. He left without declaring his love but a few days later his coachman arrived in Jassnaia Poliana with a handsome horse which, for no given reason, Urussov had sent as a gift to my father. Together with the horse the coachman brought a letter for Aunt Tania. In this letter Urussov suggested to her that she go abroad with him. The plan for the elopement was fantastic: she was to meet him aboard some steamer and they would go off together to an unknown destination. In his letter he contemptuously called the most respectable Alexander Kusminski, Aunt Tania's husband, ' that gentleman '.

The coachman tactlessly handed the letter to Aunt Tania in the presence of ' that gentleman '. A family scene ensued and my aunt had to explain her prank. To begin with Kusminski would not believe that it was only a prank and wanted to challenge Urussov to a duel, but later, being a man of some intelligence, he came to understand that it was not a serious matter and forgot about it.

Urussov's wife, Tatyana, was rather short and it was strange to see her beside her tall husband. For some unknown reason he used to call her ' Temir '. It was rumoured that their ways of life were completely different. He got up very early, at four or five in the morning, whilst she went to bed late, after midnight. They had a daughter, Lydia, a rather tall, narrow-chested girl, pale and delicate. Urussov was very fond of her. She was born in 1853 and died at the age of sixteen. Tatyana Afanasyevna died— still in the prime of life—in 1881.

The death of his daughter and of his wife affected Urussov very deeply: it was said that it even affected his mind. He spent the last years of his life in solitude on his estate, Spasskoye, refused to see anyone and whiled away the days in thought and silence.

During this period of his life he became very devout, spent much time in prayer and in reading the Psalms, knew to perfection all the church services and frequently took the place of the reader in the church or sang in the choir. He even intended to retire into a monastery, but the then well-known Archimandrite Tobias dissuaded him.

Having spent several years in this gloomy solitude he regained some of his liveliness only when he began to pay frequent visits to the numerous family of his brother, Prince Dmitri Urussov. There he discovered the family life which he himself had lacked.

My father corresponded frequently with Urussov in the sixties and seventies. He wrote more than seventy letters to him. He used to say that he could write frankly to him about matters he did not mention to anybody else. When my father turned away from the orthodox church, Urussov, in a temper, burnt these letters. By chance seventeen of them remained, but they are not the most interesting ones.

In 1870 my father wrote to Urussov about the introduction of conscription, which was being planned. From the military point of view he did not agree with this proposed reform; he believed that old soldiers who had served in the ranks for twenty-five years were better in combat than young ones on short term service. Urussov seems to have shared that opinion.

In 1876 my father wrote to Urussov ' On my arrival in Tula I found your letter and tore it up without reading it.' He did this at Urussov's own request. It appears that Urussov in a fit of temper had written an offensive letter, but had later come to his senses and had asked my father to tear up the letter without reading it.

In the eighties, in winter, when our family lived in Moscow, he became a constant visitor at our house. Our acquaintance and neighbour, V. Olsufiev, liked to play a card game called ' vint '. So did Urussov. But ' vint ' was not his only reason for visiting the Olsufievs: he was also interested in the daughters of the house. He even fell in love with one of them—I forget which one of the three—and suffered agonies of jealousy.

In 1889 my father went to stay for several days with Urussov at Spasskoye in order to rest from urban life. In his letters to my mother he described Urussov's life:

' Urussov is very charming at home with Gerasim, his servant, god-fearing, and lordly like himself, and Gerasim's sister. He gets up at four, has his tea, smokes and starts writing and working on mathematical problems which I do not understand. Yesterday I worked a little and then Urussov read me some of his work; as in everything he writes there are some new ideas but nothing is brought to a conclusion—that is so strange. But he is touching. He lives, without quarrelling with anyone around, helping many people and praying to God. For instance, before dinner he takes a walk up and down a path before the house. I went up to him the other day but saw that I was in his way and he admitted that on these walks he recites the " Hours " and the Psalms. In my opinion he has aged very much . . . I fear all his calculations are quite unnecessary. He has a lack of lucidity, a self-deception which leads him to think that he has found the solution he wished to find. Cigarettes and vodka now and then, in small quantities, and tea, serve, I fear, to dim his brain. But his simplicity and his aspirations to virtue are sincere and therefore it is satisfying to be with him. His roses are in bloom—there are many of them and he suggested I put some petals into my letter . . . '

The last years of his life Urussov spent almost uninterruptedly in Spasskoye. His financial circumstances had deteriorated. He moved from the big house into an annexe, the furnishings of which were not merely poor but almost beggarly. The furniture of the big house was sold and the trees in the park were felled. He had no manservant and had to do all the house chores himself. His faithful servant Gerasim was no longer alive.

In September 1897 he had a stroke and he died in November.

When creating his fictitious characters Tolstoy usually recalled the people he knew; and he imagined how they would act under certain circumstances. It is possible that when he wrote *Father Sergius and the Devil* he thought of Urussov.

Chapter 7

Afanasiy Afanasyevich Fet (Shenshin)

DURING our childhood we lived all the year round in Jassnaia and were usually very excited at the prospect of visitors. Visitors meant interesting conversations, indulgence over lessons, delicious hors d'oeuvres and a tasty pudding at dinner. We were even glad when the visitor was A. Fet. I say ' even ' because he was totally indifferent to us children and we felt it. Nevertheless, it was interesting to listen to the reading of his poems, to his harsh comments on other people, his frail witticisms, his complaints about public affairs and to his liberal statements. He would read his poems loudly and slowly in a deep bass voice, and would interrupt his reading by hums and haws and coughing.

Fet's appearance was very striking; a large bald head, a high forehead, black, almond-shaped eyes, red eyelids, an aquiline nose with small blue veins, a large and bushy beard, sensual lips, small feet and small, well-kept hands. His Jewish origin could be easily detected, but we children were naturally not aware of this.

There was no kind-heartedness and no immediate attractiveness in him, which, however, did not obviate the fact that he was a kind man. There was something hard in his nature and, strange to say, nothing poetical. His intelligence and commonsense, however, made themselves strongly felt.

I have always wondered: what was the basis of the friendship between Fet and my father? True, he was intelligent, well educated (mainly self-educated), his artistic taste was faultless and sensitive, and he was a sincere man with an original twist of mind. But he and my father had very different personalities. In contrast to my father Fet was calculating and irreligious—a sceptic and a heathen. He was not hostile to religion, it simply did not exist for him. Sometimes, however, he could not conceal his ironical view of church rites. I remember how Fet once spoke about the Resurrection of the Dead: ' I shall die, a burdock will grow on my grave and particles of my body will enter it; this burdock will be eaten by a cow and the flesh of the cow will be consumed by some other man; obviously the particles of my body will enter those of this man through the burdock and the cow, then this man will also die and we will both have to appear before the Supreme Judgment. Apparently either my body or that of the man who ate the meat of the cow will lack some essential particles. How, then, can we be resurrected in the flesh. ?'

At one time Fet was absorbed in Schopenhauer's philosophy and translated his *Die Welt als Wille und Vorstellung* (The World as Will and Idea). I think that this philosophy fitted in closely with his mind and character. He, like Schopenhauer, despised people and was well aware of their vices.

Notwithstanding his misanthropy Fet was vain. I even think that vanity played a certain part in his friendship with my father. However, this in no way hindered him from being sincerely fond of my father, not only as a writer but also as a man. Later, his efforts to acquire the surname Shenshin, his acquaintance with the Grand Duke Constantine and his pleasure at being made chamberlain (whereas Pushkin had only been a gentleman of the Emperor's bedchamber) revealed in him a most ordinary and naïve vanity. Fet never attempted to conceal it, either.

With other people he was always exquisitely courteous, particularly so with my mother. We even used to say jokingly that he had a weakness for her, especially after he dedicated two flattering poems to her.

In his younger days and to the end of the seventies my father shared a common interest with Fet—the farming of their estates. But their attitudes to agriculture differed. My father was carried away by what I would call the poetry of agriculture; he liked pedigree cattle, admired abundant crops, the forest and apple tree plantations, studied the life of bees, and took an interest in the life of the peasants and of the farm labourers; in general, he considered agriculture a creative task. Fet, however, as a practical man, regarded farming almost exclusively from the point of view of profit. He bought Stepanovka—a flat woodless pancake-like field in the centre of which stood the owner's house—only because it was advantageous. He did not run after picturesque views, parks, an attractive house, or anything like that. All he desired was something rewarding. Stepanovka was a profitable property and he bought it. True, later on he bought a rich and picturesque estate with an excellent park and fine house near Kursk, but then he was already so rich that he could afford this luxury; moreover, it was thrown in as a bargain with another profitable property.

In contrast to my father Fet was more or less indifferent to music. I have heard him say that music was an unpleasant noise; he only liked some Italian arias and Glinka's songs. True, in some of his poems he wrote otherwise. But it seems to me that it was not the music but the lure of a young woman's voice which inspired such poems.

In his youth Fet used to go out with Turgenev and a dog shooting snipe, blackcock and other birds; he did not, however, like hunting with borzois or hounds. I remember how he once said: 'I cannot understand what pleasure there is in listening to the baying of hounds.' I think that for him shooting was not primarily a means of communing with nature as it was for my father.

It is common knowledge that Tolstoy held a negative opinion of poets. Nevertheless, he did appreciate some of them. Fet belonged to these few.

About the well-known poem *Whisper*, father used to say: ' It's a masterly poem, there is not a single verb in it. But read it to a simple peasant, he will be bewildered and wonder why people find it beautiful and search for its meaning. It's a piece for the connoisseur in art.'

Fet's wife, Maria Petrovna, was a plain and uninteresting but very kind woman and an excellent housekeeper. It was difficult to imagine that Fet had ever been in love with her. I think that it must have been a *mariage de convenance*. They lived peacefully. Maria Petrovna looked after her husband with great solicitude and he was always very attentive to her, anyway in public.

Fet would sometimes flaunt views which showed him in an unfavourable light or were in direct opposition to commonly held opinions. I remember him saying once:

' I once loved a woman and she loved me. But I said to her: my dear, I have no money and neither have you. Only poets dream of paradise in a tent; that kind of paradise does not exist. Therefore, my love, it would be best for us to separate. And so we did.'

Fet's own marriage was a direct result of such reasoning. His wife was rich.

Fet knew the peasant well—the ordinary common peasant with all his qualities and shortcomings, and he never idealised him. He had been a justice of the peace for several years and, as far as I know, he exercised sound justice though he did not apply the law in his judgments so much as common sense. If he did not succeed in persuading the two parties to come to terms peacefully during a session, or when he lost his temper with them, he adjourned the session, took off his chain of office and called both parties to the back door; there he would reason with them and scold them and, as malicious tongues would have it, sometimes even hit them; but I do not believe this.

In general, he had the reputation of being in favour of serfdom, but I have never heard him defend it in conversation. He did, however, say that the peasant needed a strong hand to govern him and wrote articles about it in the reactionary press; the liberal papers criticised him sharply for this.

In his life, as well as in his work, poetry and prose were merged together. My father understood this. On April 6th, 1878, he wrote to Fet: ' Though I am fond of you as you are, I am always angry with you because, just as Martha was heedful about many things when only one was important, so in your case, too, this one thing is still all-important, but you, somehow, disdain it . . . You are so very attached to wordly values that, if they should fail you, you will be in a bad way . . . '

At one time Fet was on good terms with Turgenev; I do not think they were ever friends, because he criticised both Turgenev's works and Turgenev himself and took great pleasure in doing so.

I once heard him say about Turgenev's story *Asya*: ' When Asya calls out to the people moving away from the bank in a boat: " You have rowed into a pillar of moonlight,": Asya could not have seen this because if a boat enters a pillar of moonlight the pillar is broken by the ripple of water. Turgenev invented this.'

To begin with my father agreed with him, but some time later, watching from a river bank a boat entering a pillar of moonlight without dispersing it, he recalled Fet's words and admitted that it was Turgenev who had been right, not Fet.

As for Turgenev, he simply could not stand Fet's reactionary views.

When my father was trying to lead a simple life and spoke out against luxury, Fet said one day:

' I agree with you, I also do not require any luxuries. All I want is a room to myself where I can work, clean bedding, a soft mattress, plain but nourishing food like roast beef . . . ' He did not continue for at the words ' roast beef ' my father burst out laughing—roast beef is hardly compatible with the absence of luxury.

After the crisis in his philosophy my father moved further and further away from Fet. Fet regretted that they could no longer ' synchronise ', as they used to do before. He did not realise how deep was the abyss which had opened up between them. He spoke ironically of the attempt made by my father to replace popular literature and pictures of poor quality by something more edifying. Fet said to my uncle Sergei:

' Tolstoy and Chertkov want to draw pictures that would destroy the people's faith in miracles. Why should the people be deprived of their happy belief that in the guise of bread and wine they have eaten their God and been saved? It is as if a bare-footed peasant was entering a cave with the end of a tallow candle in his hand to help him find his way in the dark; and, his candle being blown out, he was told to spread the tallow on his boots . . . when he was barefoot! '

These words are very characteristic of Fet; they are witty but they express his scepticism and his contempt for the people. These were precisely the traits that my father disliked in him. Fet wrote some poems in his eightieth years in which he recalls all the women he was in love with in his youth. I heard one day what his friend, N. Strakhov, said on this subject: ' Fet is a real satyr Look at him, he even looks like one ' And there was some truth in this.

As a sceptic and heathen Fet looked courageously upon death. I believe that he was sincere in the poem addressed to death, inspired by Schopenhauer which expresses the idea that life is a mere figment of one's imagination.

Fet died in 1892. He was suffering from a disease of the respiratory organs—asthma and bronchitis—as a result of which he became very weak. On the day of his death he was still on his feet, but feeling the approach of the fatal moment he persuaded his wife to go shopping and died, sitting alone on a chair in his dining-room.

Chapter 8

Ilya Yefimovich Repin

THE first time I met Ilya Repin was in 1884 at our house in Moscow. He impressed one as being still a very young man, although he was already forty. His face was unwrinkled, he was lean and well built, with no sign of a middle-aged spread. He wore a small pointed beard and his thick hair was not as long as that of other painters in those days. He was neatly dressed without any affectation. There was a kindly, cunning smile on his face of the kind that one often sees on Ukrainian faces.

Repin came to an exhibition in Petersburg in 1884, at which his painting, *The Unexpected Guest*, was first on view. My father visited this exhibition, but the picture, which in my opinion, is one of Repin's best works, did not appeal to him at all. He even found some technical flaws in it and said that it seemed to him that the floor in the painting was sloping. Whether this is correct or not is not for me to judge. In the following year, 1885, Repin came to Moscow with the *Peredvizhniki* exhibition. His painting of Ivan the Terrible's murder of his son made a shattering impression upon the public at the time, including my father. It was much spoken of—both praised and criticised Under the immediate impact my father wrote to Repin (March 31st, 1885): ' You are a fine fellow, Repin, a fine fellow indeed! Here is something vigorous, strong and bold, something that has hit the bull's eye! . . . Good, very good. The artist wished to say something significant and said it fully and clearly and, moreover, with such skill that his mastery is not noticeable.' I also heard him say how daring it was of Repin to paint the red blood against the pink background of the son's clothing.

Later, in the nineties, when he visited the Tretyakov Gallery which had bought the painting, my father disapproved of it for some reason, probably, because it did not correspond to the views expressed by him in his article on art.

In the summer of 1887 Repin came to Jassnaia Poliana to paint a portrait of my father for the patron of the arts, Tretyakov. He painted two portraits—one of Tolstoy at his desk and another of him in an armchair. He himself was not satisfied with the first portrait. He said that there was ' no air ' in it and that the perspective was wrong. However, in this portrait Tolstoy's small, sharp, grey eyes are amazingly true to life, as in no other portrait of Tolstoy, either by Repin himself or by any other painter.

This first portrait remained in Jassnaia Poliana: Repin presented it to our family. The second, the more famous one, he sold to the Tretyakov Gallery.

Repin spent a week at Jassnaia Poliana at that time. My father was then doing all the peasant's work—mowing, ploughing, etc.—for the widow Anisya Kopylova. Repin went to the field beyond the village where my father was ploughing and made some sketches of him. To do this, he had to run from one end of the field to the other. These sketches were the origin of the famous painting and chromolithograph *Tolstoy at the Plough*. There is an error in it to which Tolstoy himself drew attention—the reins are missing.

At the end of the eighties Repin, urged by my father, illustrated several stories that Tolstoy had written for the new popular publishing house, as, for instance, *What Men Live by*, *Two Brothers and Gold*, *The Enemy Lures*, *God Steadies*, *How the Devil acquired his Bread*, as well as illustrations for *The Death of Ivan Ilyich* and *The Power of Darkness*.

In 1891 Repin stayed at Jassnaia Poliana from June 29th to July 16th. During this time he painted several pictures: *Tolstoy at Work*, *Tolstoy in the Garden*, *Tolstoy in the Forest* (barefoot), and he made a bust of Tolstoy though he had never sculpted before. At that time, too, if I am not mistaken, he did a good portrait of my sister Tatyana and a pencil sketch of Sofia Andreyevna with her youngest children. The likeness to the models is so negligible in this drawing that I would not have recognised them without the inscription.

I believe I am not mistaken if I say that his portraits of Tolstoy from 1891 onwards are not as good as the earlier ones. He painted Tolstoy at prayers; it was done in 1901 from sketches done in 1891. Tolstoy is represented barefoot in this picture with an unfamiliar expression of suffering on his face. My father was annoyed that Repin had painted him barefoot. He seldom went barefoot and said: 'I don't believe that Repin has ever seen me barefoot. He'll be painting me without my trousers next.'*

My father's words about being painted without his trousers turned out to be prophetic. In 1903 there was exhibited an allegorical painting by Bunin; it represented Tolstoy, Chekov Gorki and Repin himself as fishermen. These fishermen were in their shirts and, of course, without their trousers, tugging bare-legged at a net full of fish.†

In 1892 Repin travelled to the district where at that time Tolstoy was organising help for the famine-stricken population and was opening canteens for them. There Repin painted his *Tolstoy at the Famine* which I could not describe as a good picture.

In 1894, after a visit to the Tretyakov Gallery, my father said that he had not been able to tear himself away from Repin's picture *The Arrest* for a long time, that he liked *At Confession* very much, but he disapproved of *Ivan the Terrible* and of *An Unexpected Guest*.

In 1909 Repin came to Jassnaia Poliana with his second wife, N. Nordman. My father greatly approved of the fact that Repin and his wife were vegetarians. I think it was during this visit that Repin painted Tolstoy together with my mother. She had a photograph taken later in which she and father sat in exactly the same attitudes and surroundings as in Repin's painting; comparing the two, it can be clearly seen how poor the latter was.

After Tolstoy's death Repin painted him as an old man out of this world with 'eyes raised to heaven' against a background of

*My father had probably forgotten that Repin had seen him bare-foot. Repin writes in his memoirs that when he used to go bathing with him, Tolstoy would take off his old, home-made slippers on the way to the bathing house, stuff them into his leather belt and continue on his way barefoot.

†At the opening of the exhibition a journalist scratched the word 'filth' on the painting with his penknife. The painting was damaged and he had to pay heavily for this inscription.

pink flowers. My opinion is that this painting is based on a misconception. My father had never been a man ' out of this world ' and nothing on earth was ever alien to him. I recall how, when already a very old man he once said: ' You think that we old people no longer have any desires? We have our desires just as much as the young. I feel within me the potentiality for every kind of vice. But we, the old, have a better control over ourselves. Moses (do not think that I am comparing myself to him) said that every kind of vice lived in him but that he was stronger than they were.'

Now I should like to add a few words about the relations between my father and Repin. My father admired Repin's talent, his technique, the bold, wide sweep of his brush and valued some of his paintings very highly. I remember that he praised *The Fishermen, Farewell to the Recruit, At Confession, The Arrest, The Duel,* and his portraits; but he said that Repin sometimes did not know what, exactly, he wanted to express in his paintings. Such were his *St. Nicholas,* his ' *Get thee behind me, Satan* ' (*The Temptation*), *The Reply of the Cossacks to Sultan Mahmoud IV, What Splendour* and others. His judgment of the painting *A Religious Procession* was expressed in the following words, which I am copying from his preface to the works of Maupassant (1894): ' I remember how a famous painter once showed me his picture representing a religious procession. Everything was painted with perfection, but there was nothing to indicate the artist's attitude towards his subject. " What is your opinion," I asked the artist, " do you approve of these rites and believe they ought to be performed, or do you think them unnecessary? "

' " The artist replied a trifle condescendingly in the face of my innocence that he did not know and saw no need to know, his business was to represent life.

' " But do you, at least, admire them? "

' " I can't even tell you that."

' " Well, then, do you hate them? "

' " Neither the one nor the other," was the reply made with an indulgent smile at my stupidity by this highly cultured contemporary painter who represented life without understanding its meaning and neither loving nor hating its manifestations. Maupassant, unfortunately, behaved in the same way.'

This contention of my father's that Repin, already a famous

artist, no longer knew what to paint, was partly proved in 1898 when he insistently begged Tolstoy to suggest to him a subject for a painting.*

Repin's attitude to Tolstoy was complex. He obviously admired him as an artist of the written word, but I do not think he had any sympathy with his ethics and his philosophy.

I do not know Repin's views on the first period of my father's writings, but this is what he wrote to him about *The Power of Darkness* in January, 1887:

'Your new tragedy was read yesterday at Chertkov's house. It is such shattering truth, such a mercilessly forceful reproduction of life; and in the end, after this picture of a family den of filth and depravity, it leaves one with impression of a deep moral tragedy. This is an unforgettable lesson on life . . . and only one thing struck me unpleasantly . . . you, of course, must have thought about it and know more about it than I do, but that revolting scene with the fight between Nikita and the labourer over the rope appears to be simply impossible.'

The following conversation between my father and Repin, which has remained deeply ingrained in my memory, may serve to explain Repin's attitude to Tolstoy's ethical views. My father told him once about a letter in which a peasant compares Russia to an overturned cart being drawn by the workers. 'All of us' Tolstoy said, 'the landowners, the scientists, the writers, and the artists are sitting on the cart and the workers are pulling us. The first thing we must do is to get off the cart.'

To this Repin said, smiling his cunning smile: 'I agree with

*Concerning this my sister Tatyana noted in her diary on February 4th, 1898: Repin is still working on his *Temptation* which Papa advises him to give up. Repin is still begging him to suggest a subject for a picture. He came to Moscow with this purpose, then wrote about it to me and referred to it several times when I was in Petersburg. Yesterday Papa said that he had an idea for a subject but that it did not completely satisfy him, however. It is the moment when a group of Decembrists are being led to the gallows. Young Bestuzhev-Ryumin was more attracted by Muravyev-Apostol's personality than by his ideas and kept abreast with him all the time; only before the execution did he weaken and begin to weep. Muravyev put his arm round him and they walked together to the gallows.' Repin did not follow this advice.

you, Lev Nikolayevich. It is true that I am too, sitting on the cart, but I am like a singer who would sing to comfort those who are pulling it.'

Repin loved his art passionately. For him, people were primarily models, to be or not to be reproduced on canvas or paper. My sister Tatyana once said to him, looking at one of his sketches: ' How gifted you are, Ilya Yefimovich,' to which he replied with a smile: ' I am not gifted, I am industrious.' That he was not talented was evidently said to ' humble himself before pride ' and it is difficult to believe; but that he was industrious was proved by his whole life. Tolstoy too was for him in the first place an excellent and rewarding model, and each time he visited him he either painted or made a pencil drawing of him. However as the years passed he understood Tolstoy's spiritual life less and less and this was reflected in his later portraits: they were no longer the magnificent ones of 1887.

Chapter 9

Nikolai Gue

NIKOLAI GUÉ came to see my father for the first time in 1882. He decided to come because he considered that his own views, particularly his attitude to Christianity, were close to my father's new outlook on life.

Their similarity of ideas and Gué's admiration for my father as well as his personality immediately brought him close not only to my father but to our whole family. We were glad to see this handsome, elderly man with his lively, light-coloured eyes and fine nose, his grey beard and the long greying hair surrounding his bald pate, so full of vitality and benevolence towards all people. His appearance and his liveliness were reminders of his French origin.

Soon after meeting my father he suggested painting my sister Tatyana, but my father told him 'If you want to make me a present, paint my wife.'

Gué began painting my mother. At that time he did not yet understand her well enough and portrayed her as a society woman in a velvet dress; but he did not like this portrait and later destroyed it.

'I have done the wrong thing,' Gué said, 'I have painted a society woman and Sofia Andreyevna is primarily a mother.'

Later he painted another, more successful, portrait of my mother with a child in her arms. My mother and he were on terms of great friendship. He would say to her: 'Mamma, I'm sure you've got something delicious to eat?' She would smile and produce something 'delicious'—like home-made jam or other titbits. He would use the familiar 'thou' when addressing us, Tolstoy's children. Once he tore the knee of his trousers and turned to my sister Masha: 'Would you mend my trousers?'

Masha replied: 'Yes, I will, give me your trousers before going to bed and I will mend them.' 'No, mend them now, on me,' Gué said. Masha laughed but refused to do so.

I used sometimes to argue with him and once, in reply to one of his statements—I forget which—I said half jokingly: 'That is a hasty generalisation.' He shook his head and said: 'And you, Serezha, are a " ladivot ", a real " ladivot "!' 'Ladivot' was family slang for 'idiot'. Naturally I was not offended. I must admit that I was not much interested in his pronouncements on the gospels which were rather obscure and inspired by my father, but I was attracted by his vitality, his talent, his fondness for my father, his friendliness to all of us and, in general, his liking for all people. I sympathized with him, too, that as a true artist, he could not represent Christ otherwise than realistically, which in Russia at that time was both new and bold. Some of his judgments were correct and to the point, other were naïve. For instance, he used to say about Raphael: 'Sincere, childish faith can be felt in Raphael; he is a Christian, in contrast to his contemporary Michelangelo who was a heathen at heart.'

Before meeting my father Gué had painted hardly anything for several years. After their meeting he again started working with enthusiasm.

From 1882 until his death in 1894 Gué painted, apart from portraits and illustrations to *What Men Live By* a number of works portraying the life of Christ, like *What is Truth?*, *He must Die*, *Christ in Gethsemane*, *The Last Supper*, *Conscience*, *The Crucifixion* and others. Some of his sketches remained unfinished.

Gué was very sensitive about remarks on his paintings; he willingly discussed his subjects, liked to hear his work praised and used to praise it himself. My mother used to say; 'Nikolai Nikolayevich talks about his paintings better than he executes them.' And there was some truth in this: his brush could not keep pace with his imagination.

He spent a great deal of time thinking about his subjects, but sketched quickly on the canvas and either dropped his work or could not stop retouching it, at the same time saving on canvasses and frequently painting over a used one.

He repainted his *Crucifixion* many times and each time from a new angle. Some of his sketches for this painting made a very deep impression, yet he would remain dissatisfied with them and either destroyed them or painted them over and over again.

At last he dwelt on the moment when Christ gave up the ghost, horrifying the thief who only a short time ago had heard from him words of charity and truth.

My father had a high opinion of Gué's painting and though he used to say that it was impossible as a rule to portray Christ from a realistic angle, for some inexplicable reason he made an exception for Gué. Though he classed his *Crucifixion* very highly he said however: ' Nikolai Nikolayevich has been carried away by an imaginary romantic relationship between Christ and the thief. He has over-painted this picture (that is, he worked too much on it.) '

In the eighties Gué painted my mother, my sister Masha, and my father in oils and made a pencil portrait of my sister Tanya. I consider his portrait of my father to be the best of all the Tolstoy portraits as regards likeness and expression in spite of the downcast eyes. This portrait was particularly good because my father did not sit for it but was so intent on his work whilst Gué was painting him that he forgot the presence of the artist.

Gué had a cheerful disposition, he enjoyed a laugh and liked to tell amusing stories. For instance he once told us how he saw a woman lift her child to a fresco representing the Last Judgment in St. Sophia's Cathedral in Kiev and say:

' Kiss the Good Lord on his little tail.' This ' Good Lord ' was no other than the picture of a devil.

Gué brought us together with his family, his wife (Anna Petrovna, whom he called Anechka), and his two sons Nikolai and Piotr. Anna Petrovna had a healthy and practical mind; she protected her husband in every way and kept his infatuations under control. He valued her care for him and meekly followed her practical advice.

Gué's eldest son, his ' dearly beloved Kolechka ' (as he used to call him) had artistic leanings but the life he led was such that he failed to leave any noticeable traces in the arts. In 1886 and 1887 he was the manager of a publishing business started by my mother, but in 1887 he moved to his father's farmstead where for several years he tried to put Tolstoy's teaching into practice and worked like a peasant in the fields and on the vegetable plot, together with his half-educated woman companion (Gapka). About the middle of the nineties he drifted away from the ' Tolstoyans ', but without any bitterness or ill-feeling. Then he took French citizenship and lived abroad. He did not belong to any religion nor to any party. Kind-hearted, truthful and witty he had rare charm and was on very close terms with our family, especially with me. He was treated as one of us. We did not call him by any other name than ' Kolechka '.

I knew the younger son—Piotr Nikolayevich—very little. He lived in Petersburg and rarely visited us.

Nikolai Gué died of heart failure on his Ukrainian farmstead on June 2nd, 1894. My father felt keenly the loss of the loyal friend who had shared so many of his views. In one of his letters to a friend he described Gué in the following terms: ' He was an astonishing, pure, tender, inspired old child, overflowing with love for all and sundry, like those children whom one must try to imitate in order to enter the Kingdom of Heaven. His vexation with people who did not like him and his work, his resentment of them was childish too . . . Such a death, such a life are uplifting.'

Chapter 10

Alexander Sergeyevich Buturlin

THE Buturlins were wealthy, aristocratic landowners and had been brought up in a manner considered proper in such families.

There were three brothers: Sergei, Alexander and Dmitri. The eldest and the youngest were generals, the middle one, Alexander, was a ' political criminal.'

He was born in 1845 and completed a course in natural sciences at Moscow university. He used to tell me that as a young man he met the well-known anarchist M. Bakunin and travelled in Switzerland with him in the company of other young people, all wearing red caps. He said that, in all, he had spent three years in prison and seven in exile, all by administrative order, and had never been sentenced by a court.

He was arrested in 1869 and banished to the province of Yaroslavl for two years; in 1871 he was brought to court in connection with the Nechayev case ' for participation in a plot to overthrow the existing order.' Buturlin told me that he had never seen Nechayev himself and was only listed in one of the ' groups of five ' who, according to Nechayev's plan, were to carry out the revolution. The court acquitted him.

In 1876 he was brought to court in connection with the ' case of the 50 ' and was again acquitted. At the end of 1881 he was sentenced by administrative order to be banished to Tobolsk for five years, but he was transferred to Simbirsk before completing the period. Having served this sentence he settled down in Moscow: however, he was still considered to be ' unreliable ' and was arrested more than once. He told me that he was always arrested before the Tsar travelled through Moscow, after the attempt on the Tsar's life and on the life of other government figures, as well as for reasons unknown to him.

In March 1882 a good friend of mine, the former tutor of my

218

brother Ilya, advised me to meet Buturlin, a socialist and an expert on political economy. At that time Buturlin was in the Butyrka prison awaiting deportation. On March 5th, 1882, my mother wrote to my father: ' Buturlin has let us know that he is allowed to go home daily between four and seven and if anybody wanted to see him, they could do so. We said that you were outside Moscow and thank goodness that you are not here. Out of kindness of heart you might have gone to see him to give him a few words of consolation. Let him be, or you may again attract suspicion. Serezha wants to go but I am urging him not to do so, I do not know whether he will obey me.'

I did not obey her and went to visit Buturlin. At that time I imagined myself to be a ' radical ', and, understandably, hero-worshipped Buturlin as an old revolutionary. I was welcomed warmly by a fair, tall, handsome man who was still quite young. He was then thirty-seven. He spoke to me about the iron law of the minimum wage and the unearned income of capitalists. I listened to him spellbound.

The Buturlins had a good income but it was their mother's during her lifetime, the estates were managed badly and did not bring in much money; Alexander was married, he had three children and his income was not sufficient to make both ends meet. He was very punctilious in money matters and decided to become independent and increase his income by working as a physician. To achieve this he enrolled as a student in the faculty of medicine after his civil rights had been restored and when he was already fifty. It was strange to see this handsome grey-haired man in a student's uniform. Three years later he completed the course brilliantly.

After 1882 I did not meet him for many years. I do not remember precisely when I renewed my acquaintance with him. I believe it was towards the end of the nineties. He was already living alone, on the top floor of the Buturlin's house. Later he moved into a small apartment where he lived until his death. In the summer he did not move to the country or to a summer resort and seldom left Moscow.

As far as I know his medical training did not bring him any earnings. He treated people seldom and did not charge a fee. However, his interest in medicine continued and he kept up with new methods in this science.

He spent the major part of the day reading. Alone in his room he nearly always read aloud, a pencil in his hand. He rarely wrote down his thoughts on what he was reading but he corrected misprints in books and noted mistakes made by the authors with a sharp pencil in his clear and beautiful handwriting.* Buturlin used to speak ironically of himself, saying that his real vocation was that of proof-reader. He kept very late hours, going to bed at three or four in the morning. He smoked a great deal: stacks of boxes with cigarettes used to lie on his window-sill. ' I need many cigarettes, but few matches,' he used to say. ' I light one cigarette from another.'

He seldom went to the theatre and he described music as an unpleasant noise. Most often he spent his evenings ' at one of his good friend's ' as he used to call Maria Sklirina, with whom he had a liaison. She came from a respectable family of the gentry but led the life of a Bohemian. She was unfaithful to him but he would say: ' I am not at all jealous, I do not know what jealousy means.'

After his ' good friend's ' death he continued to lead an even more secluded life and only rarely spent his evening away from home. However, he was glad when people he liked came to see him. He was always courteous and amiable. He met my father in December 1881. Tolstoy came to see him to express his sympathy at his arrest and exile to Siberia. And in spite of my mother's advice, he visited Buturlin when the latter was allowed to leave prison for three hours daily.

In April 1888 my mother wrote to my father from Moscow to Jassnaia: ' Buturlin and Uncle Kostya came in the evening. Buturlin is very pathetic but I continue to like him. Tomorrow he is going with us to an exhibition to see Polenov's painting *Christ and the Woman Taken in Adultery* and will then dine with us.'

If I am not mistaken, Buturlin was ' very pathetic ' at that time because he and his wife had separated. He asked my father's advice about this break in their relations. My father advised him not to separate, but he did not follow this advice.

*For instance, he took my complete collection of Herzen's works, read them right through and corrected all the author's misprints and errors.

In 1902 Buturlin was in Jassnaia. In his presence Tolstoy read Chekov's story *The Darling*, and laughed until tears flowed from his eyes.

In October 1903, in Jassnaia, Tolstoy read his article on Shakespeare to Buturlin and D. Nikitin. In February 1904 Sofia Andreyevna was removing Tolstoy's manuscripts to the History Museum. Buturlin who approved of this, helped her with their transport.

On July 10th, 1910, Buturlin wrote as follows in a letter to me: ' On June 20th I visited Chertkov at his summer villa in order to see Tolstoy. He amazed me by his unusually fresh and healthy appearance, by his vitality and his intensive activity. One might think he was sixty and not approaching eighty-two. He was in excellent spirits. One has to admit that life in Jassnaia is not appropriate—excuse this barbarian neologism of the word *propice* (beneficial)—and that he feels much better when " on a visit " than at home. It is sad to have to admit it, but, regrettably, this is undoubtedly so."

It was then that Tolstoy called him in his diary: ' Dear Buturlin ... '

Usually I would come to see Buturlin at night, not earlier than ten, and frequently I would stay with him until three, so enthralling it was to talk to him. Among the subjects of our conversations were: literature, especially Pushkin and Tolstoy, criticism of the so-called Holy Scriptures, to which he devoted particular attention, and events that had laid the way for the revolution, with which he was in keen sympathy: disturbances among students, strikes, the assassinations of Sipyagin, Plehve and the Grand Duke Serge and many others.

Buturlin held Tolstoy in profound respect, waxed enthusiastic at his artistic works and supported him warmly in his criticism of orthodoxy and the contemporary state and social order.

He did not share Tolstoy's religious convictions, though he respected them. He used to say: ' Your father demands that we fulfil God's wish, the God, whom he calls Father or Master. The idea of serving any " master " is repugnant to me. I want to be free. However, let us assume that we have to carry out the will of a " master ". How can we find out what his will really is? Tolstoy maintains that it is contained in the main rules: do not resist evil, and in the five rules he has drawn from the gospels:

curb anger, do not commit adultery, do not swear, do not judge, do not fight. These rules have been uttered by people and not by the " master ". Consequently, it is possible to disagree with them. Tolstoy himself does not recognise the divinity of Christ. Is it possible to base ethics on such negative rules: do not do this or the other? Tolstoy understood correctly the basic idea of Christian ethics: do not resist evil. I do not agree with this and I think that it originated during the epoch of Roman domination when it was useless and even impossible to resist evil, that is the power of the Roman emperors. Moralists, including Christ, improved the morals of mankind but little. Wars, killings, executions, violence and poverty continue to reign as if nobody had ever called them evil.'

I retorted: 'But don't you believe that relations between people have perhaps improved owing to Christianity?'

'Relations between people improve as a result of the betterment of their social order,' Buturlin said, 'for instance, they improved after the abolition of slavery. The main cause of evil in the world is the imperfect form of the social life of mankind.'

When somebody said within his hearing that the history of the Russian people progressed along a path different from the history of West European peoples, because the Russians belonged to a different race; he retorted: ' Race does not play a large part in the history of peoples. Class distinctions are more acute than those of race.'

Buturlin read French, German and English fluently. He had read many books criticising the Old and New Testament by Reuse, Renan, Strauss and others.

Buturlin's daughter married the son of V. Istomin, head of the office of Grand Duke Serge. Istomin was known as a stubborn reactionary, an opponent of liberal reforms and an upholder of autocracy and of the persecution and execution of revolutionaries.

' You can understand,' Buturlin said to me, ' that I dislike even to be acquainted with Istomin. And now we have become kinsmen.'

As a man of manners he drove off to call on Istomin. Contrary to his expectations his visit went off well. He told me later: ' Istomin and I did not talk about politics, or about my past or about his work. We only spoke about literature. He likes Russian writers and knows them well.'

I saw Buturlin in the evening of February 4th, 1905; the day Grand Duke Serge was assassinated. Buturlin lived at that time not far from the Kremlin. He told me:

> 'When I heard the explosion I realised that this was the work of revolutionaries. A few minutes later I heard that the Grand Duke had been assassinated. My heart leapt with joy and I went to the Kremlin. The authorities had lost their heads: The Troitsky Gates had not been locked and quite a crowd had gathered in the Kremlin. I saw the broken carriage, the corpses of the horses and some of the Grand Duke's brains glued to a wall. Very little remained of his body; the explosion had been very powerful.'

In October 1905, Buturlin took part in a grandiose procession following the body of Baumann. The same evening he said: ' Going along the Tverskaya in the procession I saw with my own eyes a red flag fluttering over the doors of the Governor-General's house. I can now say like Simon " Now lettest thou Thy servant depart " and I can die quietly.'

Buturlin would often tell stories from the past. Here is one, for example:

During the Franco-Prussian War of 1870–71 a certain Nasakin, marshal of nobility and counsellor of State, was very interested in the military operations; he sided with the French and simply could not reconcile himself to the idea that General Trochu had surrendered Paris. The news in the papers did not satisfy him, and he decided to go to Paris and ask Trochu himself why he had surrendered the city. In Paris he put up at a bad hotel and ordered a French visiting card to be printed with the following inscription: ' M. Nasakin, Maréchal et Conseiller d'Etat '. In French it sounded well: ' Mr. Nasakin, Marshal and State Counsellor '. He drove to Trochu and, not finding him at home, left his card. Trochu, apparently believed that an important personage had called on him and the very next day he drove off in the full dress of a general to return the call. Nasakin was unabashed and met Trochu in the dressing-gown which he was wearing, and carrying a long-stemmed pipe. ' Ah, bonjour, Général Trochu,' he said in bad French, ' *pourquoi rendu Paris*? '

History is silent about Trochu's reply.

One day Buturlin told me about his grandfather: 'Having lived to the age of seventy, he was a witness to the history of a whole century, and not only did he himself experience, see and learn much, but he knew many old people who had been born long before his time. I remember my grandfather, Prince Gagarin, and his stories very well. Once when I mentioned Kheraskov in his presence, he said: " I knew Kheraskov—what antiquity! Doesn't it seem a long long time ago! " My grandfather was aide-de-camp to Paul I. He said that he remembered Paul as if he had seen him only yesterday. My grandfather was shortsighted and wore glasses. Once Paul asked him:

' " Do you wear concave or convex glasses ?"

' " I am shortsighted, Sire, and therefore wear convex glasses."

' "No, if you are shortsighted, you must wear concave glasses," Paul said.

' " Sire, shortsighted people wear convex glasses."

' " No, concave ones."

' " Convex ones, Sire." Paul did not like to be contradicted and his temper began to rise. Somebody pulled Gagarin by his coat-tail and made him a sign that it was time to stop. Later his friends told him: " You're mad to argue with him! He might send you to Siberia for it! " '

Buturlin began to ail in 1915. As a physician he assumed, with some reason, that he was suffering from cancer of the bladder, but he felt no pain, only his heart grew gradually weaker. He began to talk about death.

' I know,' he said, ' that I shall die soon and my mind is reconciled to it; but when I think that my body will be put into a coffin, that the lid of the coffin will be screwed down and I will be buried under earth, I am horrified. I am well aware that my horror is unreasonable, that I shall not be feeling anything by then, but I cannot overcome this feeling. Sometimes I also have the feeling—and that is also unreasonable—that I shall not die. I read somewhere that a Frenchman had begun his will with the following words: " Not *when* but *if* I should die one day . . . " That Frenchman seemed to think that one does not necessarily have to die.

' I have not been unhappy in life,' Buturlin would also say, ' my greatest joys were caused by my friends and by literature, especially by Pushkin and by Tolstoy. You will laugh at me—

I am like Pushkin's uncle, Vasiliy Pushkin, who said just before he died: " Katenin writes badly ". Then his nephew, Alexander Pushkin, went out into the next room and said: " My uncle should not say anything more after these words. May these be his last ones." May the words on my love for literature also be my last words.'

On April 4th, 1916, when he was feeling particularly weak, I was sitting in the dining-room with his niece, Marfa and the little actress Yulenka; the nurses had gone to change for the night. I was about to go home and went to say goodbye to him; Yulenka and the nurses also came into his room. He was lying very still on his back and was deathly pale. 'What have you done, Alexander Sergeyevich?' one of the nurses said, ' it is bad for you to get out of bed. Why did you not call us? "

He was silent. Suddenly a hardly perceptible tremor flitted across his face, he opened his eyes wide as if surprised by something and said ' I am dying '. No horror, no regret that his life was ending, no suffering, only amazement were heard in these words. And immediately his eyes grew dim, his body stretched out and became still. He was dead. It was a paralysis of the heart. There was no agony at all.

Music in my Father's Life

I HAVE never seen anyone who felt music so strongly and deeply as my father. It upset him, moved him, excited him, made him sob and weep. Sometimes it was even against his will, for it caused him pain and he said: '*Que me veut cette musique?*' This emotional reaction to music, quite apart from an intellectual appreciation of it, is particularly vividly described in *The Kreutzer Sonata*.

In the thirties and forties, there were few concerts and the Tolstoys, living in the country, had to content themselves with amateur performances, mostly by members of the family. Later Father began to teach himself music and took lessons from time to time. But he admitted that he had no true vocation for it: playing the piano was, for him, more a way to seduce young girls with passionate tunes. 'Then I suddenly decided,' he writes, 'that I preferred classical music, German in particular, I went into raptures over Beethoven's *Sonata Pathétique*, though to tell the truth I was pretty tired of it. In spite of all this haze and pretence I think I must have had some talent,' he went on, 'because it had such a tremendous effect on me and, had someone taught me then to look upon music as a delight in itself and not as a means of seduction, I might have grown into a good musician.' The story went that he had composed a waltz in 1849, but I have never had serious confirmation of this. He often played the waltz, but I believe he had not been alone in composing it. He also wrote a good deal about music. He enjoyed gypsy songs, for he said they were sincere and penetrating, that they were real art, even if perhaps of an inferior quality. He often wondered why music affected people so differently. He wrote: 'The purer and happier a man's past and the more he likes his memories, the stronger he feels music; on the other hand, painful memories make music unbearable and that is why some men cannot listen to it.'

He was not fond of opera and considered that two, even three, types of art—music, drama and pictorial art—could not be merged, each attenuating the effect of the other. ' I cannot bear to see a fat yelling gentleman in tights,' but he made exceptions of a few operas, like Mozart's *Don Giovanni*, and Weber's *Der Frei-schütz, The Barber of Seville, Orpheus*. Later on he wrote in his diary, quoting the words of Kant, that ' music is an irresponsible delight '. He had many friends among musicians, N. Rubinstein and P. Tchaikovsky. The latter's playing always brought tears to his eyes. One day he sent him a score of Russian folk-songs, asking him to ' arrange them in a Mozart-Haydn manner, not in the artificial manner of Beethoven-Schumann-Berlioz, which seeks to surprise.' The relationship between the two men did not last, however, partly because Tchaikovsky was disappointed not to find in Tolstoy the ' sovereign of thought ' he had expected. He wrote to Madame von Meck: ' I think that Tolstoy is a man of paradoxes, kind, straightforward, sensitive to music, but know-ing him has only brought me pain and torment, as it always does with me.' However, after reading *Death of Ivan Illyich*, he wrote: ' Tolstoy in my opinion is the greatest of all the writers the world has ever known.' But there was a strange barrier between them of which Father was aware and which at the same time he could not overcome. During various periods in his life his attitude to music changed. At one moment it even irritated him. He could not bear Wagner, he did not like concerts, con-sidering that they were only a pastime for idle people. At another period he regarded ' playing by ear ' as a more sincere way of expressing oneself in music than any other. Sometimes he would ask me to play and would sit quite relaxed, listening to my very imperfect renderings of Grieg, Chopin, Weber. He had a vast knowledge of music but it is hard to say what he liked best. He himself used to say that the music he liked best was not necessarily the best music, and he said that perhaps he was one of those people whose taste in music is distorted by a false interpretation and who accept as absolute perfection a piece simply because it might have impressed him at a particular moment. He was deeply fond of folk music of all nations and used to like to listen to my arrangements of Scottish songs. ' All folk music,' he said, ' can be understood by all people throughout the world. A Persian peasant will understand the songs of a Russian peasant and *vice versa.* But the pretentious insincerities of the great—like Richard Strauss for instance—even the great won't be able to understand. There is no doubt that all great music has used folk tunes consciously or subconsciously.'

From my own observation of his attitude to music I gathered that he liked a clear, simple melody, even if it was hackneyed. A tune for him had to be energetic, and in a major key rather than in a minor one. Harmony and counterpoint he was not really conscious of; the fugue was a form he considered artificial. He preferred the piano to orchestral music. Among composers, he liked Bach, Haydn, Mozart, Chopin, but not all their works, only fragments from their works. He liked best of all the duet ' *La ci darem* ' from *Don Giovanni.*

He wrote one day to my sister Tatiana: ' Yesterday, after Tchaikovsky's nonsensical quartet, I went to the next room and began to talk to the 'cellist, arguing that modern music seemed to have somehow gone astray, when suddenly something began to make havoc of my thoughts and drew me away, calling, demanding submission. They had started to sing ' *La ci darem la mano* ' in the music-room. I stopped talking, and just listened happily. What a terrible power music has! '

He considered Beethoven not as the climax of the greatest period of music but as the representative of its decline. He said that an artist of genius creates new forms. Haydn had created the symphonic form, Mozart the opera, Beethoven only created within old forms. About Beethoven's sonata in C Sharp, he said: ' It is like a conversation between man and wife—it is a toy sonata.' But he was a great admirer of Beethoven—he even called his story *The Kreutzer Sonata.* He loved Chopin: ' He is good even when he is banal, for he is banal in his own way,' he said. About Rubinstein: ' He knows too much foreign music, this hampers him in his own compositions.' Very often his judgments were paradoxical and contradictory. In *Childhood* he says that music is ' the memory of feelings'. Elsewhere he said that ' Music was the memory of something that had never been '. He wrote to my mother in 1905: ' Music is the stenography of the emotions '. In his old age he wrote that music helps to bring people together ' in one common emotion.' In his opinion the aim of music was to be accessible to the greatest number of people, and to satisfy their needs, not simply those of a small *élite.*

INDEX